Woodcutters and Witchcraft

SUNY series in the

Philosophy of the Social Sciences

Lenore Langsdorf, editor

Woodcutters

and

Witchcraft

RATIONALITY AND INTERPRETIVE CHANGE
IN THE SOCIAL SCIENCES

MARK W. RISJORD

STATE UNIVERSITY OF NEW YORK PRESS

Published by
State University of New York Press, Albany

For information, address
State University of New York Press,
State University Plaza, Albany, NY 12246

Production, Laurie Searl
Marketing, Anne Valentine

Library of Congress Cataloging-in-Publication Data

Risjord, Mark W., 1960–
    Woodcutters and witchcraft : rationality and interpretive change
in the social sciences / Mark W. Risjord.
        p.   cm.
    Includes bibliographical references and index.
    ISBN 0-7914-4511-9 (hc. : alk. paper). — ISBN 0-7914-4512-7
(pbk. : alk. paper)
        1. Social sciences—Philosophy.   2. Social sciences—Methodology.   I. Title.
    H61.R569   2000
    302.5′42—dc21   99-042500
                                                                                    CIP

10 9 8 7 6 5 4 3 2 1

For

Barbara

Contents

Acknowledgments

The catalyst for this book was the Luce Faculty Seminar, "Describing, Explaining, Valuing," held at Emory University in the spring of 1995. Our director and mentor, Dr. James Gustafson, guided an interdisciplinary group of scholars through an ambitious reading list. I was already developing the central themes of this essay, and the discussion of methodology stimulated the idea of structuring the book around several realistic examples. Two of the four examples in chapter 1 are drawn from the Luce Seminar. Thanks to the Luce Foundation, Emory University, and the Philosophy Department for providing the resources for this semester of research.

My colleagues and students at Emory University helped sustain progress on the manuscript in many ways. Robert McCauley, Nicholas Fotion, and Rudolf Makkreel have been excellent interlocutors throughout the process of working out these ideas and finding adequate expression for them. Graduate students in the 1997 Philosophy of Social Science Seminar, especially Eric Nelson, Michael Futch, and Bryon Cunningham provided tough-minded criticism of the manuscript at a crucial point in its development. Their comments helped shape the final form of the book.

While this work was in its final stage, I had the opportunity to attend the NEH Summer Institute, "Philosophy of Social Science 40 Years Later," directed by James Bohman and Paul Roth. Conversations with the faculty and participants—including Robert Feleppa, Jean Pederson, David Henderson, Karsten Stueber, Susan Brownell, Raymond Scupin, Mariam Thalos, William Keith, Charles Taylor, Clifford Geertz, Robert Brandom, and Alexander Rosenberg—challenged and thereby crystallized the views expressed here. My good friends David Henderson, William Keith, and Elizabeth Preston read the penultimate draft in its entirety and made both stylistic and philosophical contributions. David Henderson deserves special mention. I came to know his work intimately only after this essay was already well begun. The vast correspondence of our views has forced me to sharpen the differences. Thinking through what I have called "the Henderson Problem" (he prefers to call it "the Henderson Result") and responding to his criticism has shaped my view in important ways.

Finally, this work would have been impossible without the love of Barbara Risjord. She endured the hardships imposed by this work with grace and understanding. This book is dedicated to her.

CHAPTER 1

Introduction

1.1 BREAKDOWN AND RECONSTRUCTION

There was a time in my life when I wanted to learn how to fix cars. Reflecting back, it is striking that I learned the most from breakdowns. A properly working automobile teaches only the basic system. My understanding was deepened when something went wrong, when I tried to fix it and failed, when I ended up making things worse. Perhaps this lesson can be applied to our understanding of the sciences. In the philosophy of science, we are drawn to the ideal cases. We want to know what science would be like when all the evidence is collected or collectable, not when it is influenced by personal bias. We look at practicing scientists when they are happily engaged in normal science (or staging their bloodless revolutions), not when their projects are faltering and tenure is on the line. My faint attempt to learn auto mechanics suggests that our normal approach might be backwards. To understand science, it might be wise to look at cases where it breaks down.

A particularly interesting form of breakdown occurs when the understanding of human behavior reaches a dead end. This is not the puzzlement of someone entirely new to a culture. The informative breakdowns occur when one has enough understanding to permit a genuine conflict between the working interpretation and the new events. Then there is a breach of understanding and one is struck by something that seems completely crazy. A favorite[1]—albeit fictional—example comes from Wittgenstein's *Remarks on the Foundations of Mathematics*:

> 142. . . . People pile up logs and sell them, the piles are measured with a ruler, the measurements of length, breadth, and height multiplied together,

---

1. This is also a favorite of Richard Zaffron, to whom I owe much more than this reference.

and what comes out is the number of pence which have to be asked and given. They do not know 'why' it happens like this; they simply do it like this: that is how it is done.—Do these people not calculate? . . .

148. Very well; but what if they piled the timber in heaps of arbitrary, varying height and then sold it at a price proportionate to the area covered by the piles?

And what if they even justified this with the words: "Of course, if you buy more you have to pay more"?

149. How could I shew them that—as I should say—you don't really buy more wood if you buy a pile covering a bigger area?—I should, for instance, take a pile which was small by their ideas and, by laying the logs around, change it into a 'big' one. This *might* convince them—but perhaps they would say: "Yes, now it's a *lot* of wood and costs more"—and that would be the end of the matter.—We should presumably say in this case: they simply do not mean the same by "a lot of wood" and "a little wood" as we do; and they have a quite different system of payment from us. (Wittgenstein 1956: 43–44)

Wittgenstein's example has all the elements of what we will call a problem of apparent irrationality. An outsider is struck by unintelligible behavior. It is not merely foreign and strange. The actions are different from what rational and intelligent people *ought* to be doing. The divergence between what *is* happening and what *ought* to be is generated by some prior understanding. To see Wittgenstein's woodcutters as problematic, one must suppose that these people are buying and selling wood. One must know the language well enough to provide translational glosses like "big," "little," "more," and "less." Failure to make sense of these people is not just the failure to parse a sentence or follow a performance. The behavior seems irrational. Given the interpreter's current understanding of these people, they would have to be irrational to do what they are doing. The interpreter's smooth progress has broken down in a fundamental way.

Problems of apparent irrationality, then, arise when interpretation falters. Local action or speech seems irrational in the light of a background understanding. Of course, we know exactly what anthropologists, sociologists, and historians do when they come upon apparently irrational behavior. They rub their hands with glee and set about writing a monograph. When understood from the proper perspective, they explain, the bizarre activity makes sense. What was a breakdown in interpretation has been reconstructed into a deeper understanding. Wittgenstein himself suggests as much:

We should presumably say in this case: they simply do not mean the same by "a lot of wood" and "a little wood" as we do; and they have a quite different system of payment from us.

Since the breakdown runs deep, the changes may be radical. If we rethink the meaning of "a lot of wood" and "a little wood," we are likely to shift the interpretation of many other words too. Their "quite different system of pay-ment" may have implications for their social structure, religious life, and who knows what else. We hope that some such interpretive change will make sense of the events. If we find it, the behavior will (presumably) no longer seem irrational; the irrationality was merely apparent.

Breakdowns in understanding are interesting to philosophers for several reasons. In some cases, the behavior is unintelligible because it seems irrational. This kind of breakdown thus puts the traditional questions about rationality and interpretation into a new light. If we judge Wittgenstein's woodcutters to not only *seem* irrational, but to *be* irrational, then our questions about them become psychological and biological. On the other hand, if the interpreter tries to explain away the appearance of irrationality, there seems to be little to constrain her account. By hypothesis, nothing in her current interpretation makes sense of the behavior. Yet, some ways of reconstructing the interpreta-tion are better than others. The problems of apparent irrationality thus exhibit the role that rationality plays in interpretive change. Interpretive change itself is an issue that has seen little direct discussion. What are the criteria by which we should judge one interpretive change to be better than another? While this question is a concrete version of a general epistemological problem, it is fundamentally dynamic.[2] The question is not how an existing interpretation might be (or fail to be) justified. Rather, the problem is to specify criteria for epistemically better or worse changes in an interpretation. There is no reason to be cagey about the answer. This essay will argue that the better interpre-tation is the one with more explanatory coherence.[3] This answer seems straight-forward enough and it has plenty of intuitive appeal. One might even think it obvious. Yet articulating "explanatory coherence" in the context of the problem of apparent irrationality is far from trivial. Moreover, the study of interpretive breakdown and reconstruction should shed light on the structure of an interpretation. How do the various parts of an interpretation hang together? When do different interpretations or explanations conflict? As will become clear soon enough, the conceptions of explanation and coherence ground the answers to these questions.

Finally, two remarks about method and rhetorical style are appropriate. First, this work is not critically structured. It does not exhaustively describe the

---

2. This way of approaching the question was inspired by Gilbert Harman's approach to epistemological issues in *Change in View* (Harman 1986).

3. Explanatory coherence is no epistemological novelty. Coherence has been gaining popularity in epistemology (BonJour 1985; Lehrer 1990; Quine 1969b; Thagard 1978; Ziff 1984). Several philosophers have argued that explanation is central to justification (Harman 1973; Harman 1986; Lipton 1991b; Lycan 1988). Lycan and Harman, in particular, have pioneered the idea that coherence is to be understood in terms of explanation.

range of alternatives in the field, demolish them, and build anew from their remains. While chapter 3 comes close to this philosophical style, the general approach is constructive. Chapter 2 presents a problem—the problem of apparent irrationality—and sections 2.5 and 4.1 make the requirements for its solution clear. The body of this work presents a systematic resolution of the problem of apparent irrationality. Other philosophical views are considered in detail only when they contain arguments that directly conflict with some part of the proposed solution. Some readers may find this approach unsatisfying, since there is no attempt to argue that this solution is the only or best one. In particular, there is no comparative discussion of Foucaultian or Habermasian approaches to rationality, nor of popular alternative conceptions of explanation like the unification approach or the statistical-relevance model. Comparative discussion is essential for the ultimate evaluation of this essay. But to engage in the systematic demolition of alternatives before constructing my own would be unconvincing. Only now that the work is complete can one begin to evaluate its strengths and weaknesses as compared with other views.

Second, in this age, no work can be unselfconscious about the gender and power implications of its own language. This project faces a double problem. There is the usual challenge of finding readable, gender-neutral constructions for the personal pronouns. In addition, there is a power asymmetry between the interpreter and the subjects of investigation. The latter have often been colonized, objectified, and exploited. Social scientists have become terribly self-conscious about the language they use to describe the humans they study. "Natives" brings forward connotations of naked, stone-age folks. Even a word as apparently innocent as "subject" has become unacceptable in certain circles. Unfortunately, the proposed alternatives like "research partner" only mask the real asymmetry of power. In the philosophy of social science, it is better, I suggest, to leave the power relation explicit in the language, lest we forget it. This essay therefore deploys a number of terms to describe the persons studied: "native," "native speaker," "subject," "local," "member of the local group," and so on. To fight the negative connotations, bear in mind that *every* human is the native of some cultural milieu. In the paradigm cases, the interpreter is an outsider trying to understand persons native to an unfamiliar locale. This contrast between interpreter and interpretee is important, and thus remains in the language of this essay. Playfully disrupting the asymmetry of power, however, I have chosen to use the pronoun "she" for the interpreter and "he" for the subject of interpretation. This resolves the problem of gender-neutral language by sprinkling both pronouns evenly throughout the text. It has the additional advantage of marking the pronouns for the reader. Feminine pronouns used anaphorically will always refer to the interpreter, and masculine pronouns will refer to the persons interpreted. I fear that the trick is too clever by half, and that some readers will be annoyed. If so, my only defense can be a plea for your tolerance of a well-intentioned peccadillo.

1.2 SYNOPSIS

Chapter 2: Apparent Irrationality

To illuminate the problem with which this work is concerned, we will begin by examining four cases of apparent irrationality drawn from the social scientific literature. In each case, the interpreter was presented with prima facie irrational speech or behavior, and in each case the interpreter went on to devise a more adequate interpretation. The aim of this work is to uncover the methodological principles that govern this sort of interpretive change. Each case exposes one or more facets of the problem, and the final section, section 2.5, analyzes the problem of apparent irrationality and poses four questions that are central to its resolution:

1. What are the criteria for preferring one interpretation to another?

2. Is it possible for an interpreter to prefer an interpretation that attributes to the interpretees standards of rationality different from her own?

3. What are the epistemic grounds for claiming that a person or group adheres to a norm, rule, or standard?

4. Under what conditions are interpretations that include descriptions and evaluations from the subjects' point of view to be preferred over interpretations that employ ideas or evidence to which the subjects do not have access?

Chapter 3: Interpretive Change

Given the examples from which the problem of apparent irrationality arises, the first and second questions of section 2.5 are closely related. The four examples of chapter 2 show that whether an action appears irrational depends heavily on the interpretation from which it is understood. The content of the interpretation is at least part of the basis for evaluating the rationality of the subjects. Any methodology of interpretive change, then, must be able to adjudicate among interpretations that entail different assessments of the rationality of the agents. This means that the discussion of interpretive change involves the question of whether and to what extent social scientists need to presuppose that their subjects are rational. Most of the literature takes Peter Winch's "Understanding a Primitive Society" (1964) as the proximate origin of the position that an interpreter must identify and deploy local criteria of rationality. In response, others argued that an interpreter must presuppose her interlocutors to be rational, and thus at least some criteria of rationality are not discovered (Davidson 1984; Hollis 1967a; Hollis 1967b; Lukes 1967; Lukes 1982; Macdonald and Pettit 1981; Root 1986). Any criterion of interpretive choice that can address the problems of apparent irrationality will thus stake out a position on this issue and thereby answer question 2.

Section 3.1 addresses the principles advanced under the name "the principle of charity." This section identifies and rejects three different versions of the idea: a principle of logical charity, a principle of semantic charity, and a principle of confirmation charity. The first and third require agreement between the interpreter and the locals. The principle of semantic charity is the most satisfactory of the three, but it does little to guide interpretive choice. Explanatory grounds for choice of interpretation are usually discussed under the guise of the "principle of humanity." These principles require that the best interpretation minimize unexplained disagreement. Most defenders of this idea maintain that explanation is asymmetric. False or irrational belief is explained, while true and rational belief are interpreted. Section 3.2 criticizes the arguments that true and rational belief need to be treated differently from false or irrational belief. Section 3.3 argues that a symmetrical principle is the best candidate for a principle of interpretive change. The principle of explanatory coherence holds that the best interpretation is the one with the most explanatory coherence. According to this approach, criteria of rationality are explanatory posits. The interpreter hypothesizes that the locals adhere to one standard or another, and this hypothesis is successful insofar as it can be embedded within the interpretation that has the most coherence. The explanatory coherence position on the rationality issue, then, is neo-Winchean insofar as it gives an affirmative answer to question 2.

This book will speak at length about "interpretation." While it would beg our central questions to begin with a strict definition, something must be said about this notion. The paradigm cases of interpretation for this work are the monographs of ethnographers and historians. This kind of inquiry is distinctive because it depends on claims about word meaning and intentional action. As a first pass, interpretation is different from other sorts of theorizing because it aims at understanding meaning. Many kinds of inquiry outside of ethnography and history rely on claims about meaning, and this work will speak broadly about the "interpretive disciplines" with the intention of capturing a broad cross-section of social scientific practice. There are, however, two associations of the word "interpretation" that need to be disengaged from its use here. Artistic works are interpreted too. Whether aesthetic interpretation can be encompassed by the methodology presented here is an open question. From the perspective of this work, nothing is lost if the two sorts of interpretation turn out to be very different. Also, self-interpretation is arguably an activity in which all humans engage. At the outset, it will be an open question whether the interpretive activities of an ethnographer or historian are the same or different from the interpretive activities of her subjects. As the essay progresses, we will see that these two kinds of interpretation do not need to coincide, and that in fact they will often diverge. This book will argue for an epistemology of interpretation whereby an interpreter can represent the interpretive activities of others without necessarily engaging in the same kind of activity.

Chapter 4: Explanation

Many philosophers have argued that some aspects of human life cannot be reached by explanation. Disputants over the relative roles of explanation and understanding typically approach the problem with a conception of explanation already formed. This seems backwards. The question should be What concept of explanation is adequate to the demands of the problem of apparent irrationality and the question of interpretive change? Section 4.1 uses the explanatory coherence principle of interpretive change and the problems of apparent irrationality to establish criteria of adequacy for any conception of explanation. In particular, any adequate conception of explanation will have to give an explanatory role to claims about meaning, intentions, and norms. Chapters 5, 6, and 7 try to show how the model of explanation presented in chapter 4 satisfies the criteria of adequacy articulated in section 4.1.

Section 4.2 articulates the most promising candidate for satisfying the criteria of section 4.1. The erotetic, or "why-question," model of explanation takes an explanation to be an answer to a why-question (Garfinkel 1981; Lipton 1991b; van Fraassen 1980). This section presents the formal features of why-questions and their answers. Sections 4.2, 4.3, and 4.4 develop the model and defend it against its critics, making adjustments where necessary. The erotetic model is notorious for giving a prominent role to interest in choice of explanation. While most writers on this topic have tried to find ways of limiting the role of interest, section 4.4 argues for *laissez-faire* contextualism. There are no restrictions on the topics, foils, or relevance criteria beyond those made necessary by the presuppositions of the question and the interests of the investigator. The final section of the chapter (section 4.5) explores the way in which the erotetic model of explanation and the principle of explanatory coherence combine to provide a detailed account of interpretive change. At the end of the book, the account provided in section 4.5 is revisited in the light of the intervening chapters.

Chapter 5: Intentional Action and Social Explanation

The primary problem addressed in this chapter is whether intentional action explanations and social explanations of the same action necessarily conflict. Humans think of themselves as agents. Some explanations, however, treat actions as instances of social processes or as having a social function. The examples of chapter 2 show that such group-level explanations are sometimes useful when dissolving apparent irrationalities. An adequate account of interpretive change must provide a plausible way of resolving the apparent conflict between intentional action explanation and group-level explanations of the same action. This issue of how individual and group-level explanations are to be reconciled has been one of the pillars of discussion in the philosophy of social science. One position on this question has been that all so-called group-level explanations, insofar as they are legitimate, are ultimately reducible to intentional action explanations. The alternative view maintains that group-level explanations are sui generis. This chapter will argue for the latter position with respect to several specific forms of group-level explanation. Indeed, appeal to group-level explanations turns out to be essential to the explanatory coherence account as developed here. This leaves us with an acute form of the "invisible hand problem." That is, individuals are treated as if their intentions or motivations were irrelevant to the action at hand (Macdonald and Pettit 1981; Rosenberg 1988). Chapter 5 approaches the problem by analyzing the form of intentional action and social functional explanations, and by providing a general account of the conditions under which two kinds of explanation (or two explanations of a single event) conflict. Section 5.2 analyzes intentional action explanations and explanations of belief. Since functional explanations are the most likely to conflict with intentional action explanations, section 5.3 provides a detailed analysis of them. The final section (section 5.4) argues that there is no necessary conflict between functional explanations and reason-giving explanations, even when these concern the same event.

This chapter has two important consequences. First, the chapter shows how the erotetic model can be applied to intentional action, thus satisfying one of the criteria of section 4.1. Second, it gives part of the answer to question (4) of chapter 2: Under what conditions are interpretations that include descriptions and evaluations from the subjects' point of view to be preferred over interpretations that employ ideas or evidence to which the subjects do not have access? An interpreter may discover ways of explaining actions or social structures that draw on conceptions to which the locals have no access. The local and the interpreter's characterizations might be in prima facie conflict. Under what conditions should we prefer the interpreter's explanations or descriptions to the locals'? An adequate criterion of interpretive change must provide some plausible way of resolving the conflict between "internal" and "external" (or "emic" and "etic") characterizations. Both the political and epistemic aspects of this issue have received attention in philosophy (Bohman 1991; Feleppa 1988; Giddens 1976; Habermas 1984; Schutz 1967; Winch 1958). It is also important, if somewhat passé, in anthropology (Headland, Pike, and Harris 1990). According to the arguments of this chapter, the principle of explanatory coherence entails that many social phenomena will be best understood by interpretations that include both emic and etic perspectives. Intentional action explanations, as analyzed by section 5.2, must present the action to be explained, the alternatives, and the agent's reasons in terms familiar to the agent. This requirement anchors emic characterizations of action. At the same time, explanatory coherence may be increased by historical, functional, or structural explanations. The account of how intentional action and functional explanation can coexist in a single, coherent interpretation, then, gives us part of the account of how internal and external perspectives on human action can be reconciled. Chapters 6 and 7 also address this issue.

Chapter 6: Meaning

The importance of meaning for social life is a recurring theme among those who have taken the interpretive side of the explanation/understanding debate. The problem of meaning is whether an epistemology that sees no fundamental distinction between the interpretive and noninterpretive disciplines can capture meaning (including the self-understanding of the agents). The interpreter confronts subjects who are already engaged in the process of interpreting their own speech and action. Any methodology that grounds interpretation in simple observation of utterance and behavior can never reach the social reality at which it aims. Therefore, many have argued that the study of meaning requires a unique methodology. Section 6.1 argues that, as it has traditionally been articulated, the problem arises from an empiricist notion of observation and a foundationalist conception of justification. An explanatory coherence view of interpretive change countenances neither of these ideas. Such a view does require, however, that claims about linguistic meaning must be either explained or explanatory. Section 6.2 sketches the topics, foils, and relevance criteria of explanations that involve meaning, and thereby shows how the erotetic model of explanation satisfies yet another criterion from section 4.1. The chapter ends with a discussion of the so-called "double hermeneutic" of interpretation. Rejecting a strict theory/observation distinction and a foundationalist conception of justification shows that both natural and social inquiry are involved in something like a hermeneutic circle. Social inquiry, however, is "interpretive in a double sense" (Makkreel 1985: 239). Section 6.3 articulates the broad agreement between the explanatory coherence view and proponents of a hermeneutic methodology for interpretation. In the light of this consilience, this section criticizes the arguments that there is an additional level of interpretation unreachable by an explanatory methodology.

Chapter 7: Normativity

Rationality is normative, and it is only one particularly important aspect of the norms, rules, and values that saturate human life. The examples of chapter 2 show that hypotheses about local norms, rules, and values are crucial to any resolution of problems of apparent irrationality. An adequate account of interpretive change must therefore provide grounds for choosing between interpretations that attribute different norms, values, or rules. The examples of chapter 2 also show that there are some important wrinkles to this issue. Norms and rules are not always explicit. Where they are explicit, there may be local conflict over their authority or justification. Many have thought that, like meaning, norms cannot figure in explanations. The challenge in this case is that when norms become the subject of explanation or when they are used as explanantia, they collapse into mere descriptions. According to these arguments, the lacuna remaining in our account can never be filled by explanations.

The initial problem of chapter 7, then, is to show why claims about norms do not collapse into claims about the beliefs or dispositions of individual agents. The first step is to recognize the parallel between the problem of the loss of normativity and the long-standing issue about reductionism in the social sciences. Section 7.1 uses features of the erotetic model to argue that, in general, such reductions fail because the individual-level and the group-level explanations answer different questions. Along the way, this section characterizes the relevance relations and contrast classes of explanations that employ norms. Claims about norms answer questions about the group, not about individual action or belief. Section 7.2 unpacks the relationship between an agent's intentional action and the rules, norms, standards, or criteria that apply to it. This permits us to address a problem left over from section 2.5: articulate the difference between a common mistake and an implicit norm. The final section pulls together the remaining loose ends of the project. The answer to question (4) of chapter 2 is supplemented with an account of whether, and to what extent, the local agents need to be able to articulate the norms under which they act. This account opens a space to show how an interpretation might portray a group as systematically mistaken about their own actions or the norms under which they act. Also, it allows us to account for the fact that interpretations are often contested at the local level. Norms, rules, and values can be embedded into an interpretation without effacing local disputes about them.

A caveat concerning the notions of "norms," "rules," "standards," and "criteria" is in order here. This chapter will not ground its arguments in any specific conception of rules and rule-following. In particular, the use of these terms should not be taken as indicating a commitment to realism about norms, rules, or standards. Brandom (1994) has articulated a very powerful conception of the social character of norms. This chapter is consistent with his view, but also to the realistic alternatives that are antithetical to it. Similarly, this chapter does not presuppose that all rules, standards, or norms can be made explicit as beliefs of the person who conforms to them. Perhaps, as Dreyfus argues (1980), some aspect of rule-following must remain implicit as the agent's practical know-how. This book will argue, against Dreyfus, that rules can be represented by the interpreter (section 6.3), but this will not require that the person interpreted represent them in the same way as the interpreter does. The focus of this book is epistemological, not metaphysical. The character and ontological status of rules and rule-following are interesting philosophical issues, but they are beyond the scope of this work.

Chapter 8: Conclusion

As has already been remarked, the problem of apparent irrationality is fundamentally dynamic. In response to its demands, this essay constructs a dynamics of interpretation—an account of the forces and principles that determine how interpretations ought to change. The first section of the conclusion reiterates the essay's main points about interpretive change. The criteria for choice of interpretation articulated in section 4.5 are deepened in the light of the subsequent development of the model. The result is an understanding of interpretive change with several distinctive features: There is no unalterable core or "bridgehead" to interpretation. Claims about rationality are explanatory. Multiple explanatory perspectives are possible, even necessary, within a single interpretation. There is no knowledge of language without knowledge of culture. An interpretation does not need to homogenize local opinion. On the contrary, the most coherent interpretation will capture the real differences among the subjects. And finally, a coherent interpretation can represent some *genuine* irrationality, so there is no threat of artificial over-rationalization.

The resolution of the problem of apparent irrationality presented in this essay has ramifications for the long-standing debate over interpretation and explanation. Philosophers of social science have divided themselves into (roughly) two camps. On one side are methodological assimilationists who believe that there is a single methodology for all inquiry. On the other side are methodological separatists, who think that there are deep epistemological differences among the sciences. There are at least four issues that divide philosophers in this domain: the importance of causes or laws in explanation, the importance of understanding meaning, the relevance of normativity, and the relevance of the agents' self-interpretations. As it turns out, the explanatory coherence view does not fit easily into either camp. On each of the four issues, the explanatory coherence view articulated here either denies a presupposition of the debate or admits the significance of the phenomenon without agreeing to its purported ramifications. The position motivated in this book is globally assimilationist and locally separatist. All inquiry is explanatory, and all explanations are answers to why-questions. Therefore, there is no deep methodological divide between the social and natural sciences. At the same time, the very flexibility of the erotetic model of explanation means that there will be substantive differences among particular disciplines. The particular structure of an inquiry—the character of its explanations and their interrelations—is determined by the interests of the investigators and the facts about the domains they are investigating.

CHAPTER 2

Apparent Irrationality

Speaking of "problems of apparent irrationality" may seem to invite all of the ambiguity and vagueness that surrounds the notion of "irrationality" itself. While "irrationality" is admittedly a murky notion, it would prejudge important issues to give it a precise meaning at this point. It indicates only the broad area in which our problem lies. To get a clearer view of the issues involved, we must look at specific problems which have arisen for social scientists and the ways in which they have tried to resolve them. The four examples below are taken from anthropological, historical, and sociological monographs. They will help us identify the parameters of the problem and criteria for an adequate solution.

2.1 BLOODSUCKING WITCHCRAFT

In December 1960, Hugo Nutini had been doing ethnographic research in the Tlaxcala region of Mexico for about three months. His subjects were Nauatl speakers, descendants of the preconquest inhabitants of central and southern Mexico. At the time of Nutini's research, these people were in the midst of cultural change. The men served as laborers in textile factories and the home economy included weaving rugs and blankets for sale. While the official religion was predominantly Catholic, the folk beliefs included many preconquest elements, including the belief in *tlahuepuchis,* the bloodsucking witches. On the morning of December 9, one of Nutini's informants arrived with the news that during the night, seven infants in different houses had been killed by the *tlahuepuchis.*

Though tragic, this was an ethnographic opportunity for Nutini. Ethnographers rarely get a chance to witness witchcraft and its effects. Oral traditions typically constitute the ethnographic evidence about witchcraft. With the help of a physician who had Western training, Nutini examined the seven infants who had died in the "epidemic." They all exhibited the marks associated with *tlahuepuchis.* Telltale signs of such witchcraft are bruises on the infant's neck, chest, or face. Sometimes there are similar marks on the mother's breasts. Members of the households concurred about the circumstances. The bedroom doors had been shut in the evening, but were found inexplicably ajar the next morning. The infants were found dead on the floor, not in their cribs where they had been sleeping. Some mothers reported seeing a bright light and a turkey materialize just before falling into a deep sleep. Kinsmen who had been outside that evening reported seeing strange dogs, donkeys, or turkeys (Nutini and Roberts 1993: 144–53).

All these signs pointed toward the *tlahuepuchis.* According to traditional beliefs about the *tlahuepuchis,* blood-sucking witches are people who have the power to transform themselves into a variety of animals and insects. With an animal or insect form, a *tlahuepuchi* can surreptitiously approach and enter a house in which an infant is sleeping. If those inside the house are awake, the *tlahuepuchi* puts them into a deep sleep by emitting a vapor. After sucking the blood of the infant, the witch places the body near the door, and leaves the door ajar as she escapes. In the early 1960s, rural Tlaxcalans employed various means of protection against *tlahuepuchis.* These included leaving an open scissors, a metal cross, blessed silver medals, or garlic wrapped in tortillas near the crib (Nutini and Roberts 1993: 54–71). Nutini continued to document similar events over the next five years, collecting forty-seven cases of death attributed to the *tlahuepuchis.*

Philosophers interested in rationality have often turned to witchcraft for their examples. It has been a fertile ground for speculation about social scientific methodology (cf. Wilson 1970). Our concern is not to survey these responses, but to uncover what is problematic about the examples. What problem does the belief in *tlahuepuchis* present to a working anthropologist? It seems to have something to do with the justification of the belief. The outsider to anthropology might worry that the locals are irrationally clinging to a belief for which there is no evidence. On the contrary, however, only a little bit of the story needs to be told before we see that there is overwhelming evidence for the existence of *tlahuepuchis.* The problem lies in the relationship between the evidence and the belief system. The circumstances under which the infants died are taken to be grounds for belief in *tlahuepuchis.* These are not good grounds, so we think, because the evidence is not sufficiently neutral. The events count as "evidence" only because they fit the theory. Thus, the justification for their belief seems circular. Nutini and Roberts comment on the "self-fulfilling" character of belief in *tlahuepuchis* and take this to be a general characteristic of witchcraft.

> Given the high degree of concomitance between what people believe regarding the tlahuepuchi complex and the physical manifestations associated with it, the system is predictably efficacious despite occasional breakdowns. Epis-

temologically, then, the fact that the bloodsucking event itself, the physical antecedents to it, and the actors' perception of its aftereffects unfold according to the stated ideology is not only psychologically reinforcing, but at the same time lead the experiencing actors immediately involved to color and interpret what *really* happened, along with the entire chain of events, in terms of their a priori knowledge of the system, in terms of what is supposed to have taken place as handed down by tradition. . . . This, of course, is the very nature of any witchcraft or sorcery system. (Nutini and Roberts 1993: 79)

One reason that the belief in *tlahuepuchis,* and perhaps witchcraft in general, seems irrational, then, is that the beliefs seem to violate canons of justification for empirical claims. Beliefs about the world are rationally held when they are based (in the right way) on evidence (of the right kind). In this case, there is a conflict between the local behavior and a norm of rationality.

What is a good anthropologist to do? The locals seem to be ignoring a piece of plain common sense. If they fail to recognize how beliefs are based on evidence, how can any of their factual claims be trusted? Nutini and Roberts do what we have come to expect from anthropologists faced with such a problem. They begin filling in the details about the local system of belief, perception, and inference. Unlike some other groups who believe in witchcraft, the Tlaxcalans clearly distinguish "natural" from "supernatural" entities and causal relations. Not all deaths—not even all infant deaths—are attributed to supernatural agents. The community carefully examines each incident to determine whether it can be explained in natural terms (such as an illness or accident) or whether there are indications of supernatural forces. According to Nutini and Roberts, the persons involved attend carefully to the family and medical history, the position and condition of the body, and the reports of witnesses. Here the Tlaxcalans look for evidence to determine whether a particular infant was killed by a *tlahuepuchi* in a way that is not at all "self-fulfilling" (Nutini and Roberts 1993: 381). It is thus false to say that the Tlaxcalans fail to apportion their beliefs to the evidence. They have quite familiar ways of evaluating empirical beliefs.

On the other hand, the Tlaxcalans do not subject their belief in the existence of *tlahuepuchis* to the same scrutiny. The problem is not that they are ignoring an elementary canon of justification. Rather, they do not apply it systematically. Why is the belief that *tlahuepuchis* exist spared the investigation to which other beliefs are subjected? When Nutini and Roberts consider this question, they turn from the normative account of belief formation to a more descriptive, psychological, account:

Rural Tlaxcalans are conditioned from childhood to believe that there is such a thing as magical causation, that there are supernatural agents that affect directly their actions and lives. From childhood rural Tlaxcalans are directly exposed to inputs and outputs that the local group regards as the action of witchcraft or sorcery. These magical actions are reinforced time and again by the concentrated outbursts of verbal affirmations and elaborations of the people at large. . . . (Nutini and Roberts 1993: 380)

In their full-blown explanation, Nutini and Roberts do not rest content with this simple picture. They appeal to (presumably universal) psychological principles, such as the need to displace guilt (201, 276), belief reinforcing mechanisms (380–81), and rationalization of belief and action (279–80). What is interesting about their interpretation is the way it weaves elements internal to the conceptual scheme of the local group together with elements drawn from Nutini and Roberts's own view of the world.[1]

Such mingling of internal and external elements runs contrary to a popular view of ethnographic interpretation. One might have thought that the job of the ethnographer is to characterize the local worldview. Much ethnography has been conducted on the premise that the ethnographer's job is to present the culture in its own terms. That is, their rituals, public events, individual actions, and the like are to be understood in the way that the locals themselves understand them. Any ideas drawn from the ethnographer's own culture would only distort the interpretation. Whether this kind of ethnography is desirable (or even possible) is, of course, subject to dispute. Nutini and Roberts unambiguously stand opposed to it, and we will join this debate at the appropriate time. For now, it is worth remarking that any attempt to explain away apparent irrationality seems to involve ideas drawn from the interpreter's culture. The ethnographer and her audience believe that *there are no witches* and that *the magic doesn't work*. Indeed, this is what makes ethnographic studies of magic and witchcraft fascinating. The ethnographer needs to explain why the locals *think* that there are witches, why they keep using the magical spells. Thus, the interpretation of magic and witchcraft requires some description and conceptualization in terms drawn from the ethnographer's culture, some description of what is "really" happening. This feature of the interpretation of witchcraft may generalize to all cases of apparent irrationality.

Nutini and Roberts's explanation of why the infants died raises the issue of the relationship between internal and external characterizations of the events quite vividly. It also exposes a new wrinkle. Nutini argues that most of the infants died of asphyxiation. The infants typically die in cold weather, when the mothers are nursing them in bed under heavy blankets. Nutini and Roberts speculate that the mother dozes and unintentionally smothers the child.

---

1. Their strategy for explaining why some apparently empirical beliefs go unexamined is not unique. Horton's (1967; 1982) account of African witchcraft is similar. Where Horton appeals to social properties (the degree to which the society is "open"), Nutini and Roberts appeal to psychological mechanisms.

The infants are usually quite young—a mean age of five and a half months in Nutini's survey—and are unable to wake the mother. This kind of explanation of why the infants die obviously draws on ideas from outside of Tlaxcalan culture. The ethnographer's task is to understand how these events fit into the local belief system. Some pieces already fall into place: the marks on the mother and infant characteristic of the *tlahuepuchis* are easily explained. But the difficulty of constructing an adequate interpretation must not be underestimated. Given Nutini's explanation of the infant deaths, it follows that someone must move the infant from the mother's bed, where it died, to the door. Someone must tamper with the evidence. Who? Why?

According to Nutini and Roberts, the mother moves the infant's body. The other members of the family are (perhaps unwitting) accomplices, insofar as they distort their experiences to fit the expectations about *tlahuepuchis*. How is such tampering consistent with a belief in the existence and efficacy of the *tlahuepuchis?* Here Nutini and Roberts appeal to the functions of the system of belief to rationalize and to assuage feelings of guilt. Even though the mother must in some sense know that her child's death was not caused by a *tlahuepuchi*, she continues to believe in their existence, and apparently comes to believe that her child was a victim. The system of belief serves as a kind of elaborate social vehicle for self-deception.

In the end, we seem to have exchanged one problem of apparent irrationality for another, and this is the further wrinkle of *Bloodsucking Witchcraft*. What was a puzzle about the adequate grounds for belief has become a problem of self-deception. Notice that the latter is genuine irrationality, given Nutini and Roberts's account. Their response to a problem of apparent irrationality is not to describe a tightly sealed rational system. It is a picture of a social system with an elaborate psychological underpinning that permits a certain sort of irrationality to persist. One of the issues we must face, then, is that apparent irrationality may endure our interpretive assaults. Under what conditions may we say that the irrationality is genuine?

2.2 Sati

On September 4, 1987, Roop Kanwar mounted the funeral pyre of her recently deceased husband and was burned to death.

Suicide always skirts the fringes of rationality. While there are fates worse than death, and hence some rational suicides, they always raise questions about the person's motivation. Suicides thus provide easy examples of apparent irrationality. Roop Kanwar's death has much broader implications for this project because it has a social dimension. Her death was a *sati*. In Hindu thought, it has sometimes been deemed appropriate for a wife to immolate herself on the funeral pyre of her husband. Apparently, it was never the norm, but always the

exception (Hawley 1994: 3). The British colonials outlawed *sati,* yet it continued to surface occasionally. In India today, it is the locus of intense debate over
feminism, human rights, and the preservation of traditional Hinduism.

The mythological origins of the practice provide some illumination. "Sati"
is the name of a goddess, the wife of Shiva. Sati sacrificed herself in the fire
when her father insulted Shiva. While this story exhibits ultimate devotion of
the wife to her husband, it is not a model for the Hindu practice of *sati.* Sati's
husband does not die. The models for the practice of *sati* are found in local
mythologies. Small shrines throughout India commemorate purportedly historical *satis.* Typically, each shrine has a myth about a woman with exceptional
moral worth who became *sati* upon the untimely death of her husband. Such
women are said to become divine, and shrines to them are auspicious (Courtright
1994: 30–35). One way to understand *sati,* then, is as the ultimate demonstra-
tion of virtue available to women in this culture.[2] In some versions of Hindu
doctrine, women gain their spiritual merit through their husbands. Women's
status—both socially and in the cycle of reincarnation—is linked to their
husbands. As a widow, a woman loses her property, her social standing, and her
dharma. She does not become a widow, however, until her husband is cremated.
By performing *sati,* the woman never loses her status as a married woman,
confers merit upon her husband, and becomes divine.

The above explanation is a simplified version of a standard maneuver in
the interpretive sciences. To understand such a dramatic piece of behavior, look
inside the culture for myths, self-conceptions, and beliefs that might provide
a model for the motivation. With such material in hand, we can say that, *given*
the beliefs, immolating oneself is the rational (natural, obvious) thing to do. A
closer look, however, reveals that things are not nearly so simple and Roop
Kanwar's *sati* illustrates the hidden complexity. While thousands witnessed her
sati, there was little agreement about what happened. Observers sympathetic
to the practice of *sati* said that she calmly seated herself on the pyre, took her
husband's head in her hands, and submitted to the flames without crying out.
The last they took to be clear evidence of her divinity. Opponents, on the
other hand, said that Roop Kanwar tried several times to escape the flames,
only to be pushed back by her in-laws. They contended that members of her
husband's family, who were acting primarily on economic motives, drugged
her into submission.

The interpretive strategy that appeals to myths, conceptions, and values
relies on a particular description of the events. The description must use terms
appropriate to the conceptions and values employed by the interpretation. It
is thus important to some interpretations that the act is described as a *sati,* not

---

2. As is evident from the discussion below and in section 7.3, this is not the only way
to understand *sati,* nor is it the best.

as a suicide or murder. Careful descriptions of the events do not resolve the dispute among the partisans of different interpretations. Paul Courtright nicely expresses the difficulty facing interpreters:

> If there have been women who entered the fire out of pure devotion and a compelling confidence in the reality of rebirth and the effectiveness of self-sacrifice, these women must indeed be goddesses, worthy to be venerated by the witnessing community. But if such displays of fortitude and devotion are not possible for women on their own (owing to their abject status, to various levels of coercion, or to the fact that no woman in her "right mind" would undertake such an act of self-annihilation), then what they go through is at best suicide. More likely, in fact, it should be construed as murder at the hands of the surrounding mob. The community that venerates the supposed self-immolation of such a sati is engaging in a heinous form of collective self-deception. (Courtright 1994: 29)

The problem of how best to describe this activity might be put, again, in terms of internal and external characterizations. An internal description or explanation appeals to concepts, beliefs, and other motivating factors available to the agents. An explanation in terms of the agent's beliefs and desires is a paradigmatically internal explanation. A description of an event that uses the local conceptions is likewise internal. Internal interpretations, as we have seen, must rely on local descriptions of the events. External descriptions or explanations appeal to factors that are outside of the agents' ken. The hypothesis that a person or group is self-deceived must be external in this sense. This distinction permits us to begin sorting the alternative interpretations of *sati*. The traditionalists want to insist on internal explanations of Roop Kanwar's action. Opponents might concede that Roop Kanwar and her in-laws thought in these terms, yet insist that the event be explained in terms of oppression, coercion, or economics.

Once we recognize the difference between internal and external explanations, some new questions come to the fore. How are the two varieties of explanation/description related? Do internal descriptions always trump external descriptions? Are only the latter truly explanatory? The usual response to problems of apparent irrationality is to start talking about the "meaning" the event has for those involved. That is, we generate a more detailed internal account of the action. It is not obvious that this is always the best strategy. There may be self-deception or some kind of false consciousness involved that an internal account cannot capture. While the criteria for adopting one interpretation over another remain a mystery at this point, the construal of these problems as a choice of interpretation is helpful. Deciding whether the actions are rational or irrational, a striking but intelligible performance or a collective act of self-deception, heroic or appalling, is a matter of choosing the best interpretation.

There is a further aspect to the interpretation of Roop Kanwar's *sati/* suicide/murder that is important for us. We noticed above that the description of the events surrounding Roop Kanwar's death was disputed. The dispute runs deeper than the question of whether Roop Kanwar's action was voluntary or coerced. Whether *sati* is prescribed at all by sacred authority is itself a matter of dispute among Hindu scholars. It is this old dispute—reaching back at least into the nineteenth century (Sharma 1983)—that is now overlain with concerns about the status of women and human rights. Thus, the simple-minded interpretation that views this action as governed by local norms has to be replaced by one that is responsive to this rift among the subjects. The difference is more than a difference in opinion or belief. Competing norms seem to be in play. Roop Kanwar's *sati* might be sanctioned by some local norms and not by others. We thus cannot presuppose that the local system of beliefs and values is univocal. We have to make room for the possibility that there may be conflict among fundamental norms in a community and that the norms themselves may be disputed.

2.3 AZANDE WITCHCRAFT: THREE INTERPRETATIONS

No discussion of apparent irrationality would be complete without mentioning the Azande. The Azande were first studied anthropologically by E. E. Evans-Pritchard. His work became famous among philosophers because he claimed that Azande beliefs were formally inconsistent. There is a long-standing dispute over how to interpret Evans-Pritchard's evidence. The discussion of these alternatives provides a glimpse of the criteria that might be relevant in such choices.

During Evans-Pritchards stay among the Azande, their daily lives were permeated by witchcraft. It was a common topic of conversation, and a person guarded against the effects of witchcraft as a matter of course. Witches, for the Azande, were otherwise ordinary people who had a small blackish substance in their bellies. If a witch harbored some malevolence toward someone, the "soul" (a nonphysical aspect) of the witchcraft would leave the witch and cause the victim to fall ill, and perhaps die. The witch might not even be aware of the evil effects. In addition to illness and death, witchcraft was invoked to partially explain all manner of misfortune, from stubbed toes to failed crops (Evans-Pritchard 1937: 21–26, 33–37).

The identity of the witch causing a particular affliction was traditionally determined by "the poison oracle." A carefully prepared substance called *benge* was administered to a fowl, and a yes-or-no question was put to the oracle. The bird's survival or death constituted the answer. (Whether survival meant an affirmative or negative answer was specified in advance.) After an answer was obtained, the ritual was repeated with another fowl, reversing the question so that the opposite result confirmed the first pronouncement (Evans-Pritchard 1937: 294–96).

When the oracle determined that one person was bewitching another, the prince could authorize retribution. This ranged from a payment to the death of the witch. When the Azande were brought under British rule, the execution of witches was prohibited. During Evans-Pritchard's time, the princes would secretly authorize magical means to kill the witch. Where the accused witch later died, another oracle would determine whether a person's death was the result of vengeance magic. Before colonization, when a witch was executed, the family could demand an autopsy to determine whether justice had really been done. The autopsy consisted in making a slit in the dead person's abdomen and drawing out the intestines. If a blackish substance was found, the person was a witch and had been justly executed. If no "witchcraft substance" was discovered, then the deceased and his or her family were vindicated. The vindication of the family was important because the Azande also held that the witchcraft substance was inherited. Fathers passed it to their sons, and mothers passed it to their daughters (Evans-Pritchard 1937:21–23, 42–44).

Evans-Pritchard identified two contradictions in Azande witchcraft beliefs. He was no passive recorder of ethnographic curiosities. According to his own account, he frequently challenged the Azande to defend their claims about witchcraft. The first contradiction that he put to them involved the heritability of witchcraft. Since witchcraft is inherited, a single positive result should implicate the whole paternal or maternal line of descent. If enough autopsies had a positive result, each Azande would have some ancestor in his father's line or her mother's line who was a proven witch. It follows that all Azande are witches. But the Azande denied that everyone is a witch. Moreover, since not all autopsies have a positive result, they seem to believe this on good evidence. We might express the inconsistent triad of their beliefs as:

1. Every line of same-sex descent has one proven witch.

2. If every line of same-sex descent has one proven witch, then all Azande are witches.

3. Not all Azande are witches.

Evans-Pritchard reported that the Azande refused to draw the contradictory conclusion from (1) and (2), and apparently refused to revise any of their beliefs. He says famously: "Azande see the sense of the argument but they do not accept its conclusions, and it would involve the whole notion of witchcraft in contradiction were they to do so" (Evans-Pritchard 1937: 24).

The second contradiction concerned the use of vengeance magic and the poison oracle to determine the cause of death. The princes sponsored the oracles to determine whether a specific witch was responsible for someone's death. They also authorized the vengeance magic. Both the results of the oracle and the vengeance magic were kept a secret. Not knowing of the vengeance magic, if the intended victim died, his or her kin may suspect witchcraft. The secrecy is thus important, according to Evans-Pritchard, because if the names of those who died from vengeance magic were known, the whole system would collapse:

> If other people were acquainted with the names of those who have fallen victims to avenging magic the whole procedure of vengeance would be exposed as futile. . . . if it were known that the death of a man X had been avenged upon a witch Y then the whole procedure would be reduced to an absurdity because the death of Y is also avenged by his kinsmen upon a witch Z. Some Azande have indeed explained to me their doubts about the honesty of the princes who control the oracles, and a few have seen that their present-day system is fallacious. (Evans-Pritchard 1937: 27)

While Evans-Pritchard is not explicit on the point, the Azande must have believed that a death cannot be the result of both vengeance magic and witchcraft. A contradiction thus arises if the poison oracle pronounces that a death is due to witchcraft at one time and vengeance magic at another.

The contradictions in Azande thought are a particularly vivid form of apparent irrationality. Unlike the examples of the previous two sections, this problem explicitly concerns deductive reasoning. The Azande seem irrational because they assent to the premises and inferences that lead to a contradiction. Yet when presented with the inconsistent beliefs, they are unmoved: "So long therefore as they are able to conform to custom and maintain family honor Azande are not interested in the broader aspects of vengeance in general. They saw the objection when I raised it but they were not incommoded by it" (Evans-Pritchard 1937: 28). Evans-Pritchard's response to this problem was to suppose that the Azande system of belief was, in fact, self-contradictory in the way described. The problem was to explain why the Azande don't recognize the contradiction and how such a fallacious system of belief might be maintained.

We have already seen Evans-Pritchard's claim that the second contradiction is not recognized because the results of the oracles are a secret kept between the prince and the family. Only the princes might see the contradiction. Evans-Pritchard has no explanation of their refusal to be moved by it. Perhaps the explanation would be the same as the first case, where he contends that the Azande's interest in witchcraft is entirely practical: "Azande do not perceive the contradiction as we perceive it because they have no theoretical interest in the subject, and those situations in which they express their beliefs in witchcraft do not force the problem upon them" (Evans-Pritchard 1937: 25). Even with its contradictions, the system of witchcraft belief performs an important function for the Azande. It allows them to explain the misfortunes that afflict individuals. Moreover, it adds a social aspect to the causes of any unfortunate event. The unfortunate event happened to *me* because of someone else's hostility. If the harm is sufficient, the witch might have to be placated (Evans-Pritchard 1937: 85).

Peter Winch was among those who took issue with Evans-Pritchard's resolution of the problem presented by Azande witchcraft. In "Understanding a Primitive Society" (1964), he suggested that Evans-Pritchard missed the point of Azande witchcraft practice. Evans-Pritchard takes "witchcraft" to be an assertion about what exists—a kind of theoretical posit—and the poison oracle to be a way of finding out about such things. These are treated as analogous to the theoretical posits and methods of verification of Western science. Statements about witches and the use of the poison oracle to verify them are taken to be similar to statements about bacteria and the use of microscopes to verify them. Winch claimed that the appearance of irrationality arose out of this mistaken analogy:

> It is noteworthy . . . that the Azande, when the possibility of this contradiction about the inheritance of witchcraft is pointed out to them, do not then come to regard their old beliefs about witchcraft as obsolete. "They have no theoretical interest in the matter." This suggests strongly that the context from which the suggestion about the contradiction is made, the context of our scientific culture, is not on the same level as the context in which the beliefs about witchcraft operate. Zande notions of witchcraft do not constitute a theoretical system in terms of which Azande try to gain a quasi-scientific understanding of the world. (Winch 1964:314–15)

"Well," one wants to ask, "if it is not a theoretical system, then what?" The only proper answer is something like "a witchcraft system." The mistaken analogy between Azande witchcraft and Western science arises, Winch suggests, because Evans-Pritchard was thinking about the relationship between reality and linguistic practice in a particular way. Evans-Pritchard took reality to be something independent of linguistic practice against which any language could be measured. Language gets its sense by referring to real entities. Winch, developing some themes from Wittgenstein, wants to invert the relationship, holding that "what is real and what is unreal shows itself *in* the sense that language has" (Winch 1964: 309).

For the Azande, there is a difference between being a witch and merely being accused of witchcraft. Moreover, there are ways of finding out who is a witch. Witches are thus real and may be discovered. The problem arises when we suppose that the words "real" and "discovery" have a sense that is independent of the role they play in Azande witchcraft practices. We are tempted to treat these notions as analogous to our own. This is to forget, however, that our own conceptions of an independent reality and of its discovery get their sense from scientific practice (Winch 1964: 109). The conception of reality is crucial for both scientific practice and Azande witchcraft. These cultural practices differ, and insofar as they do differ, the cluster of conceptions in the neighborhood of "reality" and "discovery" will have different roles and different contents.

Winch's resolution of the apparent contradictions turns on his attribution of conceptions to the Azande that are different from our own. With respect to the contradictions that arise from the use of vengeance magic, he notes that the Azande have many possible explanations: the person administering the poison is ritually unclean, the oracle is itself the subject of witchcraft, and so on. One might be inclined to say that these explanations are completely ad hoc and serve only to insulate the system from any genuine test.[3] Again, this supposes that questioning an oracle is like testing a scientific hypothesis. It is not—precisely because these explanations of its failure are satisfactory to the Azande. Rather than take these as ad hoc props for inadequate explanations, Winch takes them as evidence that the Azande are not playing the game of explanation, hypothesis, and confirmation at all.

Winch's account of the inconsistency arising out of the heritability of witchcraft is somewhat more mysterious. His point seems to be this. If we take Azande beliefs about witchcraft to be like a scientific theory, then the fact that they entail a contradiction is problematic. But in their thought about witchcraft, the Azande are not attempting to draw out and test consequences. As before, their lack of interest in the consequence hints at a different form of life, not a defective version of our own. Winch does not make any positive suggestions about how we are to understand Azande reasoning about witchcraft, but it seems to amount to a different form of rationality (Winch 1964: 315).

Winch was not alone in suggesting that the contradictions in Azande thought might be resolved by attributing a different form of rationality to them. David Cooper (1975) made the more specific suggestion that the Azande were reasoning with a three-valued logic. Cooper is thus accepting Evans-Pritchard's implicit treatment of Azande witchcraft as a theoretical system. They do not recognize the contradiction because, given their patterns of reasoning, there *is* no contradiction.

A three-valued logic rejects the idea that all propositions are either true or false. Some propositions are of indeterminate truth value, where "indeterminate" is conceived as neither true nor false. The standard connectives of propositional logic can be given new truth tables with these three values. In this case, the problem turns on the conditional. Standard propositional logic holds the conditional to be false when the antecedent is true and the conse-

---

3. Nutini and Roberts's complaint that witchcraft is "self-fulfilling" is similar. See also Horton (1967) and Jarvie and Agassi (1967).

quent false, and true otherwise. This definition can be extended to three truth values as follows (Cooper 1975: 242):

P	Q	P ⊃ Q
T	T	T
T	I	I
T	F	F
I	T	T
I	I	T
I	F	I
F	T	T
F	I	T
F	F	T

The Azande beliefs about the heritability of witchcraft form an apparently inconsistent triad, which we sketched above. The form of these beliefs is:

1. P

2. P ⊃ Q

3. ~Q

If the Azande held all three to be true, they would be affirming a logical contradiction, even under the rules of a three-valued logic. However, if the Azande were using a three-valued logic and regarded one or more of these propositions as indeterminate, they would not have to make the inference that yields the contradiction. Cooper's suggestion is that the Azande regard the first, "Every line of same-sex descent has one proven witch," as indeterminate. They seem to regard the claim that "Not all Azande are witches" as true. According to the relevant row on the truth table (row 4), then, the conditional is indeterminate. No inference to a troublesome conclusion is licensed because the conditional corresponding to modus ponens—((P & (P ⊃ Q)) ⊃ Q)—is indeterminate in this case.

Cooper thus resolves the heritability contradiction by attributing a three-valued logic to the Azande. To make his claim plausible, he has to explain what the local conceptions of these three truth values might be. Following Reichenbach's discussion of the anomalies of quantum mechanics, Cooper takes "indeterminate" to mean "untestable in principle." The Azande might regard "Every line of same-sex descent has one proven witch" as untestable in principle, given their criteria of testing such hypotheses.[4] Cooper is only

---

4. Salmon (1978) rightly takes Cooper to task on this point, arguing that the available evidence about the Azande shows that they do not have a conception of an indeterminate truth value.

speculating about a possible—but interesting—interpretation, so he does not try to substantiate his attributions in detail.

We have, then, three different ways of interpreting the Azande. Our question is how one might choose among them. In this particular case, the choice among alternative interpretations raises issues that will require detailed treatment. First, two of the alternatives reinterpret fundamental conceptions. Winch suggests that our puzzlement arises because we insist on understanding the Azande practices as analogous to scientific ones. Cooper's suggestion, by contrast, is that we are underestimating the scientific sophistication of Azande thought. With typical insightfulness, Winch pinpointed the issue:

> An anthropologist studying such a people wishes to make those beliefs and practices intelligible to himself and his readers. This means presenting an account of them that will somehow satisfy the criteria of rationality demanded by the culture to which he and his readers belong; a culture whose conception of rationality is deeply affected by the achievements and methods of the sciences, and one which treats such things as a belief in magic or the practice of consulting oracles as almost a paradigm of the irrational. (Winch 1964: 307)

Are the interpretations suggested by Winch and Cooper genuine possibilities? That is, is it possible for us to formulate and test the claim that the Azande have a different conception of "reality," "empirical test," or "deductive inference"? Is it even possible to understand such a claim? Problems of apparent irrationality invite such radical changes in our interpretation. Do the criteria for interpretive change preclude some kinds of interpretation from the outset? A popular view is that they do, and in chapter 2, we will examine this position in some detail.

There is a second issue, and it may be seen by contrasting Cooper's and Evans-Pritchard's interpretation of the apparently inconsistent triad. Evans-Pritchard takes the Azande to be using inferential principles much like our own. They make some mistakes, and his task is to explain why they are so unconcerned. Cooper does not take the Azande to be making mistakes—they are properly using a different form of reasoning. The Azande do not have an articulate logical doctrine, nor (so far as I know) any tradition of reasoning about reasoning. One must wonder, then, what it means to say that they are using one kind of logic rather than another. What is the difference between mistakenly using one kind of logic and correctly using a different logic? If we are to adjudicate between Cooper's and Evans-Pritchard's interpretations, we must be able to answer this conceptual question. The problem is quite general. It arises whenever we say that the members of a group are following a rule or established practice. Such attributions require the possibility of mistakes and deviations. Whenever we attribute a rule or practice to a group, we thereby distinguish actions that follow the rule or practice from mistakes and deviations. An alternative interpretation might attribute a different rule or practice, thereby eliminating the "mistakes." Part of the burden of chapter 7 will be to address this thorny issue.

2.4 THE PURRINTON MURDERS

Sometimes we run up against events that are incomprehensible no matter which way we turn. The attempt to understand such an event and our failure can be instructive too. A gruesome example comes from Laurel Thatcher Ulrich, *A Midwife's Tale*. The work is based on the diary of Martha Ballard, a midwife in Southern Maine at the turn of the nineteenth century. Her next-door neighbor, Captain Purrinton, killed virtually his entire family with an ax, then cut his own throat with a razor. Even for us, when such events have a frightening banality, the behavior cries out for explanation. The example is instructive because the historical event is overlain with layers of interpretation. The Purrinton murders inspired Martha Ballard and her community to search for a way to understand the act. We have records of the event and the local attempts to understand it from diaries, newspapers, and sermons preached in the local churches. Ulrich, the historian, interprets these interpretations, and adds a perspective that Martha Ballard and her contemporaries could not have had. In the end, with these interpretations all in place, we seem no nearer to understanding.

Captain Purrinton bought some land near Martha Ballard's homestead in 1803. He cleared it, built a house, and in August 1805, he brought his family upriver from their previous home in Bowdoinham, Maine. Martha Ballard's diary records the neighborly comings and goings of the Purrinton family in the spring of 1806. The entry for July 9, 1806 records the horrible event:

> Clear and warm. My Husband & I were awake at 3 hour this morning by Mrs. Heartwel and Gillbard who brot us the horrible tydings that Captain Puringon had murdered all his famely Except his son James who must have shared the same fate had he not been so fortunate as to make his Escape after an attempt was made to take his life. He was wounded with an ax. He fled in his shirt only and alarmed Mr Wiman of the horrid scein who immediately ran to [Martha Ballard's] son Johnathans [house]. The two went to house where the horrid scein was perpetrated. My son went in and found a Candle, which he lit and to his great surprise said Purington, his wife, & six Children Corps! and Martha [one of Purrinton's[5] daughters] he perceived had life

---

5. The text of Martha Ballard's diary is inconsistent in its spelling of proper names. I have followed Ulrich by systematizing the name in the text, but leaving the diary spelling as is.

remaining who was removd to his house. Surgical aid was immediately Calld and she remains alive as yet. My husband went and returned before sunrise when after taking a little food he and I went to the house there to behold the most shocking scein that was Ever seen in this part of the world. May an infinitely good God grant that we may all take a suitable notis of this horrid deed, learn wisdom therefrom. (Ulrich 1990: 291–92)

Martha Ballard's diary records no further attempt to understand Captain Purrinton's behavior. The newspaper and sermons, however, leave us records of such speculation by the wider community. On Ulrich's reading, the local interpreters tried to put Purrinton's act into the context of theological debates.

As in much of New England, the first settlers in this part of Maine were predominantly Calvinist. The key doctrine of the traditional Congregationalist church was predestination. At the moment of creation, God determined who would be saved and who would be damned. During the "great awakening" in the mid-eighteenth century, this doctrine was challenged by creeds emphasizing the role of an individual's free choice in salvation. In Martha Ballard's community, this doctrinal challenge to Calvinism was reflected in the growth of non-Congregational churches. Among these, the Universalists seemed the most threatening. The Universalists preached universal salvation. All souls are saved. Captain Purrinton, it was reported, had dabbled in heterodox creeds, including Universalism. This background concern about the threat to Congregationalism and the fact about Captain Purrinton's non-Congregational inclinations formed the basis for some local interpretations of the murder-suicide. In a sermon preached ten days after the murders, the Congregationalist preacher Timothy Meritt argued:

> You all know, that for some years past, he [Purrinton] has professed to believe firmly that all mankind, immediately upon leaving the body, go to a state of the most perfect rest and enjoyment: and to my own certain knowledge he denied the doctrine of a day of judgment and retribution. Of course it was no question with him whether his family were regenerate, or born again, or in other words, whether they were prepared for so sudden a remove from this world. It was, therefore, natural, and what any one would do under the same circumstances, to endeavour to prevent the anticipated trouble of his family, and make them all for ever happy. There is every reason to believe that this was his real motive. (Ulrich 1990: 298–99)

Here we have the central elements of interpretation: an event which cries out to be explained, an explanation which draws together various, apparently disparate, facts and makes the event seem natural, rational, even inevitable. It is transformed from an unintelligible act to "what anyone would do under the same circumstances." Seen against the background of doctrinal dissent and politico-theological disputes, it is also a profoundly *interested* interpretation.

Merritt is self-consciously using the Purrinton murders as an object lesson in the dangers of heterodox creeds.

The interests lying behind Merritt's interpretation of the Purrinton murders are further highlighted by the alternative that Ulrich tentatively floats. Of Merritt's interpretation, she says:

> Merritt's method transcends his content. Interpreted with a different set of first principles, the Purrinton murders yield different lessons. Suppose the overarching concern was not the relation of believers and God but that of men and women. A feminist gloss on the murders might read: a man murdered his wife and children: in the patriarchal family all members are subject to the will of the father. (Ulrich 1990: 301)

Ulrich goes on to elaborate and support this understanding of the event. She calls different bits of evidence into service—that Purrinton left a suicide note providing for his sons, but not his wife or daughters; that his daughter had reportedly found the note, and according to a newspaper account, this sparked the mayhem, and so on. This kind of concern about gender relations is distinctly modern, and Ulrich herself highlighted the role of this interest in the interpretation by juxtaposing it with Merritt's interpretation.

What are we to make of these interests that seem to drive the interpretation? Are they blinders that can or ought to be removed in a fully justified understanding of the event? Or are they more deeply connected to the very activity of interpretations? These broad questions will occupy us below. For the moment, notice how the different interests generate widely different interpretations. Moreover, both the interpreters inside the community and the historian, looking in from the outside, generate interpretations that meet their interests. Thus we should not suppose unreflectively that the self-interpretations of a group are somehow disinterested or value free in a way that makes them different from the biased interpretations of an outsider. Indeed, this example makes it seem as if interpretation is biased always and everywhere.

For our purposes, the final point of interest in the Purrinton murders is the radical underdetermination of their interpretation. After sketching a feminist interpretation, Ulrich washes her hands of the entire matter:

> What James Purrinton believed or felt we will never know. He may have been propelled by Universalism, by an overweening patriarchy, by an unresolvable conflict between family obligation and personal despair—or by other motives we can only dimly glimpse. . . . After all the lessons are neatly argued, we are left with a dark apocalyptic vision and an inexplicable slaughter. (Ulrich 1990: 303)

There is an ambiguity to her assertion that "we will never know." To be sure, the historical record is always fragmented. There may not be enough remaining evidence to discern the reasons, feelings, or beliefs that motivated the agents. In this case, however, our failure to understand may be of a different, deeper kind. There may be no satisfactory explanation that appeals to reasons, feelings, or beliefs. After all, this man killed his wife and five of his children with an *ax*. Those who have wielded an ax know that this would make an awkward weapon. It is not likely to kill in one blow. Theological ideas or structural facts about gender relations seem far too anemic to explain an ax-murder. After reading Ulrich, I am left with the suspicion that neither a structural nor a rationalizing account will provide an adequate interpretation. In the jargon of our times, *this guy's a wacko*. This intuition of mine and its rationale will itself be grist for the mill as we continue our investigation.

2.5 PARAMETERS OF THE PROBLEM

In all of these cases, we are faced with a choice of possible interpretations. At the most general level then, the methodological question is this: By what criteria do we prefer one interpretation over another? This question arises whenever we are engaged in interpretation. It becomes profound when we are faced with a problem of apparent irrationality. In such a case, our going interpretation is incapable of providing further guidance. The behavior seems irrational precisely because nothing in our interpretation permits us to make sense of it. Moreover, since rationality (in its various guises) is deeply embedded in an interpretation, new evidence is unlikely to help. What is needed are some new attributions to the agents, a rereading of their utterances, a reinterpretation of their conceptions. For example, one of the questions about *sati* is whether the *sati* herself is motivated by religious feeling or whether she is drugged or otherwise coerced. Each of these makes a hypothesis about the mental state of the *sati*. Similarly, in the case of Azande witchcraft, the interpretations differed over what logical principles the Azande might or might not be following. What makes problems of apparent irrationality particularly deep is that they open the possibility of radical changes in our interpretation. Part of the methodological problem, then, is how such changes might be justified. The leading question of our inquiry is thus:

1.   What are the criteria for preferring one interpretation to another?

As mentioned above, the problems of apparent irrationality open the question of whether the people under study are operating with the same criteria of rational inference or good reasons for action. We also need to ask, then:

2.   Is it possible to prefer an interpretation that attributes to the interpretees standards of rationality different from the interpreter's own?

The notion of "different standards of rationality" requires careful treatment. Several points arise from the foregoing examples. First, while all of the above examples involve rationality, they do so in different ways. The Azande example appears, at least at first, to be a puzzle about reasoning. They refuse to recognize an inference. The rural Tlaxcala belief in *tlahuepuchis* also involves inference, insofar as we understand their belief as an inference from evidence. Both examples concern reasoning, the first deductive and the second inductive. In these cases, we can see what "standards of reasoning" might be like. They would be rules governing inductive or deductive inference, or (perhaps equivalently) criteria for distinguishing good inferences from bad ones.

A different kind of "standard of rationality" is at issue in the Purrinton murders and *sati*. The initial questions in these cases are about rational behavior (one might say, *practical* reasoning). Alternative interpretations attribute different motivations. The interpreter claims that such-and-such beliefs, goals, feelings, etc. were behind the action. It is crucial to the attribution to claim that the beliefs, goals, feelings, and so on were the agent's *reasons*. In such an explanation, it is essential that the agent took the beliefs, feelings, goals, etc. as a reason for the action. Hence, whenever we make claims about the motivation for action, we are implicitly relying on criteria that separate reasons from nonreasons, and perhaps good reasons from bad reasons. Moreover, it is possible for a person to act on certain grounds and for those grounds to be bad reasons for the action. Indeed, perhaps there are actions like Capt. Purrinton's for which there could be no good reasons, whatever the actual motivation. It is thus appropriate to include reasons for action within the scope of "standards of rationality."

What do "standards of rationality" preclude? If we take an action or inference to be irrational, we may be making one of several claims. It might be that the agent had a motive, and took it to be a reason for acting, but was wrong in so doing. This is perhaps the best way to understand the Purrinton example. In this case, we take the agent to be making a mistake: There is some criterion by which such-and-such motivations count as good reasons for a given action, and the agent's actual motives fell outside of its range. A parallel story may be told about inferential irrationality. In such a case, presumably, the criteria are (in some sense) the agent's own. This is not the case where we think that an action arises through self-deception. In this kind of case, the "real" motivations are hidden from the agent herself. She thinks that she has such-and-such reasons for acting, but the real reasons lie elsewhere. In a case of self-deception, the agent might reject what we take to be the "real" reasons. A deeper kind of irrationality would be action without motive at all. Actions of a drugged or deranged person might fit this description. We do not understand this kind of behavior because, in an important sense, there isn't anything to understand about it. Such action is beyond the pale of rationality insofar as it is no longer involves good or bad reasons, since the person lacks reasons entirely.

The first two questions of our inquiry press some other issues to the fore. The words "good" and "bad" have played an important role in our analysis thus far. They highlight the fact that rationality is a *normative* matter, a matter of value and evaluation. Any interpretation of belief or behavior will invoke some criteria or standards of rationality. Insofar as it does this, an interpretation is evaluative. If we interpret one belief as implied by another, we are saying that someone who believes the second *ought* to believe the first. Similarly, when we rationalize an action by saying that it followed from certain motivations, we are claiming that anyone in a similar situation with similar motives *ought* to act in a similar way. Therefore, any interpretation must attribute norms to the agents and it must evaluate their actions in the light of those norms.

Social scientists have been reluctant to evaluate the belief and behavior of their subjects, so the above argument is likely to meet some resistance. Moral judgment about other cultures has been associated with colonialism and racism, and social scientists are rightly wary. To defuse this concern, we must recognize that the evaluations in question appeal to the *local* norms and values. When an interpretation uses some criteria of rationality, these criteria are attributed to the people being interpreted. They are *their* criteria, not ours. If we are to understand a person's action in terms of such-and-such motives, the motives have to be *his* motives and their relationship to the action has to be one that *he* would recognize. A similar point could be made about the attribution of norms of deductive or inductive inference. The sense in which interpretation is always normative and evaluative, then, is that it attributes values or norms to the people being interpreted, and according to these norms, inference and behavior may be said to be good or bad. We therefore need to answer the question:

3.   What are the epistemic grounds for claiming that a person or group adheres to a norm, rule, or standard?

The normative character of rationality thus adds an important dimension to our problem space.

As already remarked, some philosophers of social science contend that the normative character of rationality limits interpretive change. For various reasons, philosophers have held that an adequate interpretation must find the subjects to have norms and values (norms of reasoning in particular) similar to the interpreter's own. This is a principle that would dictate the preference of some interpretations over others, and thus is directly relevant to our leading question. While we will take up this question explicitly (in section 3.2), the examples of this chapter show that it is part of a larger issue. The question may be put this way: Is it necessary, or even possible, to characterize the rules, criteria, or standards internally, that is, from the standpoint of the locals?

We have again come upon the problematic relationship between "internal" and "external." An internal evaluation would invoke the local standards, while an external evaluation would use the interpreter's standards (assuming that the interpreter is not a member of the local community). We noticed this difference earlier in the examples of rural Tlaxcalan belief in *tlahuepuchis, sati,* and the Purrinton murders. In these examples, the suggested interpretation mixed internal and external descriptions of the phenomena, not just evaluations. Our main problem concerns interpretive change. This suggests a way of making the question explicit. The general problem is how such disparate interpretive claims fit together.

4. Under what conditions are interpretations that include descriptions and evaluations from the subjects' point of view to be preferred over interpretations that employ ideas or evidence to which the subjects do not have access?

It could be that external descriptions or evaluations always take precedence over internal. Or it could be the other way around. More likely, each has precedence in a particular domain. If this last option is the case, we will need a systematic way to identify the conditions under which one sort of description or explanation takes precedence over the other.

These four questions will form the backbone of our inquiry. The first is the most important and the most general. The latter three spell out aspects of this question that arise when it is considered in the context of the problem of apparent irrationality. We will concentrate on the question of interpretive change as it arises in this context. Finding answers to the latter three is at least a minimal criterion for adequately answering the first.

CHAPTER 3

Interpretive Change

Apparent irrationality is a problem that historians, anthropologists, sociologists, psychologists, and other interpreters may encounter. For these inquirers, the problem is to assemble a plausible account of the problematic phenomenon. The previous chapter showed that the problem of apparent irrationality has a significant methodological dimension. The deep problem is to identify criteria for interpretive change. These hard cases vividly illustrate the prerequisites that candidate criteria must satisfy. Satisfactory criteria will have to provide plausible answers to the four questions raised in section 2.5 and permit adequate interpretations of cases like those briefly described in sections 2.1 through 2.4. While the leading question of interpretive change has received little direct attention from philosophers, the latter three questions are familiar from long-standing discussions in the philosophy of language and the philosophy of social science. The object of this chapter will be to distill criteria of interpretive change from the existing literature.

3.1 CHARITY

Wittgenstein's suggestion that the woodcutters might mean something differ-ent by "more" and "less" captures an intuition about apparent irrationality. The whole muddle might simply be the result of bad translation. Solid translation is the foundation of the interpretive enterprise. Good translators try to avoid making their subjects appear irrational. They do so by choosing charitable over uncharitable translations. One might therefore suppose that the problems can-vased in chapter 2 arise from an overly literal translation. Perhaps the Tlaxcalans do not believe that *tlahuepuchis* "exist" in the same sense that trees, chickens, and ordinary people exist. A more charitable translation of what they say about *tlahuepuchis* might read some of their talk as figurative, metaphorical, or symbolic. This line of thought suggests that our leading question might be misleading. Question (1) asks for general principles governing interpretive change. Perhaps we only need criteria for choosing the best translation. Once we have a definitive translation, the rest of the interpretation will fall into place according to the usual canons of scientific inquiry.

The idea that the problems of apparent irrationality arise from bad translation has its best foothold in problems of deductive irrationality, such as the issues surrounding Azande witchcraft. The appearance of irrationality depends on the translation of the logical particles. The difference between Evans-Pritchard's translation and David Cooper's was precisely whether the English particle "if . . . then" could appropriately render certain Zande words. In the spirit of charity, one might adopt Quine's suggestion that "fair translation preserves logical laws" (Quine 1960: 59). Or, more discursively:

> *Principle of Logical Charity:* Translate the logical apparatus of the language (sentential connectives, quantifiers, and pronouns) in a way that preserves valid inferences and consistency. Choose the translation that attributes fewer invalid inferences or inconsistencies to the translatees.

One rationale for this principle arises out of Quine's conception of translation.[1] According to Quine, the field linguist must begin by associating whole sentences of the foreign language with whole sentences of the home language. When confronting a language for the first time, the translator has only whole utterances to work with. She has not yet broken these whole utterances into their component words. The first step of a translation, then, must be to pair whole sentences of the two languages. The obvious sentences with which to begin are highly "observational," that is, where the local affirmation and denial of these sentences is strongly correlated with changes in the immediate context.[2] Noticing the conditions under which a sentence is affirmed or denied gives the linguist a rough idea of its truth conditions. One way of grounding a translation, then, is to pair sentences of the two languages when their truth conditions converge. So, a sentence of the local language is approximately translated by a sentence of the home language when they are affirmed and denied under the same conditions.

Logical particles ("and," "or," "if . . . then") join whole sentences. Epistemologically, according to Quine, they are thus some of the first candidates for word-to-word translation. Candidate words for logical particles join two sentences into one larger string. To identify the logical particle, the linguist ascertains how assent and dissent to the component sentences determine assent or

---

1. There are other rationales for this principle, too. Arguments found in Hollis (1967a; 1967b), Lukes (1967), and Davidson (1984) are scouted below.

2. The notion of observation and its relationship to word meaning will receive detailed treatment in section 6.1.

dissent to the whole. For example, the interpreter has evidence that a particle is functioning like "and" when the locals assent to the whole only if they assent to each component alone. Conversely, that the locals continue to assent to the whole even when they dissent from one component is evidence against translating the particle as "and" (Quine 1960: section 13; 1986: 82).

Given Quine's argument, the inconsistent triad of Azande beliefs about witchcraft is excellent, even definitive, evidence of bad translation. Recall (section 2.3) that the Azande assent to the following three sentences:

1. Every line of same-sex descent has one proven witch.

2. If every line of same-sex descent has one proven witch, then all Azande are witches.

3. Not all Azande are witches.

Here we have evidence that the Azande words are not well translated by "if . . . then," "not," or "all." Since the Azande (presumably) assent to all three (as expressed in Zande), and since the three are jointly inconsistent, the Azande words must not be functioning in the way their English-language translations do. The apparent irrationality is thus evidence that the translator has made a mistake of some kind. Of course, mistranslation into "if . . . then," "all," or "not" is not the only possibility—it could be that there is an unnoticed ambiguity in one of the other words. Whatever the explanation, an affirmation of inconsistency is evidence that the translation is mistaken. Quine notes:

> This approach ill accords with a doctrine of "prelogical mentality." To take the extreme case, let us suppose that certain natives are said to accept as true certain sentences translatable in the form 'p and not p'. Now this claim is absurd under our semantic criteria. And, not to be dogmatic about them, what criteria might one prefer? Wanton translation can make natives sound as queer as one pleases. Better translation imposes our logic upon them, and would beg the question of prelogicality if there were a question to beg. (Quine 1960: 58)

The principle of logical charity demands that a good translation must preserve the laws of logic. If a foreign language has logical particles at all, they will be recognizable as the connectives and quantifiers of classical logic.[3] When turned

---

3. Strictly speaking, Quine's argument applies only to propositional logic. On his view, the attribution of quantificational logic to a language community is indeterminate (see Quine 1960: 61–72). Davidson, by contrast, regards attributing the whole of first-order logic to a language as a necessary condition of translation (Davidson 1973/1984; Davidson 1974/1984). This difference in opinion is irrelevant to the argument below.

into an answer to the leading question of our inquiry, then, this principle would require that we always prefer the interpretation that attributes classical logic to the locals.

If we try to apply the principle of logical charity indiscriminately, some difficulties arise. First, it appears to preclude any disputes in the philosophy of logic. For instance, it is impossible for a philosopher to even raise the question of whether there might be a third truth value. While Quine embraced this consequence, saying that when a logician "tries to deny the doctrine, he only changes the subject" (Quine 1986: 81), it seems to be an absurd consequence in the light of actual disputes about nonstandard logics. Moreover, unrestricted application of the principle seems to eliminate the possibility of logical mistakes (cf. Cooper 1975; Gellner 1970; Morton 1970). Thus, when a student denies a tautology on a logic exam, the principle appears to demand that we reinterpret the marks on the page. Charitably interpreted, all logic exams rate As. I suggest that we recant this boon to our students. Finally, Henderson has pointed out that this sort of logical charity is at odds with robust empirical research into human reasoning (Henderson 1993: 64–68). A variety of studies have shown that humans have predictable limitations to their ability to maintain consistent belief sets and make strong inductive generalizations. Where we have reason to expect such lapses, blind adherence to the principle of logical charity seems inappropriate.

These criticisms presume that the principle of logical charity applies at all stages of the inquiry. If the principle were modified in a way that was sensitive to the growing strength of the translation, these objections would lose their force. At the very outset of a translation, the principle of logical charity seems a fair rule of thumb (cf. Henderson 1993). When the translator is just beginning, oddity is quite likely to be the fault of the translation. In *Word and Object*, Quine primarily employs the maxim that "fair translation preserves logical laws" in the opening stages of translation. Matters are different when the translation is mature and broadly based. At that point, if the native speakers persisted in following invalid forms of inference or refrained from assenting to simple logical truths, the problem could not be dissolved so lightly. Where they persisted, some kind of trade-off would have to be made. The interpreter would have to decide whether (i) the translation is appropriate, but the speaker is mistaken, or (ii) the translation needs to be modified. By itself, logical charity does not help decide between (i) and (ii). And once the interpreter has made this choice (on whatever ground), logical charity provides no support for the further interpretive choices.

The principle of logical charity, therefore, is not a good principle of interpretive change. Insofar as it is plausible at all, it simply advises that we attribute logical oddity to error in the translation when it is most likely that the error is the translator's (cf. Henderson 1993: ch. 3). Where the translator's error is rather unlikely, it gives no grounds for choice among alternatives. The problem of apparent irrationality requires the interpreter to distinguish among logical mistakes (perhaps pervasive ones), genuine differences between the interpreter and the locals, and simple mistranslations. The principle of logical charity provides no help in making these choices. Finally, as formulated above, the principle is too narrow. It applies only to problems where the apparent irrationality is deductive. Questions about inductive justification or reasons for action are left untouched. The principle of logical charity is therefore an inadequate criterion of interpretive change.

The demand that translation preserve valid inferences and consistency can be seen as a special case of the demand that a charitable translation make the utterances of one's interlocutors come out true. Donald Davidson thus took interpretive charity to be the "methodological advice to interpret in a way that optimizes agreement" (Davidson 1984: 137, cf. 169). While optimizing agreement sounds like a noble goal, what is to constitute optimal agreement is obscure. It cannot require us to maximize agreement between interpreter and interpretees. Since there are an indefinite number of possible sentences to which we might assent or dissent, little sense is to be made of counting agreements. Better sense is to be made, perhaps, of minimizing disagreement. This suggests a second principle of choice among interpretations:

> *Principle of Minimal Disagreement:* Choose the translation that minimizes disagreement between the interpreter and native speakers.

The principle of minimal disagreement already corrects what was, from the perspective of this inquiry, an important defect of logical charity. The principle of minimal disagreement applies to all of the examples canvased in chapter 1, not only to cases of apparent deductive irrationality. However, the principle of minimal disagreement as conceived here addresses the problems of apparent irrationality by determining the choice of translation. Its application to the real variety of cases is thus not entirely straightforward.

Consider those cases where apparent irrationality involves nondeductive reasons for belief. Here, the disagreement between interpreter and interpretees concerns justification or evidence. In a felicitous case, the interpreter would be presented with (i) the verbal formulation of the belief to be justified, (ii) the verbal formulation of another belief (or perhaps a set of beliefs), and (iii) the assertion that the second is good or sufficient reason for the first. Apparent inductive irrationality would manifest itself as disagreement over (ii), and the principle of minimal disagreement counsels us to translate words that indicate nondeductive epistemic support in ways that maximize agreement with the interpreter's inductive practices. Complexities arise when one or more of the elements above are not verbally formulated. In such a case, the interpreter has to attribute the belief or conception of a good reason to the locals on the basis of some other evidence. Since the relationship between nonverbal evidence and utterances is not a mater of translation, the principle of minimal disagreement gives no guidance in such cases. It must be supplemented by some other epistemic principles. (The character of these principles need not detain us for reasons that will become clear below.) Once augmented, however, the principle would apply to the translation of the attributed beliefs.

Similar gymnastics are required to apply the principle of minimal disagreement to problems of behavioral irrationality. Here the rationality of an action is in question. While actions are not subject to translation, their description is crucial to their rationality or irrationality. The rationality of *sati,* for example, depends partly on whether it is described as self-sacrifice, suicide, or murder. Presumably, what is to be translated is a description of the action acceptable to the agent.[4] The agent's reason is a little more tractable. It divides into two translatable parts: a set of propositional attitudes and the claim that these are good or sufficient reasons for the action (as described). The complexities about inarticulate belief, mentioned above, arise here too. Supposing that they can be finessed, the principle of minimal disagreement applies. It would advise the interpreter to choose a translation of the reasons, the relation of being a good reason, and the description of the action with which she agrees.

The principle of minimal disagreement can therefore provide guidance in the various problems of apparent irrationality. Yet, why should lack of disagreement be a criterion of choice among translations? Don't we *expect* disagreement among cultures? In the face of these questions, the principle of minimal disagreement is made plausible by some powerful arguments. Davidson's well-known arguments for charity were foreshadowed by Martin Hollis and Steven Lukes (Davidson 1984; Hollis 1967a; Hollis 1967b; Lukes 1967). These three authors used two distinct arguments to support the principle of minimal disagreement. We will call them the "belief-meaning circle" and the "massive error" arguments.

The circle of belief and meaning is a predicament endemic to the practice of translation. Davidson plausibly maintains that an adequate theory of interpretation must apply to those situations where the interpreter knows nothing of the language or culture of the people she is trying to understand (Davidson 1984: 128, 143). When concerned with the epistemology of translation, we cannot rely on an interpreter's previous knowledge of some parts of the language, since this would beg the question at issue. (This is what Quine and Davidson mean by "radical" translation or interpretation.) This requirement seems to result in a conundrum:

> A central source of trouble is the way beliefs and meanings conspire to account for utterances. A speaker who holds a sentence true on an occasion

---

4. This too is problematic, since the agent might be self-deceived or have a vested interest in a particular description. This point is discussed further in chapters 5 and 7.

does so in part because of what he means, or would mean, by an utterance of that sentence, and in part because of what he believes. If all we have to go on is the fact of honest utterance, we cannot infer the belief without knowing the meaning, and have no chance of inferring the meaning without the belief. (Davidson 1984: 142)

Suppose, for example, that a completely naive interpreter hears a local utter the sentence "Coca-Cola is a fine soft drink," and let us suppose that the speaker takes this sentence to be true. There are three interdependent features of this event. First, the speaker has some beliefs in virtue of which he holds the sentence true. Second, there is the meaning of the sentence. Finally, there is the speaker's act of uttering the sentence. The three features are interdependent insofar as the speaker uttered the sentence and holds it true in virtue of what it means and what he believes. The interpreter, by hypothesis, knows nothing of the speaker's beliefs nor the meaning of the sentence. Her evidence is "the fact of honest utterance." It seems that she can go no farther. Any guess about the meaning of the sentence will depend on attributions of belief to the speaker; and any attributions of belief would depend on knowledge of the speaker's language. The interdependence of belief and meaning seems to block interpretation from the outset.

The principle of minimal disagreement makes interpretation possible by permitting the interpreter to break into the interdependence of belief and meaning. In this context, Davidson presents the principle as the policy ". . . to choose truth conditions that do as well as possible in making speakers hold sentences true when (according to the theory and the theory builder's view of the facts) those sentences are true" (Davidson 1984: 152). The principle of minimal disagreement and "the fact of honest utterance" give the interpreter a way of fixing on the speaker's belief. The speaker has uttered "Coca-Cola is a fine soft drink" under certain conditions (say, sweating profusely on a hot day, reaching into his pocket and counting his change . . .). The principle says that the speaker's beliefs should be interpreted so as to make them true (by the interpreter's lights). The speaker's true beliefs now limit the possibilities for translation of his utterances. Whatever reading the interpreter gives to the sentence, it has to be one that would produce the "fact of honest utterance" when accompanied by the true beliefs.[5]

The principle of minimal disagreement is thus supposed to be a necessary precondition for interpretation: we could not break into the circle of belief and meaning without it. The argument, however, turns on the claim that the principle is the *only* way to break the interdependence of belief and meaning. Davidson argues (correctly, I think) that a naive interpreter cannot have a

---

5. While this presentation has relied on Davidson, Hollis presented very similar, if somewhat less elaborated, arguments (Hollis 1967a: 265–66; Hollis 1982: 73).

sufficiently detailed knowledge of the speakers' intentional states to fix belief independently. The other alternative—that we get a fix on the sentence independently of beliefs—has not yet been so thoroughly treated. There is a way to exploit this alternative. To do so, the edge of our wedge must be inserted into a tiny crack in the argument. Davidson begins by characterizing the speech event as an utterance. This is correct, since a truly naive interpreter has no way of knowing whether the speaker's vocalization is a sentence, a sentence fragment, or a belch. The tripartite analysis of the event, however, requires that the utterance be a sentence (or other expression of a proposition). It must do so, for only sentences or propositions can be the object of the attitude of "holding true" which is central to the analysis. Davidson slips between these two without comment, but as we will see, the difference between utterances and sentences is important in this context.

A sentence is a grammatical unit. It is a string of morphemes conforming to the syntactic and semantic regularities of the language. An utterance is a vocalization, or, by polite convention, a string of written characters. To distill sentences from utterances, a linguist has to apply the techniques of phonological and morphological analysis and devise a grammar. This is profoundly nontrivial, both linguistically and epistemologically. The key question is whether such analyses could be performed without knowing the meaning of the morphemes. If Davidson's interpreter is to rely on "the attitude of holding a sentence to be true," Davidson has to hold that a phonetic, morphological, and syntactic analysis can be performed without semantic knowledge. It seems to me that an adequate syntactic analysis would be impossible without knowledge of meaning, but this is not the place to develop the claim. Since there are well-known morphological techniques for conducting such analyses—e.g., Zelig Harris's (1960)—we may grant that a naive interpreter could get a reasonable first pass.

Davidson's naive interpreter then, must already have a good guess about how to segment the utterances into morphemes. The interpreter must also have a rudimentary syntax in virtue of which she can assemble the morphemes into sentences. The morphological and syntactic analyses will typically depend on utterances drawn from a variety of speakers under a range of circumstances. The interpreter therefore already has a source of evidence that is independent of the particular speaker in question. The speaker, in choosing to express himself in this way, has drawn on the public language, using words that are already in common currency. This gives the interpreter a grip on meaning that is independent of the particular speaker's beliefs. The interpreter's hypotheses about the speaker's belief must be consistent with the public use of the words uttered. Thus, Davidson's own analysis of the interdependence of belief and meaning presupposes that the interpreter has evidence that will allow her to break the interdependence without the principle of minimal disagreement.

The circle of belief and meaning is a real problem for any interpreter. The principle that we choose the translation that minimizes disagreement does serve to fix belief, and hence break the circle. It is not, however, the only way. Standard techniques of morphological analysis give the translator an independent grip on the public language, making her translation relatively independent of what a particular speaker might mean or believe. Therefore, the circle of belief and meaning does not show that the principle minimal disagreement is a necessary condition of interpretation.

The second argument for the principle of minimal disagreement concerns the very possibility of error. It seems prima facie likely that a cross-cultural investigation will uncover differences in belief. We thus expect the best translation to portray the locals and the interpreter as differing on many points. From the interpreter's point of view, the locals will be wrong about some things. Davidson (1984: 168–69), Hollis (1967b: 34), and Lukes (1967: 261) argued that the very possibility of identifying error depends on the principle of minimal disagreement. A belief can be erroneous insofar has it has a determinate content. An erroneous belief must be about something, and it must falsely attribute some property or relation to that thing. For these authors, belief content is holistic. That is, a belief is about a particular object because the belief plays a role in a pattern of beliefs. Suppose we attribute the belief that "the Coca-Cola Company is bankrupt" to someone. In so doing, we are implicitly relying on related attributions as well: that there is such a thing as the Coca-Cola Company; that companies are the kinds of thing that may or may not have money; and so on. The instant belief might be erroneous. But, claim these authors, if the whole network of beliefs is false, our confidence that we have correctly identified what these beliefs are about is undermined. If many of the person's beliefs about the Coca-Cola Company turned out to be false, we would lose our grip on the claim that the person had beliefs about the Coca-Cola Company at all. The greater the overlap between the interpreter's beliefs and those of her subjects', the sharper the disagreement (Davidson 1984: 168). From these considerations, Davidson concludes that:

> What makes interpretation possible, then, is the fact that we can dismiss a priori the chance of massive error. A theory of interpretation cannot be correct that makes a man assent to very many false sentences: it must generally be the case that a sentence is true when a speaker holds it to be. . . . So in the end what must be counted in favor of a method of interpretation is that it puts the interpreter in general agreement with the speaker: according to the method, the speaker holds a sentence true under specified conditions, and those conditions obtain, in the opinion of the interpreter, just when the speaker holds the sentence to be true. (Davidson 1984: 169)

The principle of minimal disagreement is thus supposed to follow from the very possibility of ascribing an erroneous belief to someone. Given the holism of belief content, massive error is impossible, and if massive error is impossible, the principle is correct.

The quotation above contains an ambiguity that is important to all versions of the massive error argument. The first sentence claims that "What makes interpretation *possible* . . . is that we can dismiss a priori the chance of massive error" (my emphasis). That is, it is impossible for a community of speakers to have beliefs or make utterances that were mostly false. This fact makes translation possible. The impossibility of massive error is a precondition of translation. In the subsequent remarks, a somewhat different claim is advanced. To say "in the end, what must be counted in favor of a method of interpretation is that it puts the interpreter in general agreement with the speaker" is to employ the principle of charity, not as a *precondition*, but as a way of *adjudicating* among competing interpretations. That is, given two translations, we are to choose the one that puts the speaker and interpreter "in general agreement."[6] The massive error argument thus depends on this pair of subprinciples. We will analyze them in turn.

Davidson expresses the first subprinciple in his claim that "it must generally be the case that a sentence is true when a speaker holds it to be" (Davidson 1984: 169). Bjorn Ramberg has made the best suggestion for unpacking this idea. On his understanding, Davidson's "principle of charity" demands only that we presume that the speaker knows his own language, and hence can reliably judge when a sentence may be appropriately uttered (Ramberg 1989: 76). That is just to say that we must take the language users to be competent speakers of their own language. Having "mostly true" beliefs thus amounts to being correct about when the utterance of a sentence is appropriate. This is a plausible candidate for a precondition of translation, which we may formulate as follows:

> *Presumption of Semantic Competence:* The speakers of the language are competent to judge whether the utterance of a sentence is appropriate.

The first part of the argument from massive error establishes this subprinciple. To suppose that a speaker had massively erroneous beliefs would be to interpret his utterances as almost always false. Such a person would typically be uttering sentences in contexts where they were inappropriate, and it would be difficult to consider such a speaker competent. A reasonable presupposition of any translation enterprise, however, is that one's informants are competent users of their own language. It is therefore a presupposition of the enterprise of translation that the speakers are competent to judge whether the utterance of a sentence is appropriate. Given this presupposition, no acceptable translation can represent the informants as widely mistaken (by their own lights) about the truth of their utterances.

---

6. This point is also made in Bar-On and Risjord (1992).

The argument from massive error has a broader conclusion than the simple observation that we must presume our informants to be competent. It is supposed to justify the claim that the interpreter must minimize disagreement between herself and her informants. Toward this end, the argument mobilizes a second subprinciple. It demands that we choose the translation that puts fewer false utterances into the mouths of the locals. To distinguish this version we might formulate it this way:

> *Criterion of Adjudication:* Given two translations of the local language, choose the one that makes fewer local beliefs and utterances false (by the interpreter's lights).

This criterion is one way of fulfilling the demand that interpretation theories be testable. We might suppose that a translation theory makes predictions of a sort. Where the interpreter takes a sentence of her own language, S, to be true, she may predict that the locals will take the translation of that sentence, $S^\star$, to be true as well. If they do not regard $S^\star$ to be true under the conditions she takes S to be true, then her prediction fails. Given this kind of prediction, the criterion is no more than the demand that we reject translations that are disconfirmed.

What is the relationship between these two subprinciples and the ultimate conclusion that the best interpretation will minimize disagreement between interpreter and interpretees? One might suppose that, given the way in which Davidson presents them, the criterion of adjudication is supposed to follow from the presumption of semantic competence. This would be a mistake, since we can easily imagine the second true and the first false. Suppose an interpreter has two translations and neither attributes widespread error. Such a situation satisfies the presumption of semantic competence. Yet, it is consistent to suppose that one of these translations attributes to the speakers many more errors than the other. Even fully competent speakers make mistakes. In the right epistemic conditions, they might make many mistakes. Why choose the translation that attributes fewer errors? Since both interpretations satisfy the presumption of semantic competence, it is consistent to suppose that the interpretation attributing more errors is the better one. Therefore, since there are conditions under which we could affirm the presumption of semantic competence and deny the criterion of adjudication, the first does not follow from the second.

Since the criterion of adjudication does not follow from the presumption of semantic competence, there must be independent motivation for the criterion. The criterion of adjudication is an instance of a common strategy for testing theories. The interpretation theory makes predictions, and it is falsified insofar as these predictions fail. While I have no complaint about the general strategy, the proposed application to interpretation is problematic. The root of the problem is that treating a false belief or utterance as a disconfirmation of the interpretation is an oversimplification. One can imagine cases where the criterion of adjudication would be positively misleading. The interpretation of a language is notoriously malleable. Given one reading of the local sentences, we can always construct another that is consistent with the recorded utterances. One way to minimize disagreement is to reinterpret sentences that are purportedly about spirits, witches, and so on as being "really" about something more mundane—say, intestinal gas, headaches, ringing in the ears, or fireflies. Such reinterpretations will always attribute more truths to the natives, and hence always be better according to the criterion. This seems quite absurd (Bar-On and Risjord 1992: 174–75; Henderson 1993: 34ff; Macdonald and Pettit 1981). The argument from the impossibility of massive error, then, does not support the principle of minimal disagreement. At best, these reflections support the claim that we must presuppose our interlocutors to be competent language users. The larger argument requires the criterion of adjudication, and we have lately seen reasons why it is unsatisfactory as a general criterion for interpretive choice. Indeed, the considerations that weigh against the criterion of adjudication also cast doubt on the principle of minimal disagreement itself. There might be conditions where an interpreter has good grounds for choosing the interpretation that does not minimize disagreement.

The upshot of these arguments is that the problems of apparent irrationality cannot be resolved by the charitable principles. Their distinctive feature is that they guide interpretive choice by constraining the possible translations. The above arguments have shown that there may be conditions where translations that maximize agreement are trumped by other considerations. To substantiate Wittgenstein's intuition that his woodcutters might mean something different by "more" and "less," we have to look beyond translation to the wider interpretation of their behavior.

3.2 HUMANITY

Wittgenstein does not just claim that the woodcutters mean something different by their words. He suggests that they have a "quite different system of payment." It seems sensible to ask how the woodcutters sustain their economy, if they sell by area covered, not volume. Answers to this question ought to influence our choice of translation. Davidson and the others who have taken charity as a principle of adjudication among interpretations never intended for the principle of minimal disagreement to be the sole criterion of choice. What we want is agreement of the right sort under the right circumstances (Davidson 1984: xvii). Spelling this out has led the proponents to talk about "the principle of humanity." The principle of humanity was originally devised by Richard Grandy as an alternative to Quine's version of the principle of charity

(Grandy 1973). Grandy tried to derive the principle from the purpose of translation. The purpose, Grandy suggests, is "to enable the translator to make the best possible predictions and to offer the best possible explanations of the behavior of the translatee" (Grandy 1973: 442). Our choice of interpretation, then, is based on its explanatory power.

As a first pass, it is helpful to see the demand for explanatory power as a modification of the criterion of adjudication. Like the criterion of adjudication, the demand for explanation presupposes that at least two interpretive options are available. The criterion bases choice of translation on its predictive power. When the interpreter holds a sentence, S, to be true, the translation predicts that the locals will hold the translation, S*, true. The criterion of adjudication requires that we choose the translation with the fewest false predictions. The demand for explanation simply expands the range of relevant predictions. We are now permitted to predict that they will hold a sentence false under conditions where we would hold it true. Thus, disagreement between interpreter and interpretees counts against the interpretation only if the interpreter cannot explain why the interpretees hold the sentences false.

In one of its most common formulations, the "principle of humanity" is a demand that we minimize inexplicable disagreement (Macdonald and Pettit 1981: 29). We might state it this way:

> *Principle of Humanity:* Choose the interpretation that maximizes agreement and minimizes unexplained disagreement between interpreter and interpretees.

The principle is asymmetric because it treats true beliefs or utterances differently from false ones. Disagreement needs explanation. Where local beliefs and utterances are false by the interpreter's lights, or when their beliefs or utterances are irrational in the context of their other beliefs, the better interpretation will explain why the beliefs are held. If true and rational belief is really *explained* at all,[7] it is explained as the rational consequence of the facts and their other beliefs.

Why should we suppose that false belief or utterance is to be explained in a way different from true belief? Hollis, one of the strongest proponents of asymmetry, has argued in this way:

---

7. Whether true belief is explained depends on the conception of explanation adopted. Those who take explanation to be necessarily causal will not take true and rational belief to be explained. Here the asymmetry holds between explanations and interpretations (e.g., Macdonald and Pettit 1981). Alternatively, if rationalizing explanations are admitted, the asymmetry is between rationalizing and causal explanation (e.g., Hollis 1982). These differences among proponents of a principle of humanity are not relevant to the arguments below.

The asymmetry in explanation . . . arises because beliefs are woven into a
system by actor's beliefs about their own beliefs. These are the actors' own
reasons for belief and so their own explanations of why they believe what
they do. Schematically someone, who cites p as his reason for believing q,
believes not only p and q but also that p is a good enough reason to believe
q. One of the enquirer's tasks is to discover these connections, not merely
because his list of actors' beliefs will be incomplete without them, but also
because his list must add up to a system. But he must also produce his own
explanation of why the actors believe what they believe. In so doing, he
cannot fail to endorse or reject the actors' own reasons or, where the actors
are not of one mind, to side with some against others. (Hollis 1982: 77)

Hollis is right to stress that the interpreter's list of the agents' beliefs (as well
as their values, desires, aspirations, aversions, intentions, and so on) must add
up to a system. An interpreter who wishes to fully understand must think
about the reasons the locals have for their beliefs and actions. This requires the
interpreter to attribute some criteria of rationality to the locals, criteria according to which one kind of belief will count as a good reason for an action
or another belief.

Hollis distills the asymmetry of explanation out of the attribution of
criteria of rationality to the native speakers. It emerges from a tension between
the interpreter's explanation of the local belief, and the locals' own understanding of their reasons for belief. The interpreter will explain a belief or action
by citing some other beliefs (desires, and so on) and asserting that the latter
are taken by the locals to be a reason for the former. There are two alternatives.
Either these criteria of rationality are the same as the interpreter's or they are
different. This is the sense in which the interpreter must endorse or reject the
locals' own reasons. If their criteria are the same as the interpreter's, then the
locals hold their beliefs (or act) for good reasons (according to the interpreter's
criteria). If the criteria are different, then the locals hold their beliefs (or act)
for bad reasons (according to the interpreter's criteria). The asymmetry of
evaluation, according to Hollis, forces an asymmetry of explanation. That a
belief is true and rationally held is sufficient for understanding why the agent
holds it. Where a belief is not held for good reason, some explaining needs to
be done.

One may object to the above argument on the grounds that the interpreter's
endorsement of the local criteria of rationality is irrelevant. The question of
good and bad reasons for belief concerns only the local criteria of rationality.
Where the agent had such and such beliefs and values, and where these are
locally considered to be sufficient reasons for belief or action, the belief (or
action) is rational. It is also thereby explained: the agents believe (or do) such-
and-such because they have these beliefs (etc.) and such beliefs (etc.) are taken
by them to be sufficient. Where the agent is mistaken or irrational by *local*

standards, a different explanation is needed. Whether the local standards are the same as the interpreter's standards does not seem to figure in the account. Whether or not the interpreter endorses them, some criteria of rationality need to be attributed to the locals. Once identified, the local criteria figure in the explanation of both rational and irrational belief (and action). While true, the fact that the interpreter's criteria of rationality may match the locals' seems irrelevant to the question of symmetry.

The asymmetry built into this principle of humanity is the assumption that false belief or irrational action (or belief) requires special treatment. Only *disagreement* needs explanation. These are the facts that might count against the interpretation and thereby need to be explained away. Another sort of motivation, then, for the principle of humanity is drawn from the same intuition that motivated the charitable principles: the best interpretation ought to ensure some kind of agreement between the interpreter and the interpretees. Grandy's original demand for explanation captured this intuition. When looking for a model of the beliefs and desires of the agents, Grandy suggested that "we use ourselves in order to arrive at the prediction: we consider what we should do if we had the relevant beliefs and desires" (Grandy 1973: 443). The consequence is a "pragmatic constraint" on interpretation: "that the imputed pattern of relations among beliefs, desires, and the world be as similar to our own as possible" (Grandy 1973: 443). Rationality has to do with the pattern of relations among our beliefs, desires, and the world. By requiring that we attribute a pattern of belief similar to our own, Grandy is requiring that we treat our interlocutors as rational in our sense of "rational." Of course, perfect rationality is an impossible goal. Grandy proposes to fill the gap with explanations. Again, the demand for agreement produces an asymmetry of explanation.

Why must we suppose that the interpreter's pattern of beliefs, desires, and so on is in any way similar to the locals'? The question of similarity becomes quite vivid when we reconsider the examples of *sati* and the Purrinton murders. These cases are problematic because it is very difficult to see how any of the plausible motivations could have been a good reason for acting. Even if I held the suggested beliefs, I am not sure that *I* would jump into a flaming pyre. While I can imagine having the relevant beliefs, I cannot imagine having a faith that strong. Given my own history and predilections, it is simply impossible for me to model such action by looking to my own case.

Grandy was not concerned to argue for his claim about similarity, since the goals of his essay lay elsewhere. Others have picked up this question and provided some very powerful arguments. These philosophers, who David Cooper first called "neo-rationalists" (1985–86), want to show that the interpreter must presume substantial overlap in principles of rationality between herself and her interpretees. I have elsewhere called this the "congruence thesis" (Risjord

1993). There have been two[8] lines of argument for this thesis (cf. Cooper 1985–86: 54–55).

In their contributions to a 1967 symposium, Hollis and Lukes developed the first argument for congruence. Hollis argued as follows. If the natives have different concepts of truth, coherence, or rational interdependence of beliefs, then the interpreter has to know them prior to interpreting the natives' language. This is because the native principles will be needed for the interpreter's attributions of belief and meaning. Prior to the interpretation of the native language and the discovery of the native principles or concepts, only her own principles are available to the interpreter. If the interpreter's principles of rationality are used to justify the attributions of belief and meaning, then any native principles of rationality different from the interpreter's principles could not be discovered. They would be inconsistent with the interpreter's grounds for attributing beliefs, concepts, and principles to the natives. Hollis concludes that "if anthropology is to be possible, I have argued, the natives must share our concepts of truth, coherence, and rational interdependence of beliefs" (Hollis 1967a: 218).[9]

The presuppositions of Hollis's argument are similar to the foundationalist theory of epistemological justification.[10] According to a foundationalist, justification is a relation of linear dependence. Where a belief, P, is justified by Q, the subsequent justifications of Q cannot ultimately return to P. Justifications form a chain where prior elements are typically more certain or probable than the elements that depend on them. The important feature of foundationalism in this context is that when some belief is undermined (say, by new evidence), all of the beliefs that depend on it are undermined as well. Hollis's argument, then, is that criteria of rationality play a foundational role in the justification of all the interpreter's attributions. If they are undermined, then the whole structure is undermined. No foundationalist believes, of course, that when a fundamental belief is undermined, we are left helpless. The structure of our belief may be shored up by finding a replacement or making other suitable adjustments.

To get Hollis's argument off the ground, we must make a distinction between the interpreter's norms of rationality and the local norms of rational-

---

8. A third motivation for the congruence thesis will be discussed at the end of section 7.1. That argument emphasizes the evaluative character of claims about rationality, and supports Habermas's contention that interpretation requires the interpreter to take a position on her subjects' justification of their actions.

9. Compare Lukes: "It follows that if S [the culture under study] has a language, it must, minimally, possess criteria of truth (as correspondence to reality) and logic, which we share with it and which simply *are* criteria of rationality" (1967: 210).

10. While he never put the point in these terms, he seemed conscious of the analogy. See Hollis (1982: 73–74).

ity. The interpreter's norms are those found in her culture and presumably are binding on the interpreter as she does her work. The local norms are those attributed to the subjects by the interpreter, the norms that are presumably binding on them. These norms systematize their beliefs, values, actions, and so on. The conclusion of Hollis's argument is that the interpreter's norms and the local norms must be presumed to converge (at least in large part). On pain of begging the question, we must presume at the outset that there is a distinction, even if this distinction is shown to be merely verbal. Hollis's argument is dubious, however, if we keep this distinction clearly in mind throughout his argument.

Suppose the interpreter begins with the hypothesis that the locals share her conception of a good reason. At this point in the investigation, then, there is a hypothesized correspondence between the interpreter's and the locals' conceptions. Hollis claims that the interpreter is not able to revise the hypothesis at a later point in the investigation because any revision would be inconsistent with the going interpretation. Notice, however, that such a revision would not involve the norms of rationality binding on the interpreter. It requires only hypotheses about the local principles. Even if the hypothesized conception is inconsistent with the interpreter's, there is no conflict because the conception is attributed to the locals and binding only on them. The revision is thus consistent with the interpreter's principles. The new hypothesis would presumably be inconsistent with the previously attributed conceptions. This inconsistency is not a problem because the old hypothesis is being replaced. Revising a fundamental hypothesis—and a principle of rationality is certainly fundamental—will no doubt require significant revision of the interpretation. Such revision may be difficult, but we have been given no reason to think it is impossible. If it is possible, then Hollis's argument for congruence fails.

There is a second line of argumentation for the congruence thesis presented by Michael Root (1986) and by Macdonald and Pettit (1981). These authors draw heavily on Davidson's ideas in semantics and action theory, going beyond his claims about charity. Root argues (1986: 278–79) that the congruence thesis follows from two features of interpretation. First, interpretation is normative. Our discussion has already made this apparent, although the character and ramifications of this normativity have not yet been explored. For the purposes of Root's argument, it is sufficient to note that interpretation is normative because norms of rationality guide hypotheses about local belief and meaning. Second, interpretation is "constitutive" in the sense that the norms of rationality constitute what a rational agent might be. They constrain the application of the concept of a rational agent. Putting these two points together, we may say that the natives must be bound by norms of rationality insofar as the interpreter understands them to be rational agents.

On first look, this conclusion appears to establish everything the neo-rationalists wanted. However, there is a subtle difference between the congruence thesis and the claim that the natives must be bound by norms of rationality insofar as the interpreter understands them to be rational agents. Root concludes that "the norms that guide an interpreter in describing an agent's actions reflect the norms that guide the agent in performing the actions" (1986: 283). This is what we have called the congruence thesis. The normative and constitutive character of interpretation only requires that some norms of rationality bind both interpreter and locals. The normative and constitutive character of interpretation does not, by itself, require that the norms be the same. The principles of rationality guiding the locals in their speech, belief, and behavior might be different from those that guide the interpreter. Some additional premise is therefore necessary to show that the norms governing the interpreter's theory formation must be the same as those binding on the locals. Root's argument fills the gap by relying on an ambiguity in the phrase "the norms that guide an interpreter." On one reading, these are the norms binding on the interpreter. In an obvious sense, they must guide the interpreter. The interpreter's work will also be guided by norms that she has attributed to the locals. When she explains their belief and behavior, the explanation will rely on the attribution of certain norms to them. Given hypotheses about these norms, the interpreter will make some attributions of belief and meaning and rule out others. Thus, these norms also guide the interpreter's theory. It does not follow, however, that the two sets of norms must be the same. Root's argument for congruence thus simply conflates the interpreter's and the (hypothesized) local norms of rationality.

Neither argument for the necessity of congruence between the interpreter's and the locals' norms of rationality is sound. These arguments have been the most powerful and persuasive in the literature. Their demise undermines a common presupposition about interpretation. Proponents of explanatory criteria for interpretive change have wanted to emphasize the continuity between the "principle of charity" (however it is construed) and the principle of humanity (Davidson 1984: xvii; Macdonald and Pettit 1981: 32). In the end, explanatory principles are supposed to preserve some central domain of agreement between the interpreter and interpretees. As we have seen, this motivation underwrites the asymmetry of explanation. If we reject the idea that a principle of interpretive change must preserve or guarantee some agreement, the problematic of interpretive change is radically altered.

3.3 EXPLANATORY COHERENCE

Proponents of the principle of humanity have rightly emphasized three points. First, like all theorizing, interpretation is systematic. Interpretive claims do not stand or fall individually. Each claim gains plausibility insofar as it is woven into a satisfactory cluster of interpretive hypotheses. Second, the systematicity of an interpretation is at least partly constituted by relationships of explanation. At least some interpretive claims earn their place in the interpretation because they explain a phenomenon. Finally, principles of rationality are crucial to the systematicity of interpretation. This is what makes interpretation different from other sorts of theorizing. In the asymmetric conception of interpretation produced by the principle of humanity, explanation and rationality worked independently to bind interpretive claims together. Each was given its own domain. The parts of the interpretation that concerned true and rational belief were made systematic by principles of rationality. Those that concerned false or irrational belief were united by explanation.

The obvious alternative to the asymmetric principle of humanity is a symmetrical explanatory principle. A symmetrical explanatory criterion of interpretive change would explain both rational and irrational belief or action, true and false utterance. In the current literature, a good example of a symmetrical criterion is Henderson's "principle of explanation" (Henderson 1993: 75–76):

> *Principle of Explanation*: Interpret so as to attribute explicable beliefs and actions to one's subjects.

If, as the previous section has argued, there is no reason to treat true and rational belief differently from false or irrational belief, then the principle of humanity collapses into the principle of explanation. However, because it was forged in a somewhat different context, Henderson's principle of explanation does not address the issue of interpretive change. We need to reformulate the principle so that it provides a criterion of interpretive change.

Let us begin by considering the way in which explanation makes an interpretation systematic. The term "system" captures the fact that elements of a theory or interpretation are interrelated. Thus to ask what makes a theory systematic is to ask what makes it coherent. Minimally, a coherent theory is logically consistent. It may not contain or entail any contradictions. More substantively, in a coherent theory each claim bears some relationship to the others in virtue of which they form a whole. Entailment would be one such relationship. For instance, consider the following sets of propositions:

a. $\{P, Q, P \text{ if and only if } Q\}$

b. $\{P, Q, \text{If } P, \text{then } Q\}$

c. $\{P, Q, R\}$

Each of these is coherent in the minimal sense of being consistent. Sets (*a*) and (*b*) are more coherent than (*c*), since each of their members either entails or is entailed by some others. Set (*a*) is more coherent than (*b*) as well. In both (*a*) and (*b*), the proposition Q is entailed by the other two propositions. In (*a*), both propositions P and Q are entailed by the other two propositions. Moreover, each is necessary for the entailment of the other (in conjunction with "P if and only if Q"). Thus, (a) is more coherent than (b) insofar as there is a greater number of entailment relations among its members.

A symmetrical principle of explanation is concerned, not with sets of propositions made coherent by entailment, but with interpretations made coherent by explanation.[11] While interpretations have not been conceptualized in this way, this sort of view has been explored in epistemology and the philosophy of natural science. This "explanatory coherence" view takes coherence to be the basis of a theory of justification, and explanation as the relationship that constitutes the coherence of belief (Harman 1973; Harman 1986; Lycan 1988; Thagard 1978; Thagard 1992). Like other coherence epistemologies (e.g., BonJour 1985), explanatory coherence denies that a special realm of experience is the basis for all knowledge. In principle, every belief is revisable in the light of other beliefs or experiences. A belief is justified if it coheres with a system of belief. And roughly, a belief coheres with a system of belief if it either explains or is explained by some other belief in the system. There is thus precedent for combining explanation and coherence in our understanding of human knowledge. What no one has recognized is that it might be particularly helpful in resolving some long-standing problems in the philosophy of social science.

What would interpretations look like if explanations made them systematic? Following the analogy with the explanatory coherence theory of justification, we may say that an interpretation is coherent insofar as each element either explains or is explained by some other interpretive claim. The phrase "interpretive claim" needs to be understood broadly, since interpretations cover such a wide variety of phenomena. An interpreter may make claims about the psychological states of the locals (beliefs, desires, wishes, ambitions, dislikes, sensitivities, etc.), their values, their language (including the syntax, semantics, phonology, morphology, and pragmatics), their economy, their religion and ritual life, their social organization, their political structure, and so on. While any particular interpreter will focus on some aspect of this whole, there is no limit on the way in which she may draw on other aspects of the culture to help understand her area of investigation. An "interpretive claim," then, will be any claim that an interpreter makes about the subjects of her inquiry.

The most articulate analysis of explanatory coherence available is found in Thagard's *Conceptual Revolutions* (1992). Thagard presents seven principles of

---

11. If all explanations are deductions, then these are equivalent. For the purposes of this section, we need to remain neutral on the question of how best to understand explanation. The adequacy of a hypothetico-deductive conception of explanation will be briefly assessed in section 4.1, below.

explanatory coherence and implements them with a computational model. The successful application of this model to cases of theory change is a compelling argument in favor of his analysis and an important confirmation of the explanatory coherence approach. The analysis of explanatory coherence on which we will rely will be broadly consonant with Thagard's. Painting with a somewhat broader brush, we may begin by pointing out that if explanation makes an interpretation systematic, then an interpretive claim will have one of four explanatory roles:

> *Explanans.* The claim explains, or is part of the explanation of, some other claim.

> *Explanandum.* The claim is explained by one or more other claims.

> *Explanans and explanandum.* The claim is explained by another and is in turn part of the explanation of a third.

> *Neither explanans nor explanandum.* The claim is neither explained by another nor is part of the explanation of any other claim.

One of Thagard's important points is that these roles contribute differently to the overall coherence of the interpretation. Some explanatory roles contribute to the coherence of the interpretation more strongly than others. Moreover, some explanatory relationships—for instance, competition among explanans—can reduce the coherence of an interpretation.[12]

The final category of interpretive claim, those that neither explain nor are explained, might seem a bit strange. These claims have no explanatory role at all, so why include them in the interpretation? There are two reasons, one theoretical and the other practical. First, if we simply ignored such claims because they did not fit into the interpretation, interpretive coherence would be far too easy to achieve. An interpreter could have an unassailable theory with exactly three claims, each of which explains and is explained by one other. Data that conflict with any of the three could simply be ignored. Proponents of explanatory coherence have thus insisted that observations retain some degree of acceptability even if they are neither explained nor explanatory (Lycan 1988; Thagard 1992). Second, the dynamics of interpretation are central to our problem. As the interpreter increases her understanding of the culture under study, she can explain more of their speech and behavior.

---

12. Some differences between this analysis of explanatory coherence and Thagard's are motivated by my use of the erotetic model of explanation. In particular, the analysis of explanatory conflict presented in chapter 5 differs significantly from Thagard's. These and other differences will become clear as we proceed.

That means that there was something left unexplained in the earlier interpretations. This suggests that we should treat the unexplained claims as part of the
earlier interpretation. An interpreter cannot simply ignore whole segments of
the lives of the interpretees. If the interpreter is aware that the locals say or
do something, then the claim that they said it or that they did it is a part of
the interpretation. Such claims are far from trivial. Not only are they fresh
input to the interpretation, they will have to be given an interpretive gloss.
Utterances must be translated; actions must be described. The bare events
taking place around the interpreter thus enter the interpretation fully clothed.
While we should expect every real-world interpretation to have some unexplained and unexplanatory claims, diminishing the number of such claims
marks a strong increase in explanatory coherence.

Closely related to the claims that neither explain nor are explanatory are
those that get explained without themselves doing any explanatory work.
Descriptions (in the interpreter's language) of what the locals do will generally
fall into this category. These play a role in interpretation analogous to the role
played by experience in epistemology. This is not to suggest that they are
somehow basic, certain, or indisputable. An interpreter may decide that the
best way to systematize her interpretation is to explain away some of these.
That is, they are explained as mistakes by the agent. Unlike the claims that are
neither explained nor explanatory, the existence of this sort of claim does not
count strongly against the overall coherence of an interpretation. On the
contrary, the capacity of an interpretation to explain what the locals say and
do strengthens the interpretation. In the remaining two roles, the claim figures
as explanans. Claims that both get explained and are part of another explanation are the most helpful from the standpoint of coherence. Claims of this sort
unify the interpretation. On the other hand, claims that merely explain, without themselves being explained, disrupt coherence of an interpretation. No
doubt, some unexplained explainers must be tolerated. But if there are too
many, the interpretation begins to look ad hoc. If one interpretation has more
unexplained explainers than another, then, the first is prima facie less coherent
than the second.

The foregoing discussion suggests that Henderson's principle of explanation can be transformed into a criterion of interpretive change by adding the
notion of relative coherence. What makes one interpretation better than another is that it is more coherent, and explanation is the relationship that
constitutes coherence. In principle form:

> *Principle of Explanatory Coherence:* Choose the interpretation with the most
> explanatory coherence.

According to the earlier discussion, one interpretation, *A*, has more explanatory coherence than another, *B*, when

1. *A* has fewer claims that are neither explained nor explanatory than *B*.

2. *A* has fewer claims that explain without themselves being explained (unexplained explainers) than *B*.

The order is important because, as suggested above, claims that have no explanatory role at all count more strongly against the coherence of an interpretation than those that do some explanatory work.[13]

Like Henderson's principle of explanation, the principle of explanatory coherence is symmetrical. It presupposes that true and rational beliefs and utterances stand in as much need of explanation as false or irrational beliefs and utterances do. Any symmetrical criterion of interpretive change faces an important challenge. Criteria of rationality appear to be central to interpretation. Yet, principles of rationality are generally taken to be either not explanatory at all or explanatory in a distinctive way. This is what motivated the asymmetry of the principle of humanity. A symmetrical principle forces these two parts of the interpretation together, and requires claims about rationality to be explanatory. There are two ways to address the challenge. One might, as Henderson (1993) does, diminish the role of normative principles in interpretation. His principle of explanation assimilates the charitable principles and the principle of humanity insofar as these are plausible. In so doing he strips away any imposition of a "normatively derived structure" (1993: 58–60). He also argues against rationalizing explanations (1993: chs. 5, 6). In Henderson's view, normative principles are not explanatory, and therefore a fully explanatory conception of interpretation must minimize their role.

The alternative to Henderson's strategy is to hold that criteria of rationality are explanatory. This is the approach I have taken (Risjord 1993; Risjord 1998). It has a prima facie advantage over Henderson's approach insofar as it captures the apparent contribution that local standards of rationality make to the coherence of an interpretation. Section 3.2 distinguished between the standards of rationality binding on the interpreter and the standards binding on the persons being interpreted. These are important for coherence in different ways. For theories of all types, standards of rationality binding on the interpreter determine the coherence of the theory. Physicists and anthropologists alike rely on criteria of rationality to choose theories and test hypotheses. Indeed, this investigation is an inquiry into the standards of rationality binding on interpreters. Where the objects of the theory are *merely* objects, the standards of rationality binding on

---

13. This sketch simplifies Thagard's analysis of explanatory coherence. He counts explanantia of different but analogous explanations as cohering with each other. Also, various explanantia of a single explanation cohere with each other. These seem like useful additions to the concept of explanatory coherence, but they are ignored here because they play no significant role in the problems with which we will be concerned.

the interpreter are the only standards relevant to the coherence of the theory. Interpretations, by contrast, take the thought and behavior of human beings as their subject. Unlike the objects of the physicists' inquiry, these subjects are themselves subject to standards of rationality. The subjects make their own thought and behavior systematic. An interpretation must capture this local systematicity. Therefore, the standards of rationality binding on the agents must also help determine the coherence of the interpretation.

To see the prima facie explanatory importance of criteria of rationality, let us return to the problem of Azande witchcraft. Cooper suggested that the Azande employ a three-valued logic. The claim is that they are not moved to revise their triad of beliefs because, according to their criteria, there is no inconsistency among them. The appearance of inconsistency depends on an inference not licensed by the Azande criteria of inference. A three-valued logic provides the local grounds for inference and judgments of consistency. Azande logic would thus be part of the way they make their beliefs systematic. Presumably, this is indicative of how all criteria of rationality integrate local beliefs and actions. According to the local criteria, some actions or beliefs are rational (right, good, acceptable, etc.) and others are not. Beliefs, judgments, evaluations, and actions are subject to reasons, and the criteria of rationality determines, in general, what is to count as a reason. Let us assume for the moment that, contra Henderson, this can be understood as an explanation. (This question will be addressed in chapter 7.) The apparently inconsistent triad will not be the only thing that Cooper's hypothesis explains. Presumably, it will account for a whole range of inferences that the Azande make, as well as those they refuse to make. If this can count as an explanation, and I think it does, it would substantially contribute to the coherence of the interpretation. Indeed, any criterion of rationality attributed to a group would have very broad explanatory import and therefore contribute to the coherence of the interpretation.

The principle of explanatory coherence will be understood in this work as giving rationality an explanatory role. The principle preserves explanatory symmetry by treating appeals to rationality as explanatory in the same sense that arational claims are explanatory. This gambit places a large burden on the conception of explanation. Henderson and others have argued persuasively that claims about rationality could not be explanatory. Our work on this will begin in the next chapter with a close analysis of the demands that the problem of apparent irrationality makes on the conception of explanation. The normativity of criteria of rationality is only one of the things that a concept of explanation has to accommodate. The final three chapters will be devoted to showing how the model of explanation articulated in chapter 4 can encompass all of the kinds of claims that interpreters need to make. The main argument in favor of the principle of explanatory coherence will be that it is the central tenet of a view that provides a comprehensive understanding of interpretive change in the face of apparent irrationality.

This chapter has sketched rough answers to two of the questions from section 2.5. The principle of explanatory coherence is a criterion for preferring one interpretation to another. It thus provides a direct answer to the leading question of our inquiry. The foregoing discussion of the principle, however, shows that this tentative answer raises a host of difficulties of its own. If a conception of explanation can be developed that addresses these problems, we will have an answer to the second question: Is it possible to prefer an interpretation that attributes to the interpretees standards of rationality different from the interpreter's own? This chapter has argued that an interpretation does not have to assume that the interpreter's and the interpretees' standards of rationality are the same. It has suggested that standards of rationality are explanatory claims made by the interpreter about her subjects, and that such claims are justified insofar as they are part of the interpretation with the most explanatory coherence. Under these conditions, it would be possible to prefer an interpretation that both gives rationality an explanatory role and attributes to the locals criteria of rationality that diverge from the interpreter's.

CHAPTER 4

Explanation

Explanation plays a central part in unraveling the problems of apparent irrationality. The puzzles arise when we are faced with belief or behavior that seems unintelligible. Their resolution requires some change in our interpretation that produces a satisfactory explanation. The explanatory coherence criterion of interpretive change enshrines this idea and sheds the unnecessary limitations of the principles of charity, humanity, and related criteria. There are many philosophers of social science, backed by a venerable tradition, who will refuse to follow this line of thought any further. They will insist that framing the problem in terms of explanation makes it hopelessly unsolvable. Explanation is a powerful tool in the natural sciences, such philosophers would argue, but when applied to human problems, explanation is impotent. The problems of apparent irrationality involve precisely those aspects of human life that explanation cannot touch: meanings, values, reasons, feelings, ideas, and purposes. These may be *understood*, and interpretive understanding is not explanatory.

The foregoing argument represents one side of a debate that has been the backbone of philosophical discussion about the social sciences and humanities. The other side has generally insisted on the hegemony of the natural, "hard" sciences. If some area of discourse falls outside of the paradigm given by the ever-successful natural sciences, then so much the worse for it. Chatting about reasons, norms, and so on may be edifying, but it is no gateway to knowledge. As important as this debate has been for the philosophy of the social sciences, it is completely wrong headed.

The explanation/understanding debate ultimately turns on what an "explanation" is taken to be. All parties have drawn their conception of explanation from the natural sciences. When that sort of explanation fails to work in the social sciences (or some of them), there are two reactions. The failure of explanation is either celebrated as showing the uniqueness of the human studies or decried as failure of the human studies to be fully "scientific." I would like to suggest that the order of inquiry in the traditional debate is backward. The upshot of chapters 1 and 2 is that problems of apparent irrationality, and the more general question of interpretive change, demand explanations. Therefore, the question should be: What concept of explanation (if any) is adequate to the demands of the problem of apparent irrationality and the question of interpretive change? The first section of this chapter will articulate criteria of adequacy based on the problem of apparent irrationality. We will then turn to the question of what, if any, form of explanation might satisfy these criteria. The second and third sections will develop the most promising candidate, the "why-question," or "erotetic" model of explanation. Showing that this model does satisfy the criteria is a large task. Each of the next three chapters will be devoted to one aspect of the problem. If the erotetic model of explanation satisfies the criteria of section 4.1, the explanation/understanding debate will have been radically transformed. We will return to the debate in the conclusion, showing how the explanatory coherence criterion of interpretive change, armed with the erotetic model of explanation, profoundly alters the explanation/understanding debate.

4.1 CRITERIA OF ADEQUACY

What must an explanation be like if it is to be the engine of interpretive change? Chapter 3 argued that the principle of explanatory coherence is the best guide to interpretive change. Any concept of explanation thus has to suit the principle of explanatory coherence. Fortified with a model of explanation, the principle, in turn, has to address the problems of apparent irrationality in a satisfying way. The problems of apparent irrationality and the question of interpretive change thus provide the parameters for an adequate concept of explanation. It could turn out, of course, that no concept of explanation is adequate. If so, then the principle of explanatory coherence must be rejected. Spelling out the criteria of adequacy for explanation thus permits a kind of adequacy test for the principle of explanatory coherence as well.

Intentional action is one locus of the interpreter's activity. Any interpretation will make claims about what the locals do. Paradigmatically, there are two aspects to the claim that an action is intentional. First, the event must be rightly described by an action concept. The interpreter must therefore claim that the action was, for example, a murder and not an accident, or an insult rather than an unintentional offense. Second, the interpreter must claim that the agent had reasons for his action. Both of these claims involve substantial complexities. Let us begin with the second. According to the principle of explanatory coherence, a claim coheres with an interpretation if it explains or is explained by some other claims. Claims about reasons must therefore be explanatory and any adequate concept of explanation must permit reasons to explain the actions they rationalize.

The requirement that reasons explain action seems trite until we return to the problems of apparent irrationality. Recall the Purrinton murders (section 2.4). In that discussion, I was inclined to say that Capt. Purrinton's actions were deeply irrational. He was crazy. Even so, we must not lose sight of the fact that his actions were intentional. After all, it was not by *accident* that his wife and children died.[1] This example vividly illustrates the possibility of purpose or intentionality without rationality. If follows that if Capt. Purrinton's actions are to be explained as intentional actions, the model of explanation must not require that all explicable actions be rational. It follows that the requirement of rationality cannot be built into the model of explanation. An adequate model of explanation must permit a reason to explain an action and at the same time allow the interpreter to claim that the action was irrational.

It is worth noting, as we pass, that some "rationalizing" models of expla-nation yield to the temptation to identify rational action with actions that are explicable. The rationalizing model of explanation uses the principle of instru-mental rationality as a guide to the form of explanation. Intentional actions are explained insofar as the action is rational in the light of the agent's beliefs and desires (Collingwood 1946; Dray 1957; Jarvie 1964; Jarvie 1972; von Wright 1971). On this sort of view, all explicable intentional actions are rational. It follows that Capt. Purrinton's actions were either rational or inexplicable as an intentional action. Neither result seems satisfactory. Thus, prima facie, the rationalizing model of explanation will not be adequate to resolve the prob-lems of apparent irrationality.

The example of the Purrinton murders forces us to separate the expla-nation of intentional action from the judgment of rationality. In this case, we do so by focusing on what Capt. Purrinton might have had in mind when he acted. Crazy as they were, his occurrent motives were such-and-such. It is important not to overgeneralize this lesson. Not all explanations of intentional action appeal so directly to the agent's psychological states. The purpose of an action is deeply connected to the way in which the agent or those around her conceptualize the action. Describing an action in a particular way imputes typical goals and intentions. As we saw in section 2.2, quite a bit turns on whether an action is described as *sati*. *Sati* is (or would be) an act of ultimate devotion. Murder and coerced suicide are not. Whether an action is a *sati*, however, does not depend entirely on what the woman herself is thinking. It depends also on the actions of those around her, as well as the conceptual and social world in which she lives. This point has two ramifications for a model of explanation. An adequate model of explanation must not require the explanans of an intentional action explanation to refer only to what the agent had in mind. The model must give a role to the typical reasons and purposes asso-ciated with the action concept. Second, intentional action explanations will have to coexist in an interpretation with other sorts of explanation. The

---

1. I am indebted to John Pauley for discussion of these ideas.

interpretation of an event as complex as *sati* will necessarily be multifaceted, and thus it will require a number of explanations. Prima facie, there will be explanations of the social structure and the functional role of agents within it. There may be cases where an event is explained both as an intentional action and as functional within a social system. (In the example of bloodsucking witchcraft, section 2.1, the mother's action of moving the child's body might be just such an event.) Any adequate model of explanation, then, must consistently permit both social-level explanations, such as structural or functional explanations, and intentional action explanations. Notice that this criterion does not rule out a reductionist approach to the social world. One way of making functional and intentional action explanations consistent is to reduce the former to the latter. While our approach, below, will not be reductionist, such reductionism is not precluded by the criteria of adequacy.

Two more criteria arise from the foregoing discussion of intentional action. First, we have appealed to the description of an action. An interpreter will therefore need to understand the local action descriptions. This is but one part of the much larger problem of meaning. No interesting theory of interpretive change could be adequate without an account of linguistic meaning. Speech is a pervasive form of intentional action. What people say is a primary source of evidence about their values, beliefs, and conceptions. Interpreting what someone means by an utterance requires us to have some understanding of their language—the meaning of the words, the syntactic regularities, and its pragmatic effects. The principle of explanatory coherence makes a radical demand on an account of translation. The claims of a translation are parts of the overall interpretation, hence they too must be explanatory or explained. An adequate conception of explanation must therefore permit statements about the meaning of words, about the syntactic regularities, and about the pragmatic effects of speech to have a role either as explanans or explanandum.

The final criterion of adequacy arises out of the normative force of rationality. The problem of apparent irrationality arises when someone says or does something that, according to the interpretation, they ought not. The interpreter must therefore be in a position to say what the locals ought, may, or ought not to do (believe, say, etc.). In short, the interpreter must be in a position to make claims about norms. Section 3.2 argued that the relevant norms and values are those recognized by the local group. Thus, any account of interpretive change adequate to the problem of apparent irrationality must give some place to claims about values, norms, or rules. Given the principle of explanatory coherence, an adequate conception of explanation must allow values, norms, or rules to figure as either explanantia or explananda.

To summarize, the principle of explanatory coherence and the problem of apparent irrationality make the following demands on an adequate model of explanation:

Intention:

1. Reasons must explain intentional actions, but

2. an adequate model of explanation must permit a reason to explain an action and at the same time allow the claim that the action was irrational;

3. the model must allow social-level explanations (such as structural, functional, or historical explanations) that are consistent with intentional action explanations.

Meaning:

4. Claims about the meaning of words, syntactic regularities, and the pragmatic effects of speech must be permitted as explanans or explananda.

Normativity:

5. Claims that the locals adhere to certain norms, values, or rules must be permitted as explanans or explananda.

Looking over this list of requirements, one sympathizes with the explanation-skeptics. Meaning and normativity, in particular, seem as if they will resist any explanatory role. Skepticism is strengthened by the observation that, in the absence of considerable refinement, none of the common models of explanation will satisfy all five desiderata. We noticed in passing that the rationalizing model of explanation stumbles on criterion (2), and we can expect it to have difficulty with criterion (3). Another class of popular models demand that an explanation subsume the explanandum under some lawlike generalization. Attempts have been made to extend this form to intentional action explanations (Churchland 1970; Hempel 1942; Hempel 1963). Even if they were successful in this domain, it is not at all obvious how claims about local norms of rationality might be subsumed under lawlike generalizations. Another popular class of models relies on causality. To explain an event is to identify its cause or causes (Humphreys 1989; Salmon 1984). Again, while this view can encompass intentional action (Davidson 1963/1980), meaning and normativity are problematic. It is not at all obvious how a claim about the meaning of a word would fit into a causal story. Norms and values *might* have causal properties, if we were prepared to adopt an appropriate metaphysics. However, the metaphysical commitments that give norms and values a causal role seem a high price to pay for keeping causality as a necessary condition of explanation.

The above considerations are not definitive criticisms of the models of explanation mentioned. Proponents of such models might respond by showing how their favorite may indeed accommodate the troublesome class of claims. Alternatively, the argument could be turned around to show that there is no model of explanation that will work for explanatory coherence, and so much the worse for explanatory coherence. Before accepting either of these, we should explore a third alternative. If they do fail, the popular models of explanation fail to satisfy the above criteria because they require too much specific content of all explanations. If all of the above desiderata are to be satisfied, the model of explanation must allow many kinds of claim to be explanatory. What the principle of explanatory coherence needs is a *logic* of explanation, a *form* that might be given substance in various ways.

The most promising candidate for the purposes of this work is therefore the "erotetic" or "why-question" model of explanation. It has been recognized for a long time that explanations could be treated as answers to questions of the form, Why *P*? (Bromberger 1966; Hempel 1965). This idea was enriched by work on the semantics of questions and the formal relationship of questions to answers (Belnap 1966; Belnap and Steel 1976; Bromberger 1992; Dretske 1973; Hintikka 1977; Teller 1974; Tichy 1978; Travis 1978). With a formal understanding of questions at hand, Bas van Fraassen (1980) and Alan Garfinkel (1981) were able to suggest that the logic of why-questions itself could ground a model of explanation. The remainder of this essay will be devoted to showing that the why-question model of explanation satisfies the five criteria above. This chapter will articulate and defend the model. Chapters 5, 6, and 7 will be devoted to showing that intentional action, meaning, and norms respectively can be explained within the erotetic form. If successful, we will have shown that the principle of explanatory coherence, fortified with the erotetic model of explanation, can encompass the phenomena that have traditionally eluded explanatory understanding.

4.2 THE EROTETIC MODEL OF EXPLANATION

A good way to ground any discussion of explanation is by looking to accounts that the inquirers themselves take to be explanatory. In keeping with the above-stated goal of looking first to the requirements of the interpretive disciplines, let us turn to Mary Douglas's classic interpretation of the Jewish kosher laws (Douglas 1966). Interesting in its own right, Douglas's discussion is a good illustration of the basic elements of the erotetic model of explanation.

The arcane and obscure laws of Leviticus and Deuteronomy pose an ancient interpretive puzzle. While they are not irrational in any strong sense, it is difficult to see the grounds or rationale that underlies them. They thus present a problem of interpretive change of the type with which we are concerned. The kosher laws are puzzling because we already have a translation of the relevant texts and an understanding of the behavior of those who adhere to them. (Indeed, this may be self-understanding, since the kosher laws have presented an interpretive problem for Jewish scholars as well as cross-cultural observers.) Given this understanding, we run into difficulty appreciating the kosher laws. We know what they say, but we cannot see why the injunctions are made. Douglas expresses the puzzle this way:

> Why should the camel, the hare, and the rock badger be unclean? Why should some locusts, but not all, be unclean? Why should the frog be clean and the mouse and the hippopotamus unclean? What have chameleons, moles and crocodiles got in common that they should be listed together (Levi. xi, 27)? (Douglas 1966: 41)

Before presenting her own interpretation, Douglas considers and rejects several lines of response to these questions found in traditional Biblical studies.

Douglas first scouts an interpretation popular with Anglo-Saxon scholars of Hebrew Scripture. This view holds that the kosher laws are arbitrary, that there is not any rationale or underlying order unifying the kosher laws. They were important because they were *laws*. The intent behind their implementation was simply to introduce discipline into thought and behavior. Of this kind of response, Douglas says: "Needless to say, such interpretations are not interpretations at all, since they deny any significance to the rules. They express bafflement in a learned way" (Douglas 1966: 45–46). On first pass, one might feel that Douglas and her interlocutors are talking past one another. To claim that the rules are arbitrary is to claim that there is no interpretation, at least in Douglas's sense. Douglas's objection simply restates the position rejected. At a deeper level, however, Douglas is making a fair point. Saying that the rules are arbitrary does nothing at all to discriminate among the alternatives. Such an "interpretation" cannot say why the frog is clean and the mouse is not, nor does it attempt to do so. Douglas's strategy is familiar in both the sciences and the humanities. She has rejected an interpretation because it cannot account for something that needs understanding. What needs understanding in this case is a body of explicit contrasts—why some animals are "unclean" while others are "clean." The proposed answer cannot make the discrimination, and hence it is rejected.

All of Douglas's questions invoke contrasts. It is clear from her discussion that the only adequate responses to the interpretive puzzle are those that discriminate among the alternatives. Her first question asks why the camel, the hare, and the rock badger are unclean *rather than* clean. Any response that fails to articulate the grounds for this contrast will simply be irrelevant. Contemporary work on the logic of why-questions has taken this to be a universal feature of why-questions and their answers. Any why-question asks about some "topic." The topic is some statement taken to need explanation. In

Douglas's first question, the topic is the claim that the camel, the hare, and the rock badger are unclean. The topic is implicitly or explicitly contrasted with a group of alternatives. Following Peter Lipton (1991b), we will call the alternatives to the topic the "foil" or "foils." The set including the topic and the foil(s) is the "contrast class." A why-question, then, has the form

Why P, rather than $\{X_1, X_2, \ldots X_i\}$?

where P is the topic, X_1 through X_i the foils, and the set $\{P, X_1, X_2, \ldots X_i\}$ is the contrast class.

The erotetic view identifies explanations with why-questions (as analyzed above) and their answers. The explanans is the answer to a why-question, and the explanandum is the topic in contrast to the foils. This contention is open to challenge with respect to both the necessity and sufficiency of why-questions for explanation. One might argue that not all answers to why-questions are explanations. Ruben (1990), for instance, argues that some why-questions are requests for "justification or defense," not explanation. His example is the question: Why did the framers of the American Constitution insist on a system of checks and balances? He remarks that "an appropriate answer might be a justification in terms of the arguments the framers might have given for such a system, whether or not it was those arguments which actually moved them to include such a system in the constitution" (Ruben 1990: 79). This answer is a rather unstable combination of justification and explanation. If we really do not care whether the arguments moved the framers of the Constitution, then there is no reason to restrict the answer to "arguments the framers might have given." In such a case, we are interested in whether there are arguments that justify checks and balances. This is, indeed, not an explanation, but it is likewise no longer an answer to the why-question posed. On the other hand, if we are interested in the framers' reasons, then the answer provides their justifications. This does seem like an explanation for why the framers of the Constitution included checks and balances. Finally, we might combine these questions: Given that the framers of the constitution had such-and-such reasons, were these good reasons for a checks and balances system? This too asks after justification, but again, it is no longer a why-question.

While Ruben's purported counterexample is unsatisfactory, there is something useful to be learned from it. There are some uses of the English word "why" which do not ask for explanations. For example, "Why me?" asked in the face of a tragedy is not a why-question of the relevant sort. The lesson is that we should not rely too heavily on the peculiarities of English usage. Why-questions are a logical object that might be expressed in various ways. If the question asked—in any language—can be so interpreted as to satisfy the terms of the analysis of why-questions, then we will say that its answer is an explanation.

The identification of explanations with answers to why-questions has been also challenged on the grounds that there are other kinds of questions that yield explanatory answers. Questions about *how* something happened seem to be particularly suggestive (Cross 1991).[2] Two points may be made in response. First, nothing in our work here requires that why-questions alone give rise to explanations. The next three chapters will show how much work why-questions can do in the methodology of interpretation. If there are other questions that give rise to explanations, then we can add them to the arsenal of explanations that make for coherent interpretations. Second, just as we noted with respect to Ruben, we should not be misled by the surface form of the question. Many English language utterances employing the word "how" can be understood as asking why-questions as they are analyzed above. I will argue below (section 4.3) that Cross's examples of explanatory how-questions are best understood as disguised why-questions.

Before moving on, there is another sort of objection to be countenanced. The erotetic view analyzes a why-question as having the form, Why P, rather than $\{X_1, X_2, \ldots X_i\}$? Ruben (1987) and Temple (1988) have argued that the foils are unnecessary, and that as a result the erotetic view adds nothing to our understanding of explanation. They begin from the observation that explaining why P rather than Q requires explaining why P is true and explaining why Q is false.[3] There are, then, two possible cases. Either the topic and foil are logically inconsistent (e.g., why P rather than $\sim P$?) or they are not. If topic and foil are inconsistent, truth of the topic entails the falsehood of the foil. Any explanation of the topic will therefore trivially explain the negation of the foil. In the first case, then, the foil is a redundant addition to the explanation.

In the second case, the topic and foil are logically consistent. The specification of the foil is not obviously redundant in this case. For instance, explaining why Jones ate a ham sandwich, rather than a turkey sandwich, is quite different from explaining why Jones, rather than Smith, ate a ham sandwich. However, both Temple and Ruben assume that topic and foil must be mutually exclusive, even if they are logically consistent. In Ruben's terms, the topic must "eclipse" the foil. This means that there must be some feature of

---

2. There is also an important tradition that identifies explanations with wh-questions: what, where, when, how, *and* why questions. Writers in this vein include Hintikka (1977), Koura (1988), Sintonen (1984; 1989), and Tuomela (1980). Addressing this approach would require an excursion into the formal semantics of why-questions that is beyond the scope of this work. Moreover, in spite of formal differences, I conjecture that the analysis yielded by this alternative understanding of why-questions is commensurate with the analyses of specific explanatory types presented in the next three chapters.

3. This assumption is shared by Travis (1978) and Koura (1988).

the context whereby eating both ham and turkey, or both Smith and Jones having a ham sandwich, is precluded. If so, then reference to this feature of the context will suffice for a full explanation. We may simply explain why, for example, Jones ate a ham sandwich, and then add the extra premise necessary to show why "Jones ate a turkey sandwich" had to be false. Therefore, in this second case too, specification of the foil adds nothing new to the theory of explanation.

The Ruben-Temple objection contains two instructive mistakes. First, it supposes that topic and foil must be mutually exclusive. This assumption will be scrutinized a little later. Second, it assumes that explaining why P rather than Q is equivalent to explaining why P and $\sim Q$. This second assumption has unacceptable consequences. If it were true, and if topic and foil are mutually exclusive, a single explanation of P would suffice to explain any contrast. Yet, this is clearly not the case. The question, Why P rather than Q? will typically require a different answer than the question, Why P rather than R? If we want to know why Jones ate a ham sandwich rather than a turkey sandwich, the answer will presumably mention Jones's beliefs and desires. Explaining why Jones, rather than Smith, ate a ham sandwich might not mention Jones's beliefs or desires at all. The answer might be, for instance, that only Jones had enough money to buy one, or that Smith keeps kosher. In general, a single explanation of P cannot also explain every fact incompatible with P. (That Jones wanted ham does not explain why Smith did not eat a ham sandwich.) Therefore, it is a mistake to identify "P rather than Q" with "P and not Q" (cf. Dretske 1973; Lipton 1987; 1991a; 1991b; Salmon 1984: 110; Travis 1978).

With these preliminary clarifications of the form of why-questions in hand, let us return to Douglas's explanation of the kosher laws. Douglas's final question—What have chameleons, moles, and crocodiles got in common that they should be listed together?—does not have the surface form of a why-question. We have already seen that the erotetic model does not require the foils to be explicitly mentioned nor that the word "why" appear in the sentence expressing the question. To apply the model, we must identify the intended topic and foil(s) that underlie her question. Casting around for an acceptable paraphrase reveals an ambiguity. There is more than one set of foils, and hence more than one possible why-question, which corresponds to Douglas's original query. The question might ask why chameleons, moles, and crocodiles are listed together, rather than separately. Or, it might ask why the chameleons, rather than some other animal, are listed with the moles and crocodiles. Which question did Douglas ask?

Choice of contrast class depends partly on the kind of answer one expects. In context, Douglas's question, What have chameleons, moles and crocodiles got in common that they should be listed together? suggests that chameleons, moles, and crocodiles should have something in common. A relevant answer

is going to have the form: chameleons, moles, and crocodiles are listed together, rather than separately, because they all have X. The other possible
contrast class, {chameleons listed with moles and crocodiles, some other animal
listed with moles and crocodiles}, points toward a very different sort of answer.
The answer to that question would say something about the difference between chameleons and other animals. Douglas is not looking for that kind of
answer. The context implicitly specifies what will count as a relevant answer
to a question and thus rules out some alternative contrast classes.

In general, knowing what question has been asked requires knowing
what sort of answer is expected. A why-question is therefore identified by
its topic, foils, and its *relevance criterion*.[4] A relevance criterion specifies what
sort of answer will be relevant. Minimally, any relevant answer to a why-
question must discriminate between the topic and foil(s). Whether there are
other criteria of relevance for all why-questions, or whether all other criteria
are specific to different forms of explanation, is an issue we will presently
engage. For now, it is sufficient to note that the relevance criterion is closely
related to the content of the topic and contrast class. The foregoing paragraph noted that an answer mentioning a common feature obviously does
not discriminate between topic and foil of the contrast class: {chameleons
listed with moles and crocodiles, some other animal listed with moles and
crocodiles}. Given a particular contrast class, only some relevance criteria
may be employed; given a particular relevance criterion, only some topics
and foils may be asked about.

While the relevance criterion and contrast class exercise mutual constraint,
they are independent elements of a why-question. Two why-questions may
have identical contrast classes, yet have different relevance criteria. A familiar
sort of case is where the speaker's and hearer's background helps determine the
relevance of an answer. So, for example, consider the question: Why did my
African Violets die {rather than continue to live}? If I am an inexperienced
gardener, the answer that I gave them too much sun and water might be
sufficient. Of course, if I am experienced in the ways of plants, it may be
obvious that I did not treat the plant properly. The question in this case asks
not about the sequence of events leading up to their death, but about the
standing conditions that permitted them to die, given those causes. In this case,
the answer that African Violets are notoriously sensitive to too much sun
would be more relevant. There are, then, three independent components to a
why-question:

---

4. Van Fraassen (1980) uses the term "relevance relation," and I intend "relevance
criterion" to do the same work. The shift in terminology signals only an interest in the
concrete details about how particular kinds of questions and answers are related.

Topic: The event or state of affairs about which the question asks.

Foil(s): Alternatives to the topic. A why-question asks why the topic occurred/obtains rather than the foil or foils.

Relevance criterion: Relationship between a proposition and the contrast class such that the proposition is an appropriate answer to the why-question. A relevance criterion specifies criteria by which the answer differentiates between topic and the foil(s).

A fully disambiguated why-question specifies all three of these elements.

There is a concern that remains from the foregoing discussion. We have distinguished between why-questions as formal objects and why-questions as English utterances using the word "why." Since the elements of a why-question need not be explicitly specified by the person who asks the question, and since English questions are, as a result, often ambiguous among their formal counterparts, what makes it the case that an investigator is asking one why-question rather than another? Two further factors serve to disambiguate real-world why-questions. Both relate the question to elements of the context in which it is asked and may thereby be called "pragmatic." First, why-questions have presuppositions. If the presuppositions of a question are not satisfied by a particular context, then that question cannot arise. These are the subject of section 4.3. Second, questions arise in context because of the interests of those who ask and answer the question. If a particular why-question does not satisfy the interests of the investigators or their audience, then it does not arise in that context. Interests are the subject of section 4.4.

4.3 PRESUPPOSITIONS

A presupposition is some proposition that must be true if the question is to be askable. The presuppositions of why-questions are important for several reasons. First, presuppositions are one of the ways in which questions are related to the world. They bring objectivity to the erotetic account because whether a question is askable is not entirely up to the inquirers. Second, whether the presuppositions are satisfied partially determines whether the question will be answered or rejected. In the context of this work, the conditions under which a question arises are important. If a why-question arises and is unanswered by an interpretation, then the interpretation is unable to explain something that needs explanation. This would be a strike against the coherence of the interpretation. On the other hand, if the why-question does not arise at all, the lack of an answer is irrelevant. Whether a particular why-question arises in an interpretation is thus a crucial question. Finally, the relationship between the erotetic model and explanatory coherence depends on a detailed account of presuppositions. An interpretation is an interlaced set of explanations, and interpretations are to be judged by their explanatory coherence. One of the ways in which one claim can cohere with another is to be presupposed by why-questions concerning the latter. Explanatory coherence is thus partly a matter of the satisfaction of presuppositions. We will return to this point at the end of this section.

One way to exhibit the presuppositions of a why-question is the rejection test: the truth of a proposition is presupposed if and only if the question is not askable when the proposition is false. (Conversely, the falsity of a proposition is presupposed if and only if the question is not askable when the proposition is true.) The first presupposition of any why-question is that its topic is true (Garfinkel 1981: 40; van Fraassen 1980: 144–45). The topic describes the phenomenon asked about. If the topic is false, then there is no phenomenon to be explained. Falsity of the topic is therefore one of the reasons why requests for explanation get rejected. If, for instance, new translations of Biblical texts showed that the hare was *not* regarded as unclean, the question of why it *is* unclean collapses. To deny the truth of a topic is thus not to answer, but to reject, a question. A second uncontroversial presupposition is that the why-question has at least one true answer (van Fraassen 1980: 144–45). In other words, asking a why-question presupposes that there is some true proposition that satisfies the relevance criterion. The rejection test makes this presupposition vivid. Suppose one asks, "Why did Jones spill her beer into Smith's lap?" and intends that a relevant answer should describe Jones's reason or motivation. If we discover that there was no such reason—because, for example, Jones's arm was pushed—then the question is rejected. The question cannot be asked because we have discovered that there is no true proposition satisfying the relevance criterion.

The structure of the contrast class gives rise to some presuppositions of its own. It is natural to suppose that the foils must be false. Again, this presupposition is most vivid when its failure motivates the rejection of the question. If both the radio and the light are working, one cannot ask why the light is working, rather than the radio. Or, to put the point another way, responding that both work when asked, Why is the light working, rather than the radio? is to reject the question, not answer it. Beyond the rejection test, there is additional motivation for this presupposition. An answer is explanatory insofar as it discriminates between the topic and the foils. If the foil is true, the answer no longer seems to tell us why the topic is true, *rather than the foil*. Presupposing that the foils are false, then, is part of what makes the answers to why-questions explanatory.

Charles Cross has challenged the view that the foils of a why-question must be false (Cross 1991). Cross's argument arises in the context of his analysis of *how*-questions. How-questions seem to give rise to explanations, and they are semantically interesting in their own right. Cross contends that how-questions and why-questions have a similar analysis, with one important difference.[5] The foils of a how-question are not presupposed to be false. For example, consider, How do *reptiles* (in contrast to fish, birds, and mammals) reproduce? Clearly, this question is askable even though fish, birds, and mammals do reproduce. Cross suggests that the analysis of how- and why-questions can be unified by eliminating the requirement that the foils be false. To support this suggestion, Cross argued that why-questions do not always presuppose that the foils are false. Cross created the following example of a why-question with true foils. Imagine an alcohol rehabilitation session where the therapist asks each member of the group: Why did *you* start drinking too much? Each patient tells a different story. Cross analyzes the question as having the form: Why does X drink too much? He suggests that the contrast class is "the set of all propositions to the effect that X drinks too much, for each member of the therapy group" (Cross 1991: 253). Here the members of the contrast class are presupposed to be true, not false, as the standard account would have it.

It seems to me that this troublesome example is best handled by a strategy that Cross himself devised. An inquirer may be interested in the contrast among the topics of a number of why-questions, or in the contrast among answers to related why-questions. Moreover, the different why-questions might be encoded in a single utterance. In such cases, we need to tease the questions apart. Cross's strategy for doing so is to assign contrasting true propositions to the topics of different why-questions, each of which has only false foils. Let us consider the alcohol rehabilitation example in this light. The question, Why did *you* start drinking too much? seems to be asking for the events that led up to the patient's first (or most recent) drinking binge. If this is the sort of answer sought, the contrast class of the question is $\{X$ started drinking too much at time t, X did not start drinking too much at time $t\}$. The question is reiterated for each patient, and the foil is false in every case. In the place of a single why-question with true foils, we have several why-questions with false foils. What creates the illusion of true foils is that the therapist is interested in the contrast among patients. However, not every contrast of interest is something that must be built into the explanations. The contrast among the stories of the different patients is something that arises from the answers to multiple why-questions. Cross's apparent counterexample, therefore, does not compel us to think that the foils of a why-question may be true.

Another common assumption about the contrast class is that the topic and foil(s) must be incompatible (Garfinkel 1981: 40; Temple 1988; Travis 1978: 289).

---

5. While I argue against Cross's contention that the foils of why-questions may be false, these arguments do not reject his analysis of how-questions. As argued above, if distinct from why-questions, explanation-seeking how-questions can take their place in an explanatory coherence view.

This idea arises from the "rather than" locution and is reinforced by many of the standard examples. To say that "P occurred, rather than Q" is to suggest that Q could not have occurred, given that P did. However, as Lipton (1991a; 1991b) and Barnes (1994) have pointed out, there are many examples where the topic and foil of a why-question are fully compatible. Consider the shopworn example of paresis: Why did Jones get paresis, rather than Smith? The why-question presupposes that Jones got paresis and that Smith did not. Yet, Jones's paresis is both logically and nomologically consistent with Smith's lack of paresis. Since this seems like an acceptable why-question even though topic and foil are consistent, why-questions do not presuppose that their topic and foils are inconsistent or incompatible. The rejection test provides a second argument against presupposing that topic and foil must be incompatible. If one asks, Why P rather than Q? and later finds out that P and Q could be true together (but, in fact, Q was false), the question is still askable. Contrary to received opinion, then, why-questions do not presuppose that topic and foil(s) are incompatible.

A different kind of presupposition will also prove important for our work. Alan Garfinkel, who was the first to notice these, called them "structural presuppositions" (Garfinkel 1981: 41). Structural presuppositions emerge when why-questions are asked about the properties of a group or about the behavior of individuals in group contexts. Consider the behavior of individuals at an auction. Joe, Margaret, and Sam are bidding on a vintage lava lamp. Joe offers $100 and wins the bidding. We may ask why Joe won the bid, rather than Margaret or Sam. Suppose the answer is, that Joe bid $100. This answer is misleading insofar as it suggests that anyone who bid $100 would have won. On the contrary, there is exactly one winner at an auction. What explains Joe's win is that his bid of $100 was the *highest*. In this context, the question, Why did Joe, rather than Margaret or Sam, win? cannot be answered by facts about Joe alone. Garfinkel tried to make this sort of presupposition explicit with the "given that" locution, for example: Given that there is one winner, why was it Joe (rather than Margaret or Sam)? This way of asking the question makes it clear that an adequate answer will have to compare Joe with Margaret and Sam.

When a structural presupposition is present, some relationship among the individuals is relevant to the explanation. This much is relatively clear. What is unclear, and remains unclear in Garfinkel's seminal discussion, is the relationship between explanations and facts about the individuals in the group. Is a structural presupposition a feature of an explanation? Or is it a social fact? Under what conditions does an explanation have a structural presupposition? Garfinkel tried to clarify the notion of a structural presupposition by appeal to "possibility space" (Garfinkel 1981: 44). The possibility space for a group or an individual is the set of possible states, properties, or values that it may have in a given domain. Garfinkel's example of a classroom grade distribution is apposite. The possibility space for each student is the set of twelve possible grades (A, A−, B+, . . .). The possibility space for the class is the set of possible grade distributions. If the grading is noncompetitive, any student can get any grade. So, the set of possible grade distributions is the Cartesian product of the possibility spaces for all of the individuals. If the grading is competitive, possibility space for the class will be much smaller. When the teacher imposes a strict curve (10% As, 15% Bs, and so on), the only possible grade distributions are those consistent with the curve. Garfinkel calls phenomena that limit the possibility space for a group "structural conditions" (1981: 44). A strict grading curve, the fact that only one person can win the bid at an auction, and even the law of the conservation of energy (Garfinkel 1981: 70) are all structural conditions.

A structural condition, then, is a fact about a group of individuals. (Notice that these "individuals" need not be humans—the point applies equally well to molecules or plants.) Such facts about a group cannot *themselves* constitute the structural presuppositions of a why-question. A presupposition is a linguistic object. It is a proposition that must be true if the question is to be answered. What is the relationship, then, between the structural *conditions* and structural *presuppositions?* Garfinkel's ploy was to identify the contrast class of a question with the actual possibility space for the individual or group in question. Structural conditions limit the possibility space, so a structural *presupposition* is the corresponding limitation on the contrast classes of why-questions about the group or individual (Garfinkel 1981: 44, 48).

Unfortunately, this suggestion will not do, even for Garfinkel's own paradigm examples. Garfinkel imagines a class graded on a curve where exactly one student will get an A, 50% get Cs, and the rest Bs. Mary gets the A, and we ask why. Garfinkel writes:

> The true contrast [class] for the question about *Mary* consists of the number of ways a set of 50 people can be subdivided into a set of 1, a set of 24, and a set of 25, in other words, only those grade distributions consistent with my policy. (Garfinkel 1981: 44)

The right contrast class for "Why did Mary get an A?" is thus *not* {Mary gets an A, Mary gets a B, Mary gets a C . . .}. That is:

1. Why did Mary get an A, rather than a different grade?

Rather, the contrast class should be {Mary got the A, Joe got the A, Cindy got the A...}. That is:

2. Why did Mary, rather than Joe, Cindy, . . . get the A?

If the contrast class of a question has to be the same as the actual possibility space of the group, then "Why did Mary get an A?" has to be understood as asking question (2) and not as (1). Given the structural condition of the curve, question (1) is not askable according to Garfinkel. This result does not seem correct. Question (1) is askable and answerable, just so long as the answer does not mention facts about Mary alone. Mary got an A because she had the *best* performance. The contrast class of question (1) is thus not obviously precluded by the structural condition of the curve.

In Garfinkel's example, question (1) and question (2) can have the same answer, namely, that Mary did the best. This helps create the illusion that only question (2) is askable in this context. When we look to more typical examples of grading curves, the answers to questions (1) and (2) may be different in instructive ways. Suppose we ask questions (1) and (2) in a context where the top 10% of the class gets As. As before, any answer to (1) will have to be comparative. It will have to discriminate between Mary and the 90% of her classmates who did not get As. However, in this case, questions (1) and (2) may require different answers. That she did the best does not explain why Mary got an A rather than any arbitrarily chosen classmate. Perhaps Mary got an A, rather than Joe, because Joe has the intellect of a stone, rather than Cindy because Mary had a better math background, and so on. Both questions are askable, and each may have a different answer. In general, then, we cannot require that a question about an individual in this context have a contrast class that is identical to the possibility space for the group.

Garfinkel tried to express the idea of a structural presupposition by a direct restriction on the contrast class. The idea is better expressed in terms of the relevance criteria for a why-question.[6] Some why-questions ask for answers that describe nonrelational, atomic facts about an individual. If one wants to know why a billiards ball bounced off of the bumper at a particular angle, it is sufficient to cite the ball's spin and angle of incidence (plus some math and the laws of motion). Spatial or causal relationships between the topic ball and its fellows are irrelevant to the explanation. This sort of question presupposes that facts about the ball are alone sufficient for the answer. Let us call this an "atomistic presupposition." It is the proposition that all combinations of individual action (relevant to the topic) are jointly possible. If there is a structural condition that limits the possibility space of the group, an atomistic presupposition will not be satisfied and the question will not be askable. Under such conditions, a relevant answer will have to mention some relationships among individuals in the group. (The specific sort of relation to be mentioned will depend on the structural conditions present.) This relevance criterion presupposes that *not* all combinations of individual action (relevant to the topic) are jointly possible, and this proposition is true when there is a structural condition present.

---

6. It should be noted that Garfinkel did not use the notion of a relevance relation (criterion). It was introduced by van Fraassen slightly later.

Where Garfinkel understood structural presuppositions as restrictions on the contrast class, I am proposing that structural presuppositions arise from the relevance criteria of why-questions. This proposal aligns structural presuppositions with the other presuppositions of a why-question. All presuppositions are propositions that must be satisfied if the question is to be askable. Like other presuppositions, the impact of a structural presupposition is that, in a given factual context, some questions will be precluded because their presuppositions are not satisfied. Only questions with the appropriate sort of contrast class and relevance criterion will be askable. In spite of the differences, my way of conceptualizing structural presuppositions shares an important consequence with Garfinkel's. Where there is a structural condition in play, explanations of an individual's behavior will have to describe some relationship between the topic individual and other members of the group. Garfinkel noticed that this result has profound consequences for the issue of reductionism in science. We will pursue this consequence in chapter 7.

Presuppositions make the erotetic model of explanation objective in the sense that whether one proposition explains another depends on the facts, not only on the investigator. The proposition A explains P, if and only if A is the relevant answer to the question, Why P rather than Q? In addition to the truth of A and P, this explanation requires the falsity of Q and the truth of either an atomistic or structural presupposition. If these presuppositions are not satisfied, the question, Why P rather than Q? cannot be asked. And if the question cannot be asked, A is no answer to the question and hence A is not an explanation of P. There is, therefore, more to explanation than arranging propositions into the proper logical form. The world has to cooperate. While such objectivity clearly benefits a model of explanation, it raises a problem for the explanatory coherence criterion of interpretive change. If some of the claims in an interpretation are false, then why-questions that presuppose them cannot be asked. If they cannot be asked, then there is no explanatory relationship between such false claims and the true claims of an interpretation. Only true claims, therefore, can cohere with each other. From an objective point of view, this is a result to be celebrated. Interpretations with all true claims will always be more coherent than interpretations with some false claims, and fewer false claims always makes for more coherence. The problem arises because chapter 3 proposed explanatory coherence as a *criterion* of interpretive change. An interpreter is to choose the interpretation with the most explanatory coherence. Presumably, when contemplating her own interpretation, the interpreter believes all of its claims to be true. It is, of course, possible for a claim to be false and yet believed true. Therefore, the interpreter has no direct access to the coherence of an interpretation. Moreover, any attempt to verify that the claims of her interpretation are true is caught in a vicious circle. Her best reasons for believing that the claims of her interpretation are true are that they cohere with each other and that her interpretation has more explanatory coherence than any alternative of which she is aware. If coherence is determined by truth, then she cannot judge the coherence of her interpretation without knowing the truth of the claims, and she cannot judge the truth of the claims without knowing whether her interpretation is coherent. As a criterion of interpretive change, explanatory coherence seems either impotent or circular.

To recover explanatory coherence as a criterion of interpretive change, we need to distinguish between *objective* coherence and *epistemic* coherence. An interpretation is coherent insofar as its claims explain, are explained by, or are presupposed by others. Where the presuppositions of the explanations are in fact satisfied, the coherence may be said to be objective. Whether the presuppositions of our explanations are, in fact, satisfied is something to which an interpreter has no independent access. The best she can do is to judge that they are satisfied. The coherence of an interpretation is epistemic when the presuppositions of each explanation are believed to be satisfied. Objective coherence requires that the presuppositions of the explanations be true, epistemic coherence requires only that they be taken to be true. The distinction between epistemic and objective coherence is homologous to the distinction between potential and actual explanations (cf. Salmon 1984: 107). The actual explanation of an event is the true, relevant answer to a why-question with all true presuppositions. If the answer is false or if another presupposition of the why-question fails, the best we can say of an answer to it is that it *would* be an explanation if the presupposition *were* satisfied. That is, that it is a potential explanation. In this latter sense, we can say that while both accounts were false, Copernicus and Ptolemy explained the motions of the planets.

When using explanation to judge the relative coherence of two interpretations, all we can demand is potential explanations and epistemic coherence. An interpretation will contain no claims that the interpreter judges to be false. When an interpreter tries to explain a new phenomenon, all she can do is to see whether the presuppositions of the why-question are satisfied by her current set of claims. If they are, then she has a potential explanation. Similarly, when judging the explanatory coherence of an interpretation, an interpreter can only say that the various claims are potentially explained. Therefore, judgments of explanatory coherence are judgments of the epistemic coherence of an interpretation. The objection presented above, then, does not vitiate the explanatory coherence criterion of interpretive change. Used as a criterion, explanatory coherence demands only that an explanation has no presuppositions that are already known to be false. The coherence it yields is internal.

4.4 Interests and Laissez-Faire Contextualism

There is a pair of serious problems with the erotetic model of explanation. We will call them the green cheese problem and the red herring problem. Both seem to indicate that the erotetic model as presented so far is too permissive. It permits many "explanations" that ought not to be countenanced. The green cheese problem is quite simple. Thus far, the only restriction on foils for a why-question is that they be false. The proposition "the moon is made of green cheese" is false, so it seems that we can construct a why-question by contrasting an arbitrary topic with it:

*. Why was Clinton elected to a second term, rather than the moon made of green cheese?

Once the principle has been noticed, an infinite number of examples can be generated. Questions like (*) are obviously absurd, yet given what has been said, (*) is a perfectly legitimate request for explanation. Some restriction on the foils of legitimate why-questions seems necessary.

While the green cheese problem points toward a need to restrict the contrast classes of legitimate why-questions, the red herring problem indicates a need to restrict relevance criteria. Without further restrictions, anything can explain anything. Philip Kitcher and Wesley Salmon expressed the difficulty in an elegant proof (1987: 319). Consider any two true propositions, P and A. A why-question is identified with its topic, contrast class, and relevance criterion. Let P be the topic. For the foils to P, take any set of false propositions, $\{X_1, X_2, \ldots X_j\}$. The contrast class, C, is then the set $\{P, X_1, X_2, \ldots X_j\}$. If A is to answer the question, Why P, rather than $\{X_1, X_2, \ldots X_j\}$? A must bear a relevance relation to $<P,\{X_1, X_2, \ldots X_j\}>$. A relevance criterion can be expressed as a relation between possible answers and the contrast class. Formally speaking, a relation is a set of ordered pairs. A relevance criterion, then, can be expressed as a set of ordered pairs, the first member of which is a possible answer and the second an ordered pair of topic and contrast class. Let R be the set $\{<A,<P,C>>, <Z_1,<P,C>>, <Z_2,<P,C>>, \ldots, <Z_n,<P,C>>\}$. If we further specify that $\{Z_1, Z_2, \ldots, Z_n\}$ are all false, A becomes the only true answer to the why-question. Hence, for any two true propositions, A and P, there is a question—defined by $<R, P, C>$—with P as topic and A as the only true answer. So, for any arbitrary pair of true propositions, each is the explanation of the other. At best, this result trivializes the erotetic model, at worst it constitutes a *reductio*.

It is worth pointing out that the same problem can be generated without the technicality. Without further restrictions on the relevance criteria, things like "adequate answers must have twenty-seven words" are admissible. Something has gone awry.

There are two kinds of response to these difficulties. Since the problems arise because the model admits of too many foils and relevance criteria, it is natural to seek general restrictions. This approach has been the most popular among philosophers of science.[7] The alternative is to deny that there are universal restrictions on the content of contrast classes or relevance criteria. It was dubbed "laissez-faire" contextualism by David Henderson (1993). For a laissez-faire contextualist, the work of distinguishing appropriate from inappropriate explanations is done entirely by the context in which the why-question arises.

I would like to argue for laissez-faire contextualism. Since laissez-faire contextualism and its alternative are disjoint, a customary strategy is to argue by elimination. One would elucidate the proposed restrictions, run up counterexamples to each, and conclude that only laissez-faire contextualism is possible. That does not seem to be the best strategy here. At best, counterexamples would show that the existing proposals for universal restrictions on contrast classes and relevance criteria were flawed. They could not show that there are no such universal restrictions. Moreover, from the perspective of laissez-faire contextualism, there is no need to argue against particular restrictions on contrast classes or relevance criteria. In a given context, there are always limitations on appropriate contrast classes and relevance criteria. A laissez-faire contextualist insists that the interests of the investigators and the presuppositions of the why-question will determine whether the proposed explanation is appropriate. There are no restrictions on contrast classes or relevance criteria that transcend all possible interests or factual contexts. Thus, once we have a positive argument for laissez-faire contextualism, the alternative, more restricted, views of why-questions can be assimilated. In their arguments for particular restrictions on why-questions, the able philosophers who resist laissez-faire contextualism have discovered contrast classes and relevance relations that are appropriate to a specific domain of inquiry.

I propose to argue for laissez-faire contextualism in two phases. First, I will argue that laissez-faire contextualism has the resources to resolve the green cheese and red herring problems without appeal to universal restrictions. Second, I will argue that the common reasons for rejecting laissez-faire contextualism are based on a misunderstanding of the role of interest.

Let us begin with the red herring problem. According to the Kitcher-Salmon argument, any red herring proposition can count as an explanation. According to laissez-faire contextualism, whether one proposition, A, explains

7. While they do not all take themselves to be responding to the green cheese or red herring problems, the following philosophers can be read as proposing universal restrictions on the content of contrast classes or relevance criteria: Barnes (1994), Henderson (1993), Hitchcock (1996), Humphreys (1989), Garfinkel (1981), Kitcher and Salmon (1987), Lipton (1991a; 1991b), Salmon (1984), Sober (1986), Travis (1978), and Temple (1988).

another, P, depends on three factors: (1) the structure of the why-question with P as topic and A as answer, (2) whether the presuppositions of the why-question are satisfied, and (3) whether the why-question satisfies the interests of the investigators. The second and third are the contextual factors that preclude many why-questions. The laissez-faire contextualist response to the red herring problem is that *in a given context,* it is not the case that anything can explain anything. Kitcher and Salmon defined their relevance relation and contrast class so that the presuppositions are trivially satisfied in any context. This leaves only the interest of the inquirers to preclude the red herring why-questions. It is quite plausible to claim that in most contexts, the why-question constructed by Kitcher and Salmon would be uninteresting. A relevance relation that permits anything to explain anything would be completely useless in most situations. So, in most contexts, A does not explain P in virtue of the Kitcher-Salmon why-question.

The laissez-faire contextualist response relies on the contingent fact that the Kitcher-Salmon relevance criterion is uninteresting. Kitcher and Salmon suggest that an adequate response must do more. The erotetic view needs to draw a distinction between those relevance criteria that are "genuine" and those that "ought not be allowed in any context" (Kitcher and Salmon 1987: 325). Trivializing relevance criteria should be ruled out in principle. It is easy to show, however, that such a principle is entirely unnecessary. Either there is a context where the Kitcher-Salmon relevance relation is interesting or there is not. If the latter, then the a priori restriction is unnecessary. Alternatively, if we discovered a real context where the Kitcher-Salmon relevance relation generated interesting explanations, then the a priori restriction will have been defeated by counterexample.

The green cheese problem is amenable to similar treatment. As far as the presuppositions go, "the moon is made of green cheese" is a foil that could be appropriate in any context. (Unless, of course, the moon *is* made of green cheese.) Again, the burden of precluding such absurd foils falls to the interests of the investigators. Mostly, we are not interested in questions that take this proposition as a foil. Because of the interdependence of the contrast class and the relevance criteria, there is an additional resource for the resolution of the green cheese problem. If any arbitrary proposition is to serve as a foil in a legitimate why-question, there must be some relevance criterion that discriminates between it and the topic. In a real context, we are not only interested in certain sorts of contrast, but particular kinds of answer as well. If the relevance criterion is relatively fixed by interest, then only a select few false propositions will be appropriate as foils. Once the interest in relevance relations and foils is taken into account, it is quite clear that not just any false proposition will do.

The laissez-faire contextualist response to these problems puts an enormous burden on interests. One might well think that interests are far too soft to be the foundation of hard-nosed philosophy of science. Philosophers tend to think of interests as passing fancies or whims. They seem subjective in a problematic sense. One can be interested in anything. So, if Jones happens to be so interested, then "light is electromagnetic radiation rather than the moon is made of green cheese because there are no red herrings" is a perfectly good explanation. There must be more to scientific explanation than this (Grimes 1987: 89; Salmon 1984: 131–32). The appropriate response to this objection is that it relies on an impoverished conception of interest. While some interests are no more than passing fancies, others are built into practices and ways of life. Interests are shared, and not accidentally, by groups of people. Shared environment, experience (including education), and common problems all contribute to the interests of a group. There is much to say about what the interests of a group are and ought to be.

For the philosopher of science, the *interesting* interests are those shared by groups of inquirers. These fall roughly into two kinds, and we will call them generic interests and constitutive interests. Generic interests are not specific to particular domains or disciplines. They arise generally in the project of empirical inquiry and are found, in one degree or another, in a wide range of disciplines. Below, we will briefly explore the interests in stability and causality. While I expect that there are others, discussing them is outside of our purview. Constitutive interests are specific to particular domains of inquiry or disciplines. They are constitutive in the sense that failure to have the interest entails that one is not working in the discipline. It is no distortion to regard the training of students as an education of their interests. I will argue in the next chapter that an interest in the agent's point of view is one of the constitutive interests of the interpretive disciplines. The distinction between generic and constitutive interests is not meant to be exclusive. What is a constitutive interest of one domain may be so widespread that it is plausibly regarded as generic.

Let us turn to some of the *generic* interests that underpin explanation in empirical inquiry. Garfinkel made the interesting suggestion that some explanations are better than others because they are more stable (1981: 57). An explanation is stable insofar as it is unaffected by small changes in the causal or structural conditions which underlie the event. A stable explanation would remain correct even if the underlying facts had been slightly different. To illustrate, consider Garfinkel's original example. Imagine that Jones awakens early one morning to go for a drive in her Nissan 300ZX. She has breakfast, jumps in the car and hits the highway. She is going about 105 M.P.H. when she rounds a bend and rear-ends a slow moving truck. Suppose we ask why Jones had an accident. One answer is that she was going too fast. Now, Jones might sidestep this answer by pointing out that there were a very large number of causally necessary conditions for her accident. Had she spent a little more time over breakfast, perhaps making an omelet and reading the paper, she would have been at the curve a little later and missed the truck. Or again, if she had just gone a little *faster* she would have met and passed the truck before the blind curve. The problem was not that she was speeding; it was her timing.

It should be clear by now that these explanations answer different questions. On one reading, the question "Why did Jones have an accident?" asked why Jones had an accident that day, rather than no accident. In Jones's attempt to sidestep this explanation she answered a different question: Why did you have an accident at time *t*, rather than some other time that day, or no accident at all? Given the second contrast class, minute differences in timing *do* discriminate among the alternatives. This contrast class is, however, very unstable. If other things had been slightly different, Jones's leisurely breakfast may not have mattered (the trucker may have had a leisurely breakfast too, etc.). The first contrast class—an accident that day rather than no accident at all—is much more stable over these small causal permutations. Speeding raises the likelihood of having an accident at some time or other.

This interest in stable explanations has its roots in the value of prediction. If very small changes in the answer would keep it from discriminating between the topic and other elements of the contrast class, then its usefulness for predicting future events is limited. Stable explanations identify factors that remain explanatory over a range of cases. Therefore, the answers to questions that are stable have more predictive value than answers to questions that are unstable. Prediction is normally associated with the natural sciences, but it is just as important for interpretation. A necessary part of understanding another person or group is the ability to anticipate their actions. If one were clueless about what would happen next in a ritual, or about how a person would respond to a situation, one could hardly be said to have understanding. While prediction is not quantitative in the interpretive disciplines, it is no less an interest for that.

Another interest that appears in a variety of contexts is the interest in causes. This interest has its roots, perhaps, in the value of control. One of the reasons we engage in empirical inquiry is that we want to control our environment. Knowing the causes of a phenomenon can give us some measure of control. Thus, we are generally interested in why-questions where the answer discriminates causally between the topic and the foil(s). Those philosophers who have wanted to put general restrictions on relevance criteria and contrast classes have typically emphasized causal explanations (Henderson 1993; Humphreys 1989; Lipton 1991a; Lipton 1991b; Salmon 1984; Sober 1986). According to a laissez-faire contextualist, these philosophers have identified a class of why-questions that are of generic interest to empirical inquiry. Because there has been so much good work on causality, I will have little to say about it here. This does not imply that causal explanation is irrelevant or that interpretation precludes it. Any interpretation will be loaded with causal explanations. As the argument of section 4.1 showed, interpretation also needs some other forms of explanation. We will be concerned with these other forms because they are the critical cases for the development of an explanatory coherence view of interpretive change.

One might worry, again, that interest in causality is an interest more appropriate to the natural sciences than the social. The value of control, after all, is suspect when we are concerned with human beings. The warning is well taken, but we must remember that these are generic interests, not necessary conditions. Interests need not be, and typically are not, fully consistent. They may conflict with each other or with other principles we hold. An interest may be trumped, in a context, by more pressing concerns.[8] In some cases, we resolve the conflicting interests by pursuing the phenomenon from different explanatory frameworks. Where the conflict is more direct, we may have to make some hard decisions. Chapter 5 will explore an apparent explanatory conflict that is directly relevant to our project.

Laissez-faire contextualism thus commits the philosopher of science to a wide-ranging program. The full understanding of explanation requires a careful look at contemporary and historical inquiries to see what kinds of interests ground them, and what sorts of relevance criteria and contrast classes are deployed. Kitcher and Salmon rightly insist that this is a nontrivial task, and that it is not enough to merely wave in the direction of its completion (Kitcher and Salmon 1987: 326). The remaining chapters of this essay will be devoted to domains of particular importance to the question of interpretive change and the problems of apparent irrationality. We will identify some of the constitutive interests of the interpretive disciplines. Showing how norms, action, and meaning can have an explanatory role will require exhibiting the contrast classes and relevance criteria of the appropriate why-questions. Moreover, the presuppositions of these why-questions will have to be satisfied by the contexts of interpretive inquiry, and the questions will have to satisfy the interests of the inquirers. It is a tall order, but not impossible to fill.

4.5 EXPLANATION AND COHERENCE REVISITED

According to the principle of explanatory coherence, an interpretation is an interlaced body of explanations. The problems of apparent irrationality are striking forms of interpretive incoherence where beliefs or behavior cry out for explanation. Finding the explanation in these cases may require revising or rejecting other, existing explanations in the interpretation. The goal is to revise

---

8. Indeed, the pressing concerns might be moral or political. I explore this idea in "The Politics of Explanation and the Origins of Anthropology" (forthcoming).

the interpretation in a way that provides the best overall explanation of the community under study. In other words, the interpreter should choose the interpretation with the most explanatory coherence. In section 3.3, we distinguished four roles that an interpretive claim might have: explanans, explanandum, both explanans and explanandum, neither explanans nor explanandum. The erotetic model of explanation requires us to refine this preliminary account of explanatory coherence.

A consequence of wedding the erotetic model of explanation to an explanatory coherence view of interpretive change is that why-questions mediate the relationships among interpretive claims. Why-questions provide three explanatory roles. A proposition may be the answer, the topic, or a presupposition of a why-question. A claim thus coheres with an interpretation insofar as it plays one or more of these explanatory roles. The four possible explanatory roles identified in section 3.3 have multiplied to eight. A claim might be the

1.   answer to a why-question,[9]

2.   topic of a why-question,

3.   presupposition of a why-question,

4.   answer to one why-question and topic of another,

5.   topic of one why-question and presupposition of another,

6.   answer to one why-question and presupposition of another,

7.   answer to one why-question, topic of another, and presupposition of a third, or

8.   neither answer, nor topic, nor presupposition of any why-question.

This list enumerates *kinds* of explanatory role. Clearly, a particular claim might be the topic, answer, or presupposition of any number of why-questions (each with different foils or relevance relations). A claim, then, coheres with an interpretation insofar as it plays at least one of these explanatory roles. Also, here and below, when a proposition is identified as the topic of a why-question, we must presume that that why-question has an answer and that its presuppositions are satisfied by claims in the interpretation. In the absence of this assumption, interpretations could be made coherent by simply *asking* "Why?" about each of their claims. This two-year-old's strategy for inquiry surely will not suffice to create coherence.

---

9. Also, it is not the presupposition or topic of any why-question. Roles 1 through 6 assume that the proposition is not playing the unmentioned roles in a why-question.

The proliferation of explanatory roles requires us to modify our earlier characterization of explanatory coherence. Section 3.3 argued that one interpretation, *A*, has more explanatory coherence than another, *B*, when:

1. *A* has fewer claims that are neither explained nor explanatory than *B*.

2. *A* has fewer claims that explain without themselves being explained (unexplained explainers) than *B*.

These two criteria were ranked. Claims that neither explained nor were explanatory—explanatory danglers—count more strongly against the coherence of an interpretation than unexplained explainers. Both of these categories remain parts of our more refined analysis. However, we need to find a place for the new explanatory roles revealed by the erotetic model.

The greatest threat to coherence is the presence of claims that cannot be explained. Such claims indicate an important inadequacy of the account. The goal of inquiry is to understand why things happen, why people do and say what they do, why social arrangements are as they are. The erotetic model of explanation identifies this goal of inquiry with explanation. The failure to explain something, then, is a profound failure to understand. This means that explanatory danglers—type (8), above—again count most strongly against coherence. Claims that are only answers or presuppositions—types (1), (3), and (6), above—and are not themselves explained also count against coherence. Unexplained answers and presuppositions count against coherence less strongly than the explanatory danglers do because these claims contribute to the interpretation. They do some explanatory work. The reason that they count against coherence at all is that an excess of unexplained answers and presuppositions makes the interpretation ad hoc. An interpretation that can answer why-questions about such claims is clearly a better interpretation than one that leaves them unexplained.

The eight explanatory roles can thus be divided into those that contribute to the coherence of an interpretation and those that detract from it. One interpretation is *less* coherent than another insofar as it has more claims, *P*, such that:

1. *P* neither answers, nor is the topic, nor is presupposed by any why-question.

2. *P* either answers a why-question or is presupposed by a why-question, but not both, and is not the topic of any why-question.

3. *P* answers one why-question and is presupposed by another, but is not the topic of any why-question.

One interpretation is *more* coherent than another insofar as it has more claims, *P*, such that:

4. *P* answers one question, is the topic of another, and is presupposed by a third.

5. *P* answers one question and is the topic of another, or *P* is the topic of one question and the presupposition of another.

6. *P* is the topic of a why-question.

Each of these lists is ranked, with the first counting most strongly for or against coherence. In addition, the positive and negative criteria are themselves ranked. Because of the importance of explanation to understanding, failure to explain something is a more important defect than additional explanatory roles is a benefit. Therefore, judgments of relative coherence should first consider criteria (1–3). Other things being equal with respect to (1–3), a judgment of relative coherence should consider criteria (4–6).[10]

In addition to these refinements in our conception of explanatory coherence, the erotetic model of explanation permits a novel conception of interpretive dynamics. Interpretations change as claims are added to or subtracted from an interpretation. These changes go well beyond mere accretion. They can force profound structural changes in the interpretation. Since why-questions constitute the coherence-making relationships among interpretive claims, a claim has an explanatory role only if there is a why-question wherein the claim is the topic, answer, or presupposition. Why-questions, in turn, are appropriate only if their presuppositions are satisfied and the interpreter is interested in such questions. It follows that removing a claim from an interpretation will force the rejection of any why-question that presupposes it. This, in turn, will cause the topic, answer, and other presuppositions of that why-question to lose one of their explanatory roles. Denying one claim in an interpretation can thus potentially cause a widespread loss of coherence.

For example, suppose we are interpreting a teacher and his class, along the lines of the examples in section 4.3. We have observed the grade distribution and know that Mary and Holly got As; Joe, Fred, and Sarah got Bs, and so on. We find that ten percent of the class got As. Against this background, we begin to interpret the behavior, and that means asking why-questions. So, we ask

---

10. This ranking is intended only to be a rough sketch. In real interpretations in the social sciences, it is unlikely that we will be faced with fine-grained decisions about coherence. I expect that these criteria could be quantified, appropriately weighted, and an algorithm created for judging relative coherence. Thagard has been successful in similar projects (Thagard 1992). This kind of work is important for the development of explanatory coherence epistemology. While it would increase the clarity and precision of the analysis, we will go no further towards an explicit model of relative coherence. The larger and more pressing problem is to show that explanatory coherence is a plausible candidate for a criterion of interpretive change.

why Mary got an A (rather than another grade). Section 4.3 argued that this question was ambiguous between a question that asked for an answer that mentions facts about Mary alone and one that asks for facts about Mary's relation to her classmates. In the first case, the why-question has an atomistic presupposition. In this context, the atomistic presupposition is the claim that there is no predetermined curve imposed on the grades. Let this be the presupposition made when we ask why Mary got an A (rather than another grade), and let the best answer to this question be that Mary worked hard. To add a bit more structure, suppose we also ask why ten percent of the students got As, and that the best answer is that ten percent of the students worked hard, and everybody who worked hard got an A. We have, then, a fragment of an interpretation that looks something like this:

Claims:
    Mary got an A.
    Ten percent of the students got As.
    There is no predetermined curve.
    Mary worked hard.
    Ten percent of the students worked hard.
    Everyone who worked hard got an A.

Explanatory relationships:
    Why did Mary get an A (rather than another grade)?

        Topic: Mary got an A.
        Presuppositions: Mary did not get another grade; there is no
            predetermined curve.
        Answer: Mary worked hard.

    Why did ten percent of the students get As (rather than a
    different percentage)?

        Topic: Ten percent of the students got As.
        Presuppositions: Neither more nor less than ten percent of the
            students got As; there is no predetermined curve.
        Answer: Ten percent of the students worked hard, and
            everyone who worked hard got an A.

This is a tidy and relatively coherent interpretation. Every claim has some explanatory role.

    Consider how this interpretation would have to be revised in the face of two possible changes. First, suppose that we discover that, contrary to the previous finding, twelve percent of the students got As. The claim that twelve percent of the students got As replaces the previously held claim that ten

percent got As. Since its topic is no longer part of the interpretation, we
cannot ask the second why-question. This leaves two claims without an explanatory role. The first why-question is unaffected and the other propositions
retain their roles. Second, suppose we discover that there is a predetermined
curve, and this claim replaces its contrary. In this case, there is a dramatic loss
of coherence. Both why-questions presuppose that there is no predetermined
curve. If this claim is denied, then neither why-question can be appropriately
raised. The result of this revision is that none of the claims have any explanatory role in this tiny fragment of an interpretation. Clearly, the second possible
revision does much more damage to the coherence of the interpretation than
the first does. Notice that in both cases, exactly one claim has been revised.
Notice also that neither revision forces us to reject any other claims. That
Mary worked hard remains one of the interpretive claims, even if it no longer
explains why she got an A.

Let us continue this simple example of interpretive dynamics by considering how coherence could be increased after each discovery. In the first case,
coherence can be restored to its former level very simply. We may ask why
twelve percent of the students got As (rather than a different percentage). This
question may still be atomistic, since the presupposition that there is *no* predetermined curve has not been disrupted in this, first, example of revision. The
claim that ten percent of the students worked hard, however, cannot be the
answer without accounting for the additional two percent of the As. Answering
this new question, then, requires us to either revise another claim (for example,
that twelve percent, not ten percent, of the students worked hard) or to
supplement the interpretation with new a claim (for example, that two percent
had previous experience with the class material). In this case, the revision of
one claim resulted in an interpretation with a very similar structure and
slightly different content.

One would expect the second possible revision to force more drastic
changes. In this case, we were left with no explanations at all, because a
presupposition shared by both why-questions failed. We can again ask why
Mary got an A, but the relevance criterion for this question has to be different
from the question asked earlier. The presence of a predetermined curve means
that relevant answers have to compare Mary to her classmates. We have to
claim not only that Mary worked hard, but that she worked harder than ninety
percent of her peers. Reconstructing this explanation, then, requires adding
claims to the interpretation. The other why-question could be reconstructed
as well. The question of why ten percent of the students got As can be directly
answered by noting that there is a predetermined curve whereby ten percent
of the students always get As. The claim that there is a predetermined curve
again does double duty, this time as the presupposition of the first why-
question and answer to the second. Even so, there is a net loss of coherence.
The claims that ten percent of the students worked hard and that everyone

who worked hard got an A are left without any explanatory role. While they might still be true, they are explanatory danglers in this interpretive fragment.

The foregoing examples have been greatly simplified. Clearly, any one of the claims in this fragment might be the topic of a why-question, and their answers would require more interpretive claims. Moreover, in a realistic case these changes would have been motivated. Perhaps they result from new observations or new explanatory hypotheses. These explanatory relationships would be open to evaluation, and the interpreter would have to decide whether the increase to coherence warranted their adoption. The point of the foregoing examples is only to illustrate the interpretive dynamics made possible by the explanatory coherence view of interpretive change. Because why-questions structure interpretations, small changes in content can have enormous ramifications for coherence. The addition of a single new hypothesis might permit the explanation of a whole range of phenomena that were heretofore inexplicable. If it is widely presupposed, the elimination of a single claim might sever explanatory relations throughout the interpretation. Powered by the erotetic model, the simple device of choosing the interpretation with the most explanatory coherence becomes the engine of interpretive change.

CHAPTER 5

Intentional Action and
Social Explanation

In the social sciences, interpretation is associated with a first person, experiential perspective. It is natural to think that an adequate interpretation must capture the agent's point of view. Intentional action explanations do so by appeal to the agent's intentions or reasons. Such explanations provide a view of how the agent saw the situation, what she regarded as important, what she was trying to achieve, and so on. There are limits, however, to the sort of internal understanding that intentional action explanation yields. The examples of chapter 2 illustrate two. First, a full understanding may require claims that the members of the social group do not or cannot recognize. If Nutini and Roberts are right, for example, the Tlaxcalan system of belief preserves a kind of self-deception (cf. section 2.1). If the cultural system is to work, participants cannot normally recognize its true properties. Second, not all irrationality is merely apparent. We want to preserve the possibility that some forms of behavior really are irrational (cf. section 2.4). In both of these cases, an external point of view is necessary for understanding the behavior. Therefore, an interpretation must not be limited to explanation from the agent's point of view.

There is a second, rather different, reason why an interpretation must include both internal and external explanations. Chapter 4 presented and defended the erotetic model of explanation. On that model, explanation is sensitive to the interests of the investigators. Section 4.4 distinguished between generic and constitutive interests. A constitutive interest is necessarily shared by inquirers in a particular domain. Having the interest is part of what identifies an inquirer as working within a given discipline or subdiscipline. The interpretive disciplines have at least two constitutive interests. The first is an interest in the agent's point of view. A cultural anthropologist, sociologist, or historian wants to know how the agents understand their own actions, values, social structures, and so on. This concern to see the world from the local point of view is the hallmark of the interpretive disciplines. It marks them off from the physical sciences on one hand and from other sorts of social science, such as biological anthropology or cognitive psychology, on the other. The interest in the agent's point of view demands that an interpretation include an agent's reasons for his actions or beliefs. This, in turn, means that claims about the agent's reasons must have some explanatory role. The obvious role for claims about reasons is the explanation of belief and intentional action. The second interest constitutive of the interpretive disciplines is an interest in social phenomena, including institutions, rituals, economic and political relationships, and other organized forms of behavior. An interpretation of a group of individuals must therefore include claims about the enduring social structures that mediate relations among individuals. Explanatory coherence requires that interpretive claims be either explained or explanatory. Therefore, if the interpretive disciplines are interested in both the agents' point of view and their social relations, an interpretation must have both individualistic and social explanations.[1]

Both of the arguments above entail explanatory pluralism. There is more than one form of explanation and an adequate interpretation will typically need more than one kind. Pluralism raises some important problems. How can different forms of explanation be integrated into a single, coherent interpretation? Are there cases where the different forms of explanation are incompatible? The latter question is particularly pressing in light of the two constitutive interests discussed above. A single action might be explained by appeal to the agent's reasons and by appeal to social factors outside of the agent's awareness. In such a case, the two interests seem to motivate incompatible explanations of the same event. In *Semantics and Social Science* (1981: 125–26), Macdonald and Pettit argued that intentional action and social explanations conflict, and that such conflict should always be resolved in favor of intentional action explanations. If sound, this argument would have important ramifications for an explanatory coherence criterion of interpretive change. Interpretations could be made coherent only by intentional action explanations, and the interest in social phenomena would have to be discharged by studying individuals and their motivations alone. Moreover, when confronted with the kind of apparent irrationality exhibited by the Tlaxcalans, an interpreter would have to preserve coherence by reinterpreting the motivations of the individuals involved. The question of whether an explanatory pluralism can be consistently maintained is thus pressing.

---

1. This argument for explanatory pluralism assumes that explanations of social phenomena do not reduce to intentional action explanations. This assumption will be supported by arguments in this chapter and in chapter 6.

Macdonald and Pettit's argument begins from the premise that there are three sorts of explananda possible for social explanations, and all three explananda are also the object of intentional action explanations. The first two explananda are (1) the action of an individual and (2) any event that is the cooperative outcome of several agents' actions. Since, in both cases, the explanandum is the intentional action of one or more agents, an intentional action explanation is possible. Therefore, both a collectivist explanation and an intentional action explanation of the same event are possible. The third kind of explanandum for a collectivist explanation is institutional change or the effects of one institution on another. For example, suppose a church congregation slowly loses members until the church disappears. The dissipation of the congregation might be explained by the fact that the church's function was taken over by some secular institution. This kind of event is distinct from the first two explananda of collectivist explanations, since the event is presumably not to be explained directly as the intentional action of one or more agents. (We may suppose that no member wanted the church to dissolve.) Nonetheless, Macdonald and Pettit maintain that the institutional events must have some relationship to the intentional actions of agents. If not, the explanation of institutional change would "depict people as regularly going 'on the blink,' performing in the mode of autonomic systems rather than agents" (1981: 125). The agents did not intend the institutional change; it was the unforeseen result of their intentional action. Macdonald and Pettit therefore suggest that institutional change must supervene on the intentional actions of the participants. That is, there can be no events involving the institution that do not involve some intentional actions. If this supervenience assumption is granted, then the third explanandum shares the fate of the first two. All possible explananda of social explanations are also explananda of intentional action explanations.

Macdonald and Pettit contend that an intentional action explanation of a given event is incompatible with any social explanation of the same event. When presented with two conflicting explanations of the same event, we are forced to choose. We should always prefer the intentional action explanation, according to Macdonald and Pettit, because such explanations preserve our conception of ourselves as agents. Social explanations appeal to factors outside of the awareness of the agents. Social explanations thus conflict with the "orthodox conception of agents," roughly, the conception of persons who act rationally on their beliefs and desires. We cannot cease thinking of ourselves as agents, and therefore we must always prefer intentional action explanations to social explanations. Since intentional action explanations are available whenever a social explanation is proposed, social explanations are never acceptable (1981: 125–26).

Macdonald and Pettit's argument has two premises that deserve closer examination. First, they contend that intentional action explanations and social explanations have the same explanandum. Whether two explanations have the same explanandum depends on how explananda are individuated. This depends, in turn, on the model of explanation deployed. The remainder of this chapter will be devoted to analyzing the form of intentional action explanations and one particularly troublesome sort of social explanation. The second important premise of Macdonald and Pettit's argument is that intentional action explanations and social explanations are incompatible. This premise needs to be unpacked too, since under some circumstances different explanations of the same event are compatible. To evaluate the argument we need a clear sense of the conditions under which two explanations conflict.

When do two explanations have the same object? On the erotetic model, an explanation is the answer to a why-question. Why-questions are defined by their topic, foils, and relevance criteria, so the object of explanation must be one of these elements or some combination of them. The topic is an obvious candidate for the object of explanation. This suggestion does not seem right, however, since the topic is never explained all by itself. An answer must discriminate between the topic and foil. So, it is more plausible to suppose that the object of an explanation is the topic in contrast to the foil. Two explanations have the same object, or "explain the same thing," when they are answers to why-questions with the same topic and foil(s).

The question of whether two explanations conflict is independent of whether they explain the same thing. Answers to entirely different questions may be inconsistent, and different answers to questions with the same topic and foil(s) may be compatible. Moreover, explanations may conflict in several different ways. Let us distinguish between conflict that arises from the content of the answers and conflict that arises from the why-questions themselves. With respect to the answers, conflicting answers may be either logically inconsistent or logically consistent but not compossible. The latter could arise because the event described in answer to one why-question would preclude the event described by the answer to another or causally screen it off from the topic event. Alternatively, the two answers might ascribe incompatible predicates (for example, blue and colorless, mammal and avian) to a single event or state of affairs. The possible incompatibility of answers is no threat to explanatory pluralism. Competing answers to a single question can be incompatible. This sort of incompatibility shows only that both answers cannot be true. It does not show that the why-questions are incompatible.

To threaten explanatory pluralism, the why-questions themselves would have to be incompatible. Since questions make no claims, the incompatibility would have to arise from the content of the questions' presuppositions. Why-questions presuppose that the topic is true and that the foils are false. Thus, if one why-question takes P as its topic, and another takes P as a foil, then the two cannot both be appropriately asked. Relevance criteria have presuppositions too, as section 4.3 showed. In general, two why-questions conflict when the presuppositions of one are inconsistent or not compossible with the presuppositions of another. Explanations can be sorted into kinds on the basis of their shared presuppositions. Two *kinds* of explanation will conflict, then, if the presuppositions definitive of each kind are inconsistent or not compossible.

Macdonald and Pettit's claim about conflict does not seem well expressed by our analysis that conflict arises from incompatible presuppositions. Their concern is a bit more sophisticated. They think that the explanans of social explanations, when taken as explanatory, conflict with our conception of ourselves as agents. The content of any answer (or, perhaps, most or typical answers) to an intentional action why-question will conflict with the answer to a social why-question with the same object. We can use the resources of the erotetic model to make this concern precise. Relevance criteria serve to identify a class of propositions that could be answers to the why-question. The why-questions underlying intentional action and social explanations require different classes of possible answers. Macdonald and Pettit's argument seems to be that the members of these two classes are incompatible. Social why-questions require answers that are always or typically not compossible with answers required by intentional action why-questions. In general, then, we may say that two explanations or kinds of explanation conflict when either

1. the presuppositions of one (kind of) why-question are inconsistent or not compossible with the presuppositions of another (kind of) why-question, or

2. the relevance relation for the two (kinds of) why-questions isolate classes of answers that are always, mostly, or typically inconsistent or not compossible.

Conflicts that arise out of kinds of why-question are a significant threat to explanatory pluralism. If two kinds of why-question conflict, then an interpretation would have to limit itself to one form of explanation at the expense of the other. While this result would not undermine the explanatory coherence criterion of interpretive change, it would profoundly influence the shape of possible interpretations.[2]

To determine whether two kinds of explanation conflict, we need a close analysis of their forms. We need to understand the character of the topics, foils and relevance criteria, and the presuppositions that arise from them. We also have to determine whether the answers to which the relevance criteria direct

---

2. Thagard also points out that explanatory conflict makes a theory relatively incoherent. The forgoing discussion shows that the erotetic model of explanation permits a more elaborate analysis of conflict than the one Thagard uses in his principles of explanatory coherence (1992: 68–69).

us are compatible. The issue raised in this chapter is whether intentional action explanations and social explanations are compatible. There are, however, a variety of "social explanations." Explanations that involve meaning and norms— to be analyzed in chapters 6 and 7 respectively—are social in the sense that they neither explain individual actions nor appeal to the motivations of particular agents. We will consider their consistency with each other and with intentional action explanations at the appropriate time. The remainder of this chapter will consider whether functional explanations conflict with intentional action explanations. Traditionally, functional explanations have seemed the most threatening to the agent's point of view. An individual's action can be explained functionally. Prima facie, then, functional and intentional action explanations can have the same explanatory object. Moreover, a functional explanation of an intentional action seems to treat the action as if the agent's faculties had "gone on the blink." If we can show that functional explanations are compatible with intentional action explanations, then we will have disposed of one of the hard cases of explanatory conflict.

5.2 Intentional Action Explanations

Intentional action explanations look for the reasons, goals, plans, aspirations, and other sorts of motivations for action. An interest in the agent's reasons stands behind a why-question about an intentional action. We want to know what made the action attractive to the agent, what she was trying to achieve by doing it, and so on. Intentional action why-questions therefore require answers that describe the agent's reasons or motivations. An agent's reasons can discriminate between topic and foil only if the contrast class is properly constructed. This criterion of relevance therefore imposes restrictions on the contrast class of an intentional action why-question. These restrictions are the distinctive presuppositions of intentional action why-questions.

The first, rather obvious, presupposition of intentional action why-questions is that the topic sentence describes an intentional action. Suppose we ask, "Why did Jones order coffee?" as Jones receives her cup from the waiter. If the answer is to give Jones's reason, then the question presupposes that the order was something Jones did intentionally. This presupposition is stronger than the generic presupposition that the topic of a why-question is true. The action has to be intentional under the description employed by the topic. If the topic proposition is true but the action is not intentional under that description, then the why-question cannot be answered by describing some of the agent's motives. For example, suppose English is not Jones's native tongue and she confused the words for "coffee" and "tea." She did order coffee, but she did not do so intentionally. Jones had no reason for ordering coffee, and hence there is no answer satisfying the relevance criterion. Construed as an intentional action why-question, "Why did Jones order coffee?" deserves to be rejected in a factual context like this, say, by noting that she did not mean to order coffee.

Intentional action explanations have several other distinctive presuppositions. One way to elicit the presuppositions is to contrast questions satisfying the presuppositions with questions violating them. Consider the following set of questions where the foils have been made explicit. Let us suppose that the topic describes an intentional action in each case.

1.   Why did Jones order coffee rather than tea?

2.   Why did Jones order coffee rather than stealing it?

3.   Why did Jones order coffee rather than carving a bust of Nietzsche?

4.   Why did Jones, rather than Smith, order coffee? (Or, more canonically: Why did Jones order coffee rather than Smith order coffee?)

Clearly, not just any false proposition can be the foil for an intentional action why-question. While (1) and (2) are natural questions about action, (3) and (4) are bizarre. Answering (4) does not constitute an intentional action explanation at all. The question contrasts the actions of two different agents. The question could be answered by citing some difference between Smith and Jones (for example, that Smith did not have enough money). In the absence of an elaborate story, however, none of Jones's motives will discriminate between her ordering coffee and Smith's ordering coffee. Under ordinary circumstances, no answer to question (4) will satisfy the relevance criterion of an intentional action why-question. Question (3) is similarly absurd unless we imagine some very special circumstances. It suggests that, in this context, ordering coffee and carving a bust of Nietzsche are somehow alternatives among which Jones could choose. Telling a story that makes the foil a legitimate alternative to the topic makes the question much more acceptable. For example, suppose Jones is a sculptor in the process of carving the bust of Nietzsche. She stops to order coffee and we ask why. In the right context, question (3) could be an appropriate intentional action why-question. The contextualization of question (3) and the failure of question (4) as an intentional action why-question highlight two features of the contrast class for why-questions about intentional action.

First, elements of a contrast class for an intentional action explanation must be subject to the same sort of reason. If a reason is to discriminate between two possible actions, it must be applicable to both topic and foil. Question (4) fails to satisfy this presupposition because it contrasts the actions of two different agents. With respect to question (3), a person usually orders coffee because she likes the taste, needs the caffeine jolt, wants something to do with her hands during a conversation, or something similar. Question (3) sounds odd because none of these are ordinarily reasons for or against carving a bust of Nietzsche. When constructing a context in which question (3) makes sense, we make the alternatives subject to commensurable reasons. There is a set of considerations that count for or against the choice between continuing to work on the statue or take a break. Jones might be tired, or conversely, under deadline pressure to finish. Notice that questions (1) and (2) are both more readily intelligible and clearly satisfy this presupposition. In both (1) and (2), the reasons for or against the topic are normally relevant to the foil. It should not be concluded that every reason must count for the topic and against the foil. An agent may have motives that count against both, but is forced to choose the lesser of two evils. In realistic settings, an agent is likely to have a number of reasons that weigh differently for topic and foil. Real choice is rarely a simple matter.

Second, the foils need to be appropriate (in a sense to be determined) for the agent under the circumstances. One of the reasons why question (3) seems odd is that a choice between ordering coffee and carving a bust of Nietzsche sounds absurd. The alternative is made more plausible by the contextualzing story. Similarly, where Jones is an ordinary, morally upright citizen, question (2)—Why did Jones order coffee rather than stealing it?—would be completely inappropriate. If stealing coffee is something that the agent would not conceive of doing, she would have no reason for ordering a cup of coffee rather than stealing it. If we put the question to her, she would be offended because the question presupposes that stealing the coffee is something she might do. Someone for whom stealing is not a viable option would reject the question rather than answer it.

Spelling out the sense in which a foil must be "appropriate" is a complex matter. In the paradigm cases of deliberate action, the agent consciously chooses among alternative courses of action. It is thus tempting to require that the contrast class for an intentional action explanation describe those actions among which the agent chose. It would be a mistake to do so, since not all intentional action is deliberate in this sense. As I walk through the halls of a building, I intentionally turn right or left at each fork. Moreover, I have a reason for each choice (this is the fastest or only way to get where I am going). Yet, I do not bring the alternatives to mind and deliberate among them at each turn. Therefore, where the action is intentional and explicable by reasons, the agent need not have actually called all of the relevant alternatives to mind or explicitly chosen among them.

The context of the action is one source of appropriate alternatives. The environment itself can structure a person's choices. Thus, when walking through a building, the architecture forces one to turn left or right, choose this door or that, and so on. Cows can only be milked one at a time, so one has to be first and another second. The social environment is relevant too, including the local norms, habits, and customs. When ordering coffee in a café, one set of relevant alternatives is given by the café's menu. For any item on the menu, it is appropriate to ask why the agent preferred coffee to it. Or again, when driving up to a filling station, a person expects or is expected to make a small number of choices: the kind of gasoline, method of payment, and whether to check the oil and wash the windows. In all of these cases, the alternatives could be appropriate foils of intentional action why-questions even if the agent did not consciously deliberate among them. The reason is that in such contexts the agent is likely to have a reason for doing the topic action rather than the alternative.

Another source of plausible alternatives arises from the topic itself. When we describe the topic action as "Jones ordered coffee," the concept of an order sets the stage. Jones must be in some context where coffee (and, perhaps, other things) may be requested from others and (perhaps) paid for. The likely alternatives are those things that might be ordered in this context. Many intentional action concepts have such natural alternatives built into them. Where the action concept involves a mode, such as quickly or slowly, deliberately or carelessly, cautiously or aggressively, we can use these modes as foils. Similarly, where the action is performed on or to something, there is a normal class of objects for the action; and where the action is typically done with some tool or means, there is a normal class of instruments. In such cases, the typical objects or instruments can be appropriate foils. In all of these cases where a foil is one of the typical modes, objects, or instruments of the action, the foil may be appropriate even if the agent did not bring it to mind and consciously decide not to adopt it.

Whether a foil is "appropriate under the circumstances" is thus determined by at least four factors: (i) The alternative is one that the agent had in mind. (ii) The natural or social context forces a choice between the topic action and the alternative. (iii) The alternative is one that is customary or normally expected under those circumstances. And, (iv) the alternative is one of the typical modes, objects, or instruments of the intentional action concept deployed in the topic. These criteria are not mutually exclusive. Indeed, where the foils of a why-question are not alternatives that the agent brought to mind, the appropriateness increases as these factors are combined. Thus, asking a person at the grocery store why she bought 2% milk rather than skim or whole milk satisfies (ii), (iii), and (iv). It is very likely to elicit a response even if she did not deliberate among these alternative actions. Asking that same person why she bought 2% milk rather than a half-pound of salt cod is likely to elicit puzzlement. The second presupposition of intentional action explanations, then, is that the foils are appropriate for the agent under the circumstances, and an action is "appropriate for the agent under the circumstances" if it satisfies one or more of conditions (i–iv), above.

The way in which intentional action why-questions have been characterized thus far is open to a couple of important objections. First, the action must be intentional under the topic description, and the description is a source of appropriate foils. It is essential, then, that the topic describe something the agent did intentionally. The erotetic view of action explanation thus becomes entangled in the traditional questions about intentional action descriptions. This is a wide problematic, and we do not need to survey the entire web. The primary questions of this project are epistemological, so we are interested in how an interpreter might know that an intentional action description is the right one. How does an ethnographer or historian know that she has characterized the actions of her subjects in an appropriate way? An appeal to the larger interpretive context is the beginning of an answer. The very fact that the topic coheres with the interpretation gives grounds for believing that it is correct. Claims are made coherent with an interpretation by being explained or explanatory. So, the fact that there is an answer to the question, Why P, rather than Q? is grounds for believing the claim that P. Where the question is an intentional action why-question, we have grounds for thinking that P is an appropriate intentional action description. Of course, if this were the *only* reason for believing that the intentional action description was correct, it would be a very weak justification. We need some richer connections between the intentional action description and the other interpretive claims.

Each time a question is answered, that answer potentially becomes the topic of a new why-question. This relationship among explanations was used by G. E. M. Anscombe to probe the conception of intentionality (Anscombe 1963). The answer to an intentional action why-question may sometimes take the form "In order to X." In this kind of case, X can be itself the topic of another intentional action why-question:

> [T]here are a large number of [descriptions], in the imagined case, for which we can readily suppose that the answer to the question 'Why are you X-ing' falls within the range. E.g. 'Why are you moving your arm up and down?'— 'I'm pumping.' 'Why are you pumping?'—'I'm pumping the water-supply for the house.' 'Why are you beating out that curious rhythm?'—'Oh, I found out how to do it, as the pump does click anyway, and I do it just for fun.' 'Why are you pumping the water?'—'Because it's needed up at the house' and (*sotto voce*) 'To polish that lot off.' 'Why are you poisoning those people?'—'If we can get rid of them, the other lot will get in and . . .' (Anscombe 1963: 38).

We begin with some description of the event, X, and ask the agent: Why are you X-ing? If the agent accepts this question and answers it, then X-ing is a description under which the action is intentional. If he rejects it, then X was not an appropriate intentional action description. It was an unintended or unforeseen consequence, side effect, accidental correlation, or something of the sort. The range of appropriate intentional action descriptions can be identified with the scope of these chains of sensible why-questions. This is a further way in which coherence with other interpretive claims makes an action description appropriate.

The core of Anscombe's insight is that the topic of an intentional action why-question must be one recognized by the agent. The agent has to think of herself as acting under that description. This gives rise to a further objection. The agent has an implausible degree of authority over the characterization of what she did. If the identification of descriptions under which the action is intentional is up to the agent, it would follow that the opinion of the perpetrator alone distinguishes between first-degree murder and an accidental death. If she says that she was not "committing murder," then she did not commit a murder. This is absurd. While the agent's self-description has significant weight, it is not definitive. The problem arises because, so far, the primary grounds for determining the truth of the description is its acceptability to the agent.

To resolve this problem, we need to draw on the resources already developed for the foils of intentional action why-questions: the descriptive term itself and the context of the events. These compete with and in many cases can defeat the agent's authority over how her action is appropriately described. Consider, for example, the phrase "driving an automobile." This phrase denotes an intentional action—driving is not something that might be done either deliberately or accidentally, like "falling," or as a reflex, like "moving your arm." While "driving an automobile" is unambiguously intentional, whether someone is driving does not primarily depend on how the agent conceives of her own action. If she is making the vehicle turn, accelerate, brake, etc., she is driving. What is within the agent's awareness, what she *thinks* she is doing, is largely irrelevant. Thus an intoxicated person who has no idea what she is doing is still driving. Or again, consider the difference between pretense and action in this case. When a child sits at the wheel, flipping the switches and making motor noises, she may be pretending to drive. If the car starts an uncontrolled roll, then the child may still be pretending. If she starts the engine and makes a left onto the highway, she is no longer pretending. Regardless of her mental state she is now driving (for better or worse!).

The semantic content of the action description determines how to balance the agent's self-descriptions against her actual movements and their consequences. Semantically, action descriptions have a range of dependency on the agent's self-description. On one end of the range, there are objective action concepts, for example, walking, driving, eating, making a pot, building a house, and so on. In these cases, the events and their context determine whether a person is or is not acting intentionally under that description. If a person is moving his body in a particular way, then he is walking. In this case, it does not matter what he *thinks* he is doing. At the other end of the scale are subjective action concepts. The application of these depend more heavily on how the agent conceives of himself. Whether one is playing solitaire or just practicing is a distinction that depends on what the agent takes himself to be doing. Similarly, the difference between thinking hard and daydreaming is one that has frustrated many a philosopher's spouse because the contextual clues are so sparse. This is not to say that they are nonexistent.

Customs, conventions, and norms can also determine the applicability of some intentional action descriptions. Game rules sometimes speak to the issue of whether an action was or was not performed. In many card games, for instance, once a card has been played it cannot be recalled, even if the player put it on the table by mistake. In this case, whether an action description like "Jones played the two of clubs" is entirely determined by the rules found in the context of action. It does not matter what Jones was thinking or even whether she meant to play the card. Social norms and conventions are significantly different from game rules, but similar points can be made. Telling a ribald joke in the common room of the Philosophy Department may constitute an act of sexual harassment, even if the narrator meant no harm. To drive past a stop sign is to perform an illegal act, even if the driver did not see the sign or did not know the law. In these and similar cases, whether the action description is appropriate depends on the rules, norms, conventions, or customs in play.

The contentiousness of the sexual harassment example, above, highlights the subtle, and sometimes problematic, nature of intentional action description. The *sati* example is an excellent illustration. There were two competing explanations of why Roop Kanwar submitted to the flames of her husband's pyre. According to the first, her's was an act of self-sacrifice. This answers the question why Roop Kanwar performed *sati* rather than become a widow. The question asks for an explanation in terms of her reasons, and it presupposes that she acted intentionally. According to the second explanation, she was coerced, perhaps drugged, by her husband's family for their own base purposes. Proponents of the second are denying that a presupposition of the first is satisfied. If Roop Kanwar was strongly coerced or drugged, she was not sacrificing herself, in which case the first question does not even arise. Likewise, by denying that Roop Kanwar was strongly coerced or drugged, the proponents of the first explanation deny a presupposition of the second. What this example shows is that the appropriateness of an action description is not something to be determined by simply observing the action. It depends on how that description may be embedded within a larger explanatory framework. The dispute over Roop Kanwar's intentions or lack thereof is simply the point of contact between two far-reaching interpretations.

We may conclude that the agent does not have absolute authority over the description of her action. While the agent's self-descriptions are an important source of topics for why-questions, they are not the only source. Many intentional action descriptions will be true regardless of the mental state of the agent, and regardless of whether she accepts or admits them. Knowing what the descriptive terms mean can, in a large class of cases, help determine whether the action is intentional under that description. Knowing the norms, conventions, and customs relevant to a particular context is likewise helpful. For both subjective and objective action concepts, the final test of whether the action description is appropriate is whether the descriptions can be embedded in a larger interpretation. All of the embedding links are explanatory, and they establish several kinds of relationship. The topic description might be the answer to another intentional action why-question. Moreover, claims about the meaning of the local action words are themselves the sort of thing that can be explained, as are the norms, customs, and habits that form a relevant part of the context (the forms of these explanations will be explored in chapters 6 and 7). The interpreter thus has various grounds for judging that an intentional action description is appropriate.

It is instructive to contemplate the differences and similarities between the erotetic model of intentional action explanation and some popular alternative models. One of the watersheds in action theory has been the issue of whether action explanations are a species of causal explanation. Aligned against causality are the several versions of the rationalizing account of intentional action explanation (Collingwood 1946; Dray 1957; Dray 1963; Jarvie 1964; Jarvie 1972; Melden 1961; Ryle 1949; von Wright 1971). On the side of causality are both those who emphasize the role of laws in explanation (Churchland 1970; Hempel 1942; Hempel 1963) and those who minimize it (Davidson 1963/1980). If we adopt an erotetic analysis, the question of causality becomes moot. Causal explanations and intentional action explanations are both answers to why-questions. The answer to an intentional action why-question must be a reason. The erotetic model remains neutral on the question of whether reasons are causes. A fully causal metaphysics of human action is consistent with the erotetic model of intentional action explanations. Whether beliefs and desires are causes, and whether the norms of rational action can be embedded in a causal world view are questions that belong to metaphysics, not the analysis of explanation. On the other hand, intentional action why-questions, unlike causal why-questions, do not *require* that the answer be a cause of the topic. Therefore, on the erotetic analysis, intentional action explanations are not identical to causal explanations.

The erotetic analysis is somewhat similar to the rationalizing model of explanation. Both deny that laws are required for the explanation of human action, and both recognize a role for norms. Rationalizing explanation is often represented by a practical inference (*cf.* von Wright 1971: 96):

i. S intends to bring about P.

ii. S considers that she cannot bring about P unless she does A.

iii. Therefore S does A.

This representation of intentional action explanation was criticized by Hempel on the grounds that it is incomplete (Hempel 1963). Claims (i) and (ii) are, at best, part of the explanation of why S did A. Explanations should give some reason for expecting or predicting the explanandum. To satisfy this pragmatic interest, Hempel suggested that explanations be modeled as valid deductions. Clearly, (i) and (ii) do not entail (iii). The gap needs to be filled with a law— something like "For any person, S, if S intends to bring about P and S believes that she cannot bring about P unless she does A, then S does A." While proponents of rationalizing explanation generally agreed with Hempel that explanantia ought to entail the explanandum, they denied the necessity of laws for intentional action explanations (Dray 1963; von Wright 1971). On their view, explanation relies instead on the instrumental rationality of both the agent and the inquirer. If the agent is rational, then she will do A if she wants P and believes that A is necessary to achieve it. The interpreter recognizes that the agent is rational, and therefore expects the agent to do A. Where the norms of deductive logic constitute the relationship between explanans and explanandum on Hempel's model, the norm of instrumental rationality constitutes the relationship in the rationalizing model.

    If the arguments of this section are sound, then both of these models of intentional action explanation are mistaken. Relevant answers to intentional action why-questions neither need to deductively entail the topic nor rationalize it by appeal to a fixed norm of instrumental rationality. The root of the difference lies in the conception of the explanandum. For both Hempel's deductive-nomological model and the rationalizing model, the explanandum is taken to be a complete sentence describing an aspect of an event. Both models thus try to make the truth of the explanandum a theoretical or practical consequence of the explanantia. Because the erotetic model never explains P alone, but always P in contrast to Q, this inferential apparatus is unnecessary. The explanantia need not entail P in order to differentiate between P and Q.

    The erotetic model of intentional action explanation requires that the explanantia describe the agent's reason for acting. It thus reintroduces the norm of instrumental rationality in a somewhat different role. With respect to the way that norms function in explanation, there are two important differences between the erotetic model and the rationalizing model. Rationalizing explanations make the norm of instrumental rationality part of the form of the explanation itself. The relationship between explanans and explanandum is mediated by the norm of rationality—the action (the explanandum) is instrumentally rational in light of the agent's beliefs and desires (the explanans). The erotetic model, by contrast, makes the norm part of the content of the explanans. If an agent did A because P, then the agent must have taken P to be a reason for doing A. Part of the answer to an intentional action why-question, then, must be that the agent took her beliefs, desires, etc. *as reasons for acting*. The erotetic model is similar to the deductive-nomological model of intentional action explanation in this respect. Where rationalizing explanations use the norm of instrumental rationality as the form of intentional action explanations, the erotetic and deductive-nomological models add the norm to the content of the explanans.

It might seem as if this difference between the rationalizing and erotetic models of intentional action explanations was merely notational. On the contrary, it leads to a second, and much deeper, difference between the two analyses. Rationalizing explanations take all action to be governed by a single norm. The erotetic model can help itself to a variety of fine-grained norms, rules, and values because it includes these within the content of the explanans. For example, suppose we ask of Michael why he rides his bicycle to school every day, rather than driving his car. Let us suppose Michael rides his bike because it pollutes less than the car. This explanation seems to involve a value: pollution is bad. Analyzed according to the model of rationalizing explanations, the value that pollution is bad reduces to Michael's dislike of pollution. Michael rides his bike because he does not like pollution and believes that the bicycle will not pollute. Rationalizing explanations thus require us to view any value that informs action through the lens of the agent's attitudes. To many philosophers, this reduction of norms to individual desires or attitudes has seemed inappropriate, or even incoherent.

If we put the question to Michael, he is likely to say that pollution is bad, and not merely that he personally dislikes it. Michael takes the statement that "people should do what they can to reduce pollution" as a norm, a course of action to which all are obligated. This norm is a natural part of the explanation of his action, but it is not well captured by deflating the norm to Michael's dislike of pollution. The erotetic model can capture Michael's recognition of the norm in a full-blooded way. His reason for riding his bike (rather than driving) is twofold. First, Michael believes that the bicycle does not pollute. This constitutes a reason for riding because Michael recognizes "one ought not pollute" as a norm and takes himself to be adhering to it. The difference between the erotetic model and the rationalizing model is a trade-off of interpretive subtlety for interpretive simplicity. Rationalizing explanations would permit that an interpretation could get by with exactly one norm: Where D is desired and A is the best means of achieving D (all things considered), A is the rational course of action. Any differences between the interpreter's norms and the local norms, or differences among the agents' norms, are represented as differences in desires (or other affective states). This simplicity is gained at the price of subtlety, and perhaps accuracy. People do not always take their moral and political disputes as mere disagreements of taste. They often take them as disagreements about what is right and wrong. Moreover, they take the rightness of a course of action as grounds for doing it. The erotetic model permits the interpreter to take such claims seriously. The interpreter may postulate a variety of detailed, local norms—perhaps even norms that conflict—and use these in the explanation of action.

The foregoing discussion of the role of norms in interpretation raises many issues. Do claims about norms "reduce" in some sense to claims about individual belief or desire? Can appeals to norms and values be explanatory at all? How can a single, coherent interpretation represent norms that conflict with each other? These questions deserve a more elaborate discussion, and chapter 7 will provide it.

There is a third difference between rationalizing explanations and the erotetic analysis of intentional action explanations. Rationalizing explanations require that both the agent's belief and desire be described by the explanans. They need both beliefs and desires in order to conform to the principle of instrumental rationality. So, for an example, suppose Sam is chopping wood. In its full glory, a rationalizing explanation would look like this:

i.   Sam wants a fire (or, intends to make a fire).

ii.   Sam believes that he cannot make a fire unless he chops wood.

iii. Therefore, Sam is chopping wood.

In ordinary English, explaining Sam's action by saying "He wants a fire and believes that he could not have one without chopping wood" sounds awkward. Too much information is being provided. The erotetic analysis conforms more closely to our explanatory practices. Depending on the foil, a belief (thought, hunch, etc.) alone or a desire (aspiration, want, need) alone will suffice for the explanation. To apply the erotetic analysis, we need to identify the why-question. The topic is "Sam is chopping wood," but the foil has not yet been specified. If the asker did not know what the wood was for, he might contrast the action with another possible action, say, fetching the water. Under these conditions, answering that "Sam wanted a fire" would be sufficient to answer the question "Why is Sam chopping wood rather than fetching water?" Alternatively, suppose the asker believes that the wood-box is already filled. He might ask "Why is Sam chopping wood rather than using the wood in the wood-box?" To this question, the answer that "Sam believes that he needs more wood" or "Sam doesn't think the wood-box is full" would be sufficient. Like ordinary English, intentional action why-questions may be answered by describing one of the agent's motives. The relevant belief, desire, etc. is determined by the contrast class.

We have concluded our analysis of the form of intentional action explanations. Their distinctive features may be summarized as follows:

Topic: The topic is a description of an intentional action. The why-question presupposes not only that the topic is true, but that the action is intentional under that description.

Foils: The foils describe alternative actions that satisfy one or more of the following constraints. (i) The alternative is one that the agent had in mind. (ii) The natural or social context forces a choice between the topic action and the alternative. (iii) The alternative is customary or normally expected under the circumstances. And, (iv) the alternative is one of the typical modes, objects, or instruments of the intentional action concept deployed in the topic. Also, topic and foil(s) must be subject to the same sort of reason.

Relevance Criterion: The answer to an intentional action why-question describes one of the agent's occurrent psychological states, for example, belief, intuition, hunch, aspiration, desire, want, need, and so on. This motive is taken by the agent to be a reason for performing the topic action.

Before concluding our discussion of intentional action why-questions, it will be useful to make a short digression. Social scientists very often make claims about beliefs and try to explain why their subjects have particular beliefs. With some adjustments, the foregoing analysis of intentional action explanations may be extended to cover explanation of belief. Beliefs are held for reasons, and like actions, they may be explained by appeal to reasons. The demand for reasons as explanantia determines (in large part) the relevance relations and contrast classes of intentional action explanation. Therefore, the explanation of belief in terms of reasons is structurally similar to intentional action explanation.

The topic of a belief explanation is a description of something the agent believes. This simple point flushes a covey of issues in cross-cultural understanding. The interpreter asks the why-question in her own language, yet the person about whom she asks might not speak the interpreter's language. Thus, asking why a subject believes that P presupposes that "P" is a translation of a sentence in the local language to which the subject would assent. There is, of course, a sizable literature on the relationship between translation and description of belief. The explanatory coherence view of interpretive change expresses one aspect of that interrelationship. Why-questions about belief presuppose claims about meaning. Thus, the explanation of belief must be embedded within a larger interpretation that includes claims about meaning. The explanatory role of claims about meaning will be explored in chapter 6.

Foils for belief explanations share some features with the foils of intentional action explanations and they raise some interesting issues of their own. Thinking back to the bloodsucking witchcraft case of section 2.1, suppose we ask why a particular person believes that a child's death was caused by the *tlahuepuchis*. There are several questions that might be asked in this context:

1. Why does S believe that *this infant's* death was caused by tlahuepuchis {rather than the death of other infants}?

2. Why does S believe that this infant's death was caused by *tlahuepuchis* {rather than other causes}?

3. Why does S believe that tlahuepuchis *cause the death of infants* {rather than doing other things}?

4. Why does S *believe that tlahuepuchis exist* {rather than not believing that they exist}?

The opacity of the "believes that" sentential context creates an interesting difference between the last question and the first three. The contrast classes for the first three questions fall within the scope of "believes that." They ask why the agent believes one thing rather than believing another. In most contexts, these questions would be asking for a reason for selecting among the alternatives. In question (2), the answer is likely to be some criteria for identifying death by *tlahuepuchi* (the distinctive bruising, its placement after death. etc.) and their application to the instant case. The answer to question (1) is likely to describe those factors thought to make a child vulnerable to bloodsucking witchcraft (a lack of ritual precautions, for instance). The relevance criteria for both questions thus require that the answer be a reason for the described belief.

We saw above that where a reason discriminates between topic and foil, the foils have to satisfy some distinctive presuppositions. Like intentional action why-questions, the topic and foils of a why-question about belief must be subject to commensurable reasons. It makes sense to ask question (2), while it does not make sense to ask why S believes that this infant's death was caused by *tlahuepuchis* rather than believing that all rocks are blue. Why-questions about belief have additional presuppositions. It makes no sense to ask why Aristotle believed that water is an element rather than believing that water is H_2O. To make "Water is H_2O" comprehensible to someone who did not understand the atomic theory would require substantial education. There is thus no reason that would discriminate between topic and foil in this case. Why-questions about belief presuppose that the foils are epistemically accessible to the subject, where a belief Q is epistemically accessible if it is possible for the agent to form the belief that Q, given his language, other beliefs, and environment.

Finally, like intentional action explanations, answers to questions about belief implicitly make claims about norms of rationality. If an answer, A, is to be the reason why S believes P rather than Q, then the agent must take A to be a reason. Reasons are normative. To say that A is a reason for believing that P is to say, ceteris paribus, that anyone who believed A ought to, or is entitled to, believe that P. By taking A to be a reason, the subject is implicitly or explicitly adhering to a norm of rationality. When an interpreter makes the claim that S believes that P rather than Q because S believes A, the interpreter must also claim that S takes A to be a reason. Therefore, when explaining belief, the interpreter must invoke norms of rationality as part of the explanation. Again, the erotetic model of explanation does not require that there be one universal norm of rationality that appears within all explanations, nor that the norms invoked in the explanation of S's belief be the same as those norms to which the interpreter is committed. Detailed discussion of the explanatory role of norms must await chapter 7.

Question (4) is quite different from the first three. It asks why the agent has a particular belief rather than not having that belief. While there may be some cases where the agent has a reason for believing P rather than not believing P, we cannot require that all such questions be answered by reasons. If question (4) were posed to the subject, he would probably be puzzled by it. If answered at all, the answer might be something like "Well, my parents taught me this, and their parents taught them." The anthropologist's answer could be quite similar, supplemented, perhaps, by more detailed historical documentation. These answers are not *reasons*, yet the question and its answer are important. In anthropological and historical work, we expect historical, functional, or structural answers to this kind of question. Such explanations do not give the agent's reason for his belief. The relevance criterion requires an answer that gives the historical conditions under which the belief was formed or the social conditions that make such beliefs functional. Some kinds of belief explanation are thus social or historical, not individualistic.

Having identified these two kinds of relevance relation, we can see that question (3) is ambiguous between them. One sort of answer would provide the agent's reason for believing that *tlahuepuchis* cause the death of infants rather than, say, adults, children, or animals. This would be a plausible reading if, for instance, we expected the agent to have deliberated about the matter. When Nutini and Roberts ask questions like (3), however, they get a more traditional treatment. Nutini and Roberts abstract away from the reasons that might be given by particular persons. *Tlahuepuchis* have a place in a mythological system. Within the terms of this system, one can see why *tlahuepuchis* are supposed to suck the blood of infants, not adults, children, or animals. *Tlahuepuchis* need the blood for the rejuvenation of their supernatural powers, and the blood of infants is more "invigorating" than children's or adults' (Nutini and Roberts 1993: 59-61). In this case, the relevant answer to question (3) is much more like question (4) than questions (1) and (2).

Suitably interpreted, questions (3) and (4) ask for answers that are historical, social, or functional. The agents may not be aware of these factors, hence they cannot constitute reasons for the belief. Like intentional action explanations, explanation of belief is a site of potential conflict between social-level explanation and explanation in terms of reasons. As section 5.1 argued, whether there is conflict among these explanations depends on whether their distinctive presuppositions and classes of relevant answers are consistent. To determine whether reason-giving explanations and social explanations conflict, then, we need an analysis of the latter. It is to that project that we now turn.

5.3 SOCIAL EXPLANATIONS

The leading question of this chapter is whether reason-giving explanations are compatible with explanations that appeal to features of the group. The agent's reasons may explain why she performed an action (or holds a belief), but at the same time, the action (belief) may be explained by its role in the social system of which the agent is a part. In section 5.1, we saw some prima facie reasons to think that social explanations conflict with intentional action explanations. There are, however, many different kinds of social explanation. Presumably, the why-questions that generate historical accounts of social change are different from those that demand structural or functional answers. An exhaustive analysis of all kinds of social explanation is beyond the scope of this work. Since conflict is our focus, the best strategy is to consider those social explanations that are most likely to conflict with intentional action explanations. Functional explanations are potentially the most threatening. An individual's action or belief can be the topic of a functional explanation, and the answer may appeal to factors outside the consciousness of the individual. In the remainder of this chapter, then, we will concern ourselves with functional explanations.

The distinguishing feature of a functional explanation is its relevance criterion. To say that humans have toes in order to balance while walking upright is to explain the presence of toes by something that toes do. In general, the relevant answer tells us what role the item has in a larger system. Functional explanations are why-questions answered by function statements. A crucial prerequisite to understanding functional explanations, then, is to understand functional statements. Section 5.3.1 will analyze function statements. It will turn out that there are two complementary forms of function statement. Section 5.3.2 will argue that, as a result, there are two forms of functional explanation.

5.3.1 Functional Statements

Talk of function arises in a variety of domains. It is most robust in biology, where the effects of an organ can be identified and the cost of dysfunction is high. In social theory, early functionalists, such as Durkheim, Radcliffe-Brown, and Malinowski, conceived of social function as directly analogous to biological function. Society is like an organism, they thought, and institutions contribute to its flourishing or survival. The analogy proved problematic. Later functionalists, such as Merton and Parsons, eschewed it entirely. Philosophical work on the concept of function has yielded two ways of understanding function statements. The first relies heavily on evolutionary theory and, unsurprisingly, is most comfortable in biology. The second arose out of reflection on psychological functions. In this section, I will follow Preston (1998) in arguing for a pluralistic conception of function. Properly understood, the two conceptions of functional statements are complementary.

We will call the first conception of function the "etiological" conception because it relies heavily on the evolutionary history of the item in question. This conception was developed by Wright (1972; 1976), Ruse (1971; 1973), Millikan (1984), Neander (1991), and others. The central idea is that the functions of an entity are those effects or properties for which it was selected. For example, fish have gills in order to extract oxygen from water. According to the etiological view, this statement about the present organs of the fish commits us to an evolutionary story about the fish's ancestors. The ancestors with gills had greater fitness in their environments than those without them. To say that they had greater fitness is to say that more of them survived to adulthood and reproduced than their competitors. Moreover, the difference between the ancestors of modern fish and their competitors was the presence of gills, and the gills account for the greater fitness of fish ancestors. Gills are present in contemporary fish because they had beneficial effects on the ancestors of contemporary fish, namely, extracting oxygen from water in a relatively efficient way. In general, the proper functions of an organ are those effects or capacities that caused it to be present in current populations. Michael Ruse tidily summarized the etiological conception by saying "if A has function F, then A is an adaptation and doing F is adaptive" (Ruse 1981).

Several features of the etiological view are important for our discussion of functional statements. First, we need to distinguish between the item or organ with its function on the one hand, and the system or organism with its capacities on the other. Natural selection does not act directly on parts of organisms like hearts or lungs. Only whole organisms can be fit in a given environment. To say that an item has a function is thus to say that there is some phenotype (system, organism) of which the item is a part. According to the etiological view, the organ is present in the phenotype because the organ had some disposition that made ancestors of the organism more fit. Not every organ will effect fitness directly. Most will be hidden from the eye of selection as subsystems. The functional parts of an organism's subsystems are present because of their contribution to the organism's capacities, and those capacities make it more or less fit in its environment. On the full analysis, then, we need to speak of the organism (system) with its *capacities,* and the organ (item) with its *functions.*

The second detail arises from the conception of fitness. Natural selection requires differential survival and reproduction among a population of similar organisms. Within a population, organisms will differ with respect to many properties and capacities. Because of these differences, one part of the population can have a greater rate of survival and reproduction in a particular environment. Where a difference in fitness is correlated with the variation in a certain capacity, there is a selection pressure on that capacity. Under these circumstances, organisms are selected for that capacity. It is only against this background that the dispositions of organs contributing to the fitness enhancing capacity are *adaptations*. Therefore, on this conception of function, only items with a history of differential reproduction and survival can have functions. Finally, an adaptation must be a heritable trait. The etiological conception of function holds that the function of an organ is the contribution it made to the fitness of the organism's ancestral population. There must, therefore, be a causal link between the organism's possession of the organ and its ancestors' possession of similar organs. In biology, the causal relationship is instantiated by the underlying genetics.

These features are important because they structure the way in which the etiological conception of function may be extended to nonbiological cases. While nonbiological functions are possible, function talk outside of biology must retain the central characteristics of the biological conception. There must be a causal relationship of heritability and a history of differential reproduction and survival. This constitutes the core of Millikan's argument for a biological conception of thought and language. Her definitions of "reproduction" and "reproductively established families" forge a relationship between past and present language use that will make the etiological conception of function applicable (Millikan 1984; cf. Preston 1998). If the etiological concept of function is to be used in the social realm, similar work is required. The causal relationship between past and present social systems will have to be identified. This relationship will have to preserve structural information. The social scientific functionalist has to argue that present social systems have a particular structure *because* past systems had that structure. Also, the social systems will have to exhibit differential reproduction and survival. Robust senses of "reproduction" and "survival" for social systems thus need to be articulated. Etiological function statements can be used to describe the functions of the parts of social systems only if these requirements are satisfied.

The close connection between etiological functions and evolutionary theory strengthens the etiological conception. Ironically, therein lies its main weakness. The etiological conception entails that an organ without selection history has no function. Thus, in its inaugural use, a beneficial organ is not functional. Suppose, for example, that Swamp Man is spontaneously created from a flash of lightning in the organic soup of Dismal Swamp. He walks, eats, and terrorizes the local town. According to the etiological view, his organs have no functions because he has no ancestors. Moving from science fiction to science, some evolutionary biologists have found the conception of an *exaptation* useful. An exaptation is an effect that is useful to the system, but is not an adaptation. That is, past systems were not more fit because they contained it. The exaptation is present for some other reason. Perhaps it is required by design constraints, or perhaps it was adapted to some other purpose. It is not unreasonable to think that exaptations are important for evolutionary theorizing (Gould and Lewontin 1979).

While defenders of the etiological view have debated the cogency of such counterexamples, their role here is only to motivate an important alternative to the etiological view of function. It has been primarily championed by Robert Cummins (1975; 1983). It is important to recognize that Cummins was oriented toward issues in the philosophy of psychology, not biology. Information processing systems seem to have functional parts, but are not obviously subject to selective forces. For Cummins, functions arise out of the attempt to analyze and explain the dispositions of some system. Suppose that system S has the capacity or disposition to C. One way of explaining S's capacity is to analyze the system into component parts. The capacity to C is nothing more than the operation of the components. An item, I, has a function, F, if I is one of the components revealed by an analysis of system S's capacity to C and I's doing F contributes to S's capacity to C.

Cummins's "system" conception of function is applicable to just those examples that are problematic from the etiological point of view. If Swamp Man is able to extract energy from his surroundings by eating leaves, then this is one of his capacities. On examination, if it turns out that one of his organs turns vegetable matter into a useful form by extracting its component sugars, then the function of that organ is to digest food. His lack of selection history is irrelevant. A similar story can be told about exaptations or the novel use of an organ that was originally adapted for some other purpose. The system conception of function is also more naturally applicable to social systems. When trying to understand a person's function within a bureaucratic system, a social scientist is likely to look at the person's role in the larger system. According to the system conception, a person's function in a social system is the contribution she makes to something the system does. In other words, the social system has a capacity, and a person's function is her contribution to that capacity. There is no need to establish a causal relationship between present and past systems or uncover a selection history.

The system conception of function, however, has difficulties of its own. Indeed, they are complementary to the difficulties faced by the etiological conception. On the system view, an item can have a function only if the item actually has the disposition to perform the action. There are some problematic cases where the item has a function but cannot (for one reason or another) fulfill it. For example, the function of John's toes is to help him keep his balance. This is true even if he has never walked, and has used a wheelchair since birth. According to the system conception, John's toes have no function. This consequence is problematic because functions are what an item is supposed to do, what it ought to do, regardless of whether it can do so now. The system conception cannot capture this "normative" character of function statements, and proponents of the alternative etiological conception take this to be an important failure.

Most of the literature on function statements and functional explanations tries to argue against one of the above conceptions and in favor of the other. I would like to follow Preston (1998) and others in arguing for a pluralist view of function statements. Three facts motivate this pluralism. First, the two conceptions are consistent. It is possible for something to have a function in both the system sense and the etiological sense. The counterexamples canvased above merely show that some cases are captured by only one of the two conceptions. Second, the problematic examples are complementary. Each conception includes something that the other excludes. Finally, there is substantial overlap between the two conceptions, both in the cases they cover and in the terms of their analysis. This latter point suggests that not only can we consistently affirm both conceptions, but that a unified analysis is possible. Both conceptions take a function to be the contribution that a part makes to the capacities of a system. This forms the core of the concept of a function:

An item type I has the function F in system type S if and only if

A. I is a part of S.

B. I's doing F contributes the capacity of S to do C.

A system, for our purposes, is a stable collection of parts with the capacity to do something that is not possessed by any part alone. Biological organisms are such systems, as are bureaucracies, churches, computers, telephone exchanges, and so on. System and etiological functions may be distinguished by adding clauses to these first two. In addition to (A) and (B), the system conception of function demands that

C. I now has the disposition to do F.

Etiological functions may or may not satisfy (C). An etiological function does have to satisfy two further criteria:

D. I is a heritable trait.

E. Ancestors of current S-type systems where I did F were more fit in their typical environments than S-type systems where I did not do F.

The logical structure of this pluralistic definition of function is that something is a function if and only if it satisfies both (A) and (B), and in addition, either (C) or both (D) and (E). Where an item satisfies only (A), (B), and (C), we will say that it has a system function. And where an item satisfies only (A), (B), (D), and (E), we will say that it has an etiological function. Clearly, some functional items satisfy all five conditions (presently working eyes, for instance), and we will call these etiological functions.

5.3.2 Functional Explanations

A functional explanation is a function statement that answers a why-question. If a function statement is to provide a relevant answer, the contrast class and relevance criteria of the why-question must be constructed in the right way. Functional statements are about the parts of a system, and two kinds of why-question concern the parts of a system. We might ask why the item is present in the system, or ask why it has its dispositions. One can imagine the second sort of question arising when one is looking at the whirring and spinning parts of an unfamiliar mechanism. It is natural to point at a part and ask: Why is it doing *that*? The system as a whole has certain capacities, and we want to understand how the parts contribute to these capacities. So, we ask about the activities of the parts with the hope of an answer that says how the activity contributes to the whole. In other words, the criterion of relevance is that the answer must be a function statement.

Let us call questions of the form, Why does *I* do *D*? "disposition questions." The topic of a disposition question describes a part of the system, *I*, and its disposition, *D*. The question asks why the item is doing *D* rather than anything else. So, the foils for a disposition question are alternative dispositions. For example, suppose we are trying to understand how the shifting mechanism in a bicycle works. Among its parts is an arm holding a small gear. The gear engages with the chain. The arm moves up and down as the gears are shifted. A question that can be asked is, Why does the arm move this way? Appropriate foils for this question would include the proposition that the arm moves in some other way (say, left and right) or that it does not move at all. The answer to this question is that the movement of the arm keeps the chain tight as it moves across gears of different diameters. The answer thus characterizes the function of the item in the sense that it tells us how the dispositions of the arm contribute to the capacities of the system (shifting gears). Notice that the answer can discriminate between topic and foil only if the foil is not functionally equivalent to the topic. If moving left and right would keep the chain tight too, then keeping the chain tight does not explain why the arm moves up and down rather than left and right. Disposition questions thus presuppose that the elements of the contrast class are not functionally equivalent.

The answer to a disposition question will satisfy at least criteria (A), (B), and (C) of functional statements. The topic is the disposition of some part, and the question presupposes that the item contributes to the system's capacities. Since a disposition question asks why the part is doing something, it also presupposes that the item has the disposition to do *D*. Thus, any answer to a disposition question will be a function statement of some kind. Notice that disposition questions are neutral between system functions and etiological functions. The answer has to satisfy conditions (A), (B), and (C), and it may also satisfy (D) and (E). A disposition question does not presuppose that the answer must be a particular sort of function. Whether the answer is an etiological or system function depends on empirical facts about the system.

Answers to disposition questions explain why the item is doing what it does, but they do not explain why the item is there in the first place. Thus, we might ask, Why does S have A? We will call questions like this "item questions." Questions about items are familiar in both biology and social science. Why hearts? Why initiation rites? Again, we are looking for answers that say something about the item's contribution to the system. This sort of explanation has struck many as problematic. It is difficult to see how the effects of an item might account for its presence in the system without postulating backward causality. The erotetic model looks promising, since it does not demand that the answer to a why-question always describe an efficient or proximate cause of the topic.

In asking an item question, we want to know why the item is present rather than some alternative item. The topic is a description of a part, I, of a system, S, and the foils are parts that the system might, but does not, have. The interesting foils are items that would be functionally equivalent to I in S. This was the kind of question that originally motivated the etiological conception of function. By satisfying conditions (D) and (E), an etiological function statement discriminates between the topic and the foil by telling us how items like I got into systems like S. Etiological function statements are therefore candidate answers to item questions.

The special characteristics of etiological function statements impose restrictions on the contrast class for item why-questions. Not just any item— even functionally equivalent items—can be taken as foils. For example, there is no functional answer to the question of why humans have brains rather than functionally equivalent silicon computers in their heads. The question is unanswerable because no fact about the evolutionary history of humans is relevant to this topic and foil. Silicon CPUs just were not a possibility for us. This suggests that the truth of the topic and the falsehood of the foil must have some common cause in the evolutionary history of the system and that this common cause discriminates between topic and foil (cf. Sober 1986).[3] The common cause requirement is most clearly satisfied where both the topic and

---

3. Sober argues that all why-questions presuppose that the elements of the contrast class have a common cause that discriminates. Barnes (1994) provides some compelling counterexamples and thus argues against Sober's claim of universality. For our purposes, we need only the weaker claim that a common cause is *sometimes* presupposed by why-questions. This claim is not defeated by Barnes's counterexamples.

foil describe traits that, at some point in history, were in free variation in systems of type S. For example, present-day llamas are able to survive at high altitudes because of their peculiar hemoglobin.[4] Call this altitude enhancing property H. Suppose that among the ancestor population of llamas there was variation with respect to this trait. Some llamas had hemoglobin with H, others with H'. As long as the population remained at low altitudes, there would be no selection pressure on this trait. When llamas began to occupy niches at high altitudes, those with H were more likely to survive and reproduce than those with H'. In this case there is a common cause of the fact that contemporary llamas have H and do not have H': their ancestors with H were more fit than those with H'.

The common cause requirement does not demand that the topic and foil must always have been in free variation in the present system's ancestors. It requires only that the events in the evolutionary history of the system be causally relevant to the foil. That is, for a prospective foil, B, there has to be some event, E, such that the probability of $\sim B$ given E does not equal the probability of $\sim B$ alone. Changing the example, suppose that modern llamas were one of two daughter populations that emerged from a speciation event. The mother population had neither H nor H'. Its hemoglobin had a different property, G. Selection pressures in their respective environments caused G to evolve into H in llamas and H' in the other daughter population. In this case, there is a common cause for H and H', but no ancestor of contemporary llamas ever had H'. The why-question, Why do llamas have H rather than H'? is askable, and the account of the llama's selection history seems to answer it. By contrast, notice the question, Why do humans have brains rather than silicon computers in their heads? remains unaskable. This contrast class still fails to have a common cause.

In sum, we may conclude that there are two distinct forms of functional explanation. All functional explanations share a relevance criterion: the answer must be a function statement. They all thus presuppose that there is a system with some capacities and parts, and that the parts' dispositions contribute to the system's capacities (or have contributed to ancestral systems). The why-questions of the different forms are differentiated by their topic, and this difference gives rise to different presuppositions. Disposition questions contrast what an item does with other dispositions the item might have. The dispositions described by the foils are presupposed to be not functionally equivalent to the topic. The answers to disposition questions must satisfy the requirements for system functions, and may also be etiological functions. Item questions contrast the presence of the item with other possible items. They presuppose that the foils are functionally equivalent to the topic, and that both share a common cause. To discriminate between these topics and foils, the relevant

---

4. The example is taken from Neander (1991).

answers need to satisfy conditions (D) and (E). Item questions, therefore, require etiological function statements as answers.

Let us return, briefly, to functional explanations in the social sciences. As mentioned at the outset, early functionalists thought of social functions as analogous to biological functions. The analogy is problematic, and the foregoing analyses show why. Organisms have selection histories. We can therefore ask both item questions and disposition questions about their organs and answer both with etiological function statements. Using etiological function statements to describe social relations requires substantial ontological and theoretical commitments. If the institutions or practices within a social system had etiological functions, the social system would need a mechanism of heritability and a history of differential survival and reproduction. If these requirements are not satisfied by an institution or practice, then item questions about it cannot be asked. We could not functionally explain why that institution or practice exists. All is not lost for functionalism in the social sciences. Social institutions and practices have effects on larger institutions. A social system may have certain capacities (to defend itself against outside incursion, to distribute food among its members, etc.) that are the product of the system's parts. In such cases, the practices or institutions will have system functions. Disposition questions about social systems, at least, can be raised and answered about social institutions and practices.

5.4 THE COMPATIBILITY OF FUNCTIONAL AND REASON-GIVING EXPLANATIONS

We are now in a position to directly answer the question of whether reason-giving explanations conflict with functional explanations. Section 5.1 argued that why-questions conflict when either their presuppositions are incompatible or when their typical relevant answers are incompatible. This chapter has shown that there are two kinds of functional explanation. It has also analyzed the form of reason-giving explanations, which include explanations of intentional action and belief. What remains is to consider whether these kinds of why-questions are compatible.

Section 5.3.2 distinguished "item why-questions" from "disposition why-questions." In the social sciences, item why-questions ask about the presence of some social institution or practice. If this kind of question is to be answered by a function statement, several presuppositions need to be satisfied. The topic institution or practice has to contribute to the capacities of the social system. The foils describe functionally equivalent institutions or practices that the system does not have, and members of the contrast class must have a common cause. Moreover, the social system must be placed in a larger context where social systems of this type exhibit a history of differential survival and reproduction. Finally, there must be some mechanism of heritability for transmitting information about the structure of past systems to the present system. It seems to me that these desiderata are difficult, perhaps impossible, to satisfy. I am thus skeptical that item questions are ever appropriate in the social sciences. However, whether they are ever satisfied is largely an empirical question and we must let it pass here. Since we are interested in potential conflicts, our question is whether the presuppositions of item questions and reason-giving explanations are consistent.

There seems to be no incompatibility between the presuppositions arising from the contrast classes of item questions and intentional action or belief why-questions. The topic of an item question describes an institution or practice, whereas the topic of a reason-giving explanation describes either an intentional action or a belief. It seems obvious that the existence of institutions and practices is consistent with the existence of intentional actions and beliefs. Since no conflict arises from the contrast class, let us consider the answers identified by the relevance criteria of item questions and intentional action or belief questions. Suppose that the presence of institutions within a social system could be explained functionally. Intentional action why-questions and why-questions about belief look to reasons as answers. The existence of a particular kind of selection history for a social system does not preclude or screen off the agent's reasons for action. It seems entirely possible for a social system to have a selection history of which the participants are unaware. Moreover, this history may have profoundly shaped their institutions and practices. Within these institutional settings, agents act and form beliefs for reasons of their own. If item questions were appropriate in the social sciences, this sort of functional explanation would not portray agents as regularly "going on the blink." Item questions and reason-giving explanations are compatible.

Prima facie, disposition why-questions are much more threatening to the intentionality of action or belief formation than item why-questions. The topic of a disposition why-question can be anything that by its action contributes to the capacities of the social system. Institutions and practices can make such contributions. For the reasons discussed above, these explananda do not give rise to conflicts with reason-giving explanations. Particular actions and beliefs or action and belief types can contribute to the capacities of a social system, and thus they are also possible topics of disposition questions. It would indeed be like glimpsing the strings of the puppet-master to find that one's act could be explained functionally. The Tlaxcalan belief in *tlahuepuchis* appears to be an example. According to Nutini and Roberts, the *tlahuepuchi* system of belief serves an important social function. It assuages the mother's feelings of anguish and guilt after the loss of her child. The mother believes that *tlahuepuchis* caused the death of this infant (rather than believing that she unintentionally suffocated it) because this belief supports the system's capacity to satisfy the psychological needs of its members. The individual's belief may also be the topic of a reason-giving why-question. As analyzed at the end of section 5.2, the foils of this kind of why-question are propositions not believed by the agent. All members of the contrast class are presupposed to be epistemically accessible and subject to commensurable reasons. In this case, then, the disposition why-question and the reason-giving why-question share a contrast class: the mother believes that *tlahuepuchis* caused the death of this infant rather than believing that she unintentionally suffocated it.

The fact that we can construct an example where a functional explanation and a reason-giving explanation have the same object shows that the presuppositions arising from the contrast classes of these kinds of question are compatible. Their compatibility, however, makes Macdonald and Pettit's concern all the more acute. Functional explanations can explain the same thing as a reason-giving explanation by appealing to something of which the agent is unaware. Our analysis has thus permitted the precise reconstruction of Macdonald and Pettit's worry that the functional answers required by disposition questions are incompatible with the motivational answers required by reason-giving why-questions.

On a closer look, however, no incompatibility arises from the different classes of relevant answers. Disposition questions may be answered either by system or etiological function statements. System functions would show how the action or belief contributes to the social system. An etiological function would describe the selection history of societies that included actions or beliefs of a given type and show how they increased the fitness of the social system. Both kinds of function statement characterize the effects of the action or belief on the society or its "ancestors." Reason-giving explanations look for answers among the motives and beliefs of the agent and the norms of rationality by which he is bound. It is clearly possible for an intentional action or rationally formed belief to have effects on the social system. These effects in no way diminish the intentionality of the action or rationality of the belief. Social effects do not screen off the reasons for belief or action. Moreover, the agent may be ignorant of the functions of his action or belief. Where the effects of his action (belief) are opaque to the agent, the action (belief) has what Merton called a "latent function" (Merton 1957). If the agent is aware of the social function of his action (belief), this function may be part of the reason for his action (belief) and the function will be "manifest." Our discussion has shown that social functions are not all manifest, and that latent functionality is compatible with the intentionality of action and rationality of belief.

The foregoing discussion is subject to one important proviso. These arguments show that there is no *necessary* conflict between explanations of the various forms. The mere fact that an interpretation deploys functional explanations does not preclude the use of intentional action explanations. Nonetheless, particular why-questions may conflict. Conflict among particular why-questions is important for explanatory coherence. Conflict may preclude a particular why-question. If a why-question is to be asked appropriately, its presuppositions must be coherent with the interpretation. For example, if the interpreter thinks that the agents have been hypnotized, brainwashed, or coerced, then reason-giving why-questions about some of their actions or beliefs will not be askable. Explanatory coherence is thus decreased when the presuppositions of one why-question conflict with other claims in the interpretation. Conversely, harmony among presuppositions can increase explanatory coherence. The presuppositions of one why-question can become the topic of another, and thus be explained. Alternatively, the presupposition of one why-question might serve as the answer to another. The why-questions that constitute the explanatory relationships within an interpretation, then, can contribute to or decrease the coherence of the whole.

Functional explanations are a paradigmatic form of external explanation, where the agent is not aware of the factors that explain his action. This chapter began by arguing that interpretation has constitutive interests in both external explanations and internal explanations. Internal explanations appeal to the agents' point of view and to features of the natural and social world of which they are aware. The arguments of the intervening sections have shown that it is possible for an interpretation to deploy both internal and external explanations. Functional explanations, at least, are consistent with the use of reasons to explain action and belief. Since functional explanations have always seemed the most threatening to intentionality, we can be optimistic that other forms of social explanation are consistent as well. Explanatory pluralism is thus at least partially vindicated.

CHAPTER 6

Meaning

Human action and speech are meaningful. It has meaning for the agent and for those who witness his performance. The meaning is partially embedded in the immediate context, but it is also closely related to the language spoken by the agents and other features of their social world. When the social scientist arrives on the scene, her subjects are already engaged in a process of interpreting themselves. Many have argued that methodologies drawn from the natural sciences are necessarily blind to this aspect of the social world. A social science with an explanatory methodology would miss what is distinctive and interesting about humanity. Meaning has thus been one of the most well-fortified lines of defense against creeping empiricism in the social sciences. While the explanatory coherence criterion of interpretive change is not a flat empiricism, we need to take the objection seriously. Section 6.1 will present the problem of meaning as it arises for an explanatory coherence approach to interpretation. The section will sketch a resolution of the problem of meaning that draws on the results of chapter 5. We will then turn to the positive work of showing how claims about linguistic meaning can be explained or explanatory. Section 6.2 will be occupied with this positive work, and if successful, it will show how the erotetic model of explanation satisfies the fourth criterion of adequacy of section 4.1.

6.1 THE PROBLEM OF MEANING

The problem of meaning is whether an epistemology that sees no fundamental distinction between the interpretive and noninterpretive disciplines can capture word meaning, the meaning of individual action and social events, and the self-understanding of the agents. While this problem is clearly relevant to the explanatory coherence approach to interpretive change, it has historically been raised against varieties of empiricism. Dilthey, Schutz, Gadamer, Habermas, Taylor, and others have eloquently presented the issues, but prescient as they

125

were, none of them had much to say about explanatory coherence. This section will articulate the difficulty as it arises for our work by drawing indirectly on their arguments.

The problem of meaning arises because the discussion in chapter 3 accepted the presumption of interpretive naiveté on the part of the interpreter. On pain of begging the epistemic questions under discussion, we must presume that, at the outset, the interpreter knows nothing of the language or culture she is about to study. It follows that the clues to meaning that make translation and interpretation possible must be on the surface (Davidson 1984: 128, 143; Quine 1960). That is to say that the appropriateness of local words is determined by contextual clues equally available to the interpreter and to the native speakers. This severely limits the descriptions of utterances and their context that underlie translation. The interpreter can describe how the speakers move and the sorts of objects with which they interact. She cannot use richly intentional language, or characterize the speakers as believing such-and-such, since doing so presupposes a knowledge of the native speakers' language (cf. Davidson 1984). This seems to limit interpretive claims to very thin, behavioristic characterizations of the conditions of utterance. In Taylor's language, such commitments restrict the ultimate grounds for interpretation to "brute data," the uninterpreted building blocks of an interpretation (Taylor 1971).

Unlike traditional varieties of empiricism, an explanatory coherence view of interpretation does not require that all hypotheses be reducible to uninterpreted "brute data." Nor is such primitive evidence the ultimate justification for all interpretation. Simple, behavioristic descriptions are themselves justified by their coherence with the overall interpretation. Nonetheless, Taylor's "brute data" remains important as a kind of epistemic ideal. In the limiting case of an interpreter who knows nothing of the people to be interpreted, thin descriptions are the material with which she must begin. "Overt behavior in observable circumstances," as Quine put it (cf. Quine 1960: ix; Quine 1969a: 26; Quine 1987: 5), is the ideal epistemic origin of all interpretation. While distinct from the empiricist reliance on "brute data," the role of such epistemic primitives (even if ideal) is sufficient to generate the problem of meaning. While the interpreter has to rely (at the outset) on thin descriptions to understand the local actions, the locals themselves are not so restricted. The character of an action or the content of an utterance has immediate meaning for the native subject. The meaning of an action or utterance is much deeper than the superficial clues available to the naïve interpreter.

To vividly illustrate the problem of meaning, imagine Quine's radical translation thought-experiment performed in reverse. Imagine that *we* are the native speakers and a foreign interpreter is attempting the first translation of our language. One of us says "Smith paid Jones ten dollars." Whether Smith paid Jones is a perfectly observable event that any one of us would be able to identify. Or again: "The mayor has appointed a new police chief." This is a completely public matter. The conditions that make these sentences appropriate are perfectly overt and observable to a native speaker of English. However, they are completely opaque to an interpreter who has to describe the events in behavioristic language. A theorist who was forced to begin her interpretation with such thin claims would fail utterly to make sense of the local scene. Human societies are already structured by meaning when the interpreter begins her work. Interpretation of such meaningful structures thus requires a richer foundation than that permitted by the presumption of interpretive naiveté. The problem is, of course, the problem of the hermeneutic circle, and this is where our discussion makes contact with the arguments of Dilthey (1996), Schutz (1967), Gadamer (1975), Habermas (1984: vol. 1; 1988/1967), and Taylor (1971).

An explanatory coherence view of interpretation appears to be deeply problematic in the light of this argument. We have admitted that the epistemically ideal origin of an interpretation is a set of thin claims about behavior and utterance. The only resources available for further theory construction are explanations of these very thin observations. These thin claims and their explanation are patently inadequate descriptions of the local actions and assertions. Native speakers do not rely on the sort of uninterpreted evidence that are the only clues available to a naïve interpreter. The simplest utterances are comprehensible to members of the culture because they already understand a host of things about their social world. There is a gap between the evidence available to the interpreter (under the naiveté assumption) and the local understanding of their social world. The project of constructing an interpretation from the "brute data" of utterances in context is therefore hopeless. Like its empiricist cousins, an explanatory coherence approach will never reach a true understanding of the language or actions of the locals.

The problem with which we are faced is closely related to the problem of theory-laden observations in the philosophy of natural science. The hermeneutic circle is problematic for empiricist views of the social sciences because there is an element of social reality they cannot reach. They cannot reach "meaning" because the relevant sort of meaning cannot be constructed from the brute data available to them. To get at the real meaning of social action and language, one needs observations that are already interpreted. On pain of circularity, empiricist social science cannot appeal to preinterpreted observations. Traditional empiricism is in precisely the same situation with respect to the natural sciences. Classical empiricist epistemologies of science demanded that the scientist base her theories on theory-neutral evidence. On pain of circularity, a theory ought not to be grounded on evidence that, in turn, presupposes knowledge of the theory. Empiricist scientists and philosophers of science held that observations must be characterized in phenomenalistic terms, for example, "Red here now" or "The black line intersects the blue circle." While there are a number of problems with this view, Pierre Duhem's criticism is telling.

Duhem noticed that the observations supporting one theory depended upon theories from other domains. To take an example from astrophysics, contemporary theory holds that heavy elements like iron are the result of a chain of events that happen when stars go nova. One of the links in that chain is the isotope cobalt-56. For over twenty years, however, cobalt-56 had not been observed in any supernova. Supernova 1987A was the first wherein instruments detected 843 kilo-electron-volt gamma rays. The scientific community celebrated this result as an important *observation* of the creation of this element.[1] It is, of course, not an observation that any nonscientist could make. Moreover—and this is the problem Duhem raised—this astrophysical observation depended heavily on other theoretical results. The spectrometers that detected the gamma rays were built on the basis of knowledge of electromagnetism and the behavior of electrons in semiconductors. The calculation of the gamma rays' energy required knowledge of the physics of the atom, and so on. What counts as an observation in astrophysicists depends in turn on the theoretical results of other disciplines.

Observations in science are thus theory-laden in the sense that any observation relevant to the confirmation of a theory already depends on theoretical claims. An empiricist philosophy of science cannot accept the interesting results of real science without condemning them to epistemic circularity. There is a superficial resemblance, at least, between the problem of meaning and the theory-ladenness of observation. Where the confirmation of natural scientific theories depends on further theoretical knowledge, understanding utterance or action requires a prior knowledge of customs, roles, institutions, and so on. This is just to say that the *subjects'* observations of their own social world are theory-laden. If she is to have any hope of understanding, the interpreter's observations must be laden with the subject's own "theories." The hermeneutic circle and theory-ladenness thus present importantly similar problems to traditional empiricism. Empiricism limited its evidential foundation in such a way as to preclude a noncircular understanding of either the natural or social world.

The first step toward resolving the problem of meaning, then, is to enrich the conception of observation. Classical empiricism conceived of observations as something conceptually and epistemologically primitive. They were the starting point from which theory construction began and in which justification ended. From Kant onwards, philosophers have urged us to revise or reject this dogma of empiricism. For our purpose here—resolving the problem of meaning as it arises for an explanatory coherence view of interpretive change—the issue is best framed in broadly Quinean terms. An interpretation is a set of claims, or as Quine would have it, sentences, about a group of people. Which among them are "observation" sentences and which are "theoretical"?

---

1. Reported in *Science News*, 133, 1 (January 2, 1988).

Quine suggested that, as a minimal condition, an observation sentence must be a sentence to which we are inclined to assent (or dissent) depending on the current conditions (Quine 1960; Quine 1969b; Quine 1975). "Red here now" is a sentence to which a person will (usually) assent when presented with a red object and (usually) dissent from otherwise. By contrast, "F=ma" is a sentence to which a scientist will assent (or dissent) regardless of the present context. Quine captured this aspect of the theory/observation distinction as a difference between "standing" sentences and "occasion" sentences (Quine 1960: 36). There is no absolute difference between occasion sentences and standing sentences. It is a matter of degree. A sentence is maximally occasional if it is one to which a speaker will assent (or dissent) only after the appropriate stimulation. A sentence like "The cat is biting my hand" is maximally occasional. "The cat is hungry," by contrast, may prompt assent well after the cat is no longer in view. It is therefore somewhat less occasional. Further along the scale toward standing sentences are those that prompt assent for long periods of time, but not indefinitely, no matter what the current stimulus: "I live with two cats," or "I am reading *War and Peace.*" Maximal standing sentences command assent (or dissent) consistently and independently of the current stimulations affecting the speaker, such as "Elvis is the King," "God exists," or "Water is H_2O." By assimilating observations to occasion sentences, we can capture the fact that observationality is a matter of degree (Quine 1960: 42–43).

Using the occasion sentence/standing sentence scale to capture degrees of observationality permits us to recast the problem of theory-laden observations in terms that do not presuppose problematic aspects of empiricism. The problem is that a person's assent to a sentence depends on facts about that person as well as the present conditions. The astrophysicist will readily assent to "Gamma rays of 843 kilo-electron-volts were emitted by supernova 1987A." It is an occasion sentence for the astrophysicist, but not for the lay person. Theory-laden observation is problematic insofar as a sentence that counts as an occasion sentence for a specialist will not be equally occasional for a nonspecialist. Any attempt to justify a theory by appeal to observations that only a specialist can make seems suspect at best and circular at worst.

Framed in this way, the problem of the theory-ladenness of observation can be banished with a two-pronged move. First, we need an additional criterion of observationality, and second we need to exorcise a lingering specter of empiricism. Part of the role of an observation sentence is to be the point of entry into a theory. When trying to justify a theory to someone who does not already accept it, one needs to cite neutral evidence. This is why observations open only to the trained few seem suspect. The plausible additional criterion of observationality, then, is the degree to which a sentence is intersubjective. A sentence is intersubjective to the degree that speakers of the language agree about its application. Intersubjectivity and the occasion/standing scale are independent criteria. A standing sentence, for example, "God exists," may have a very high degree of intersubjectivity in a community. Conversely, some occasion sentences depend on discriminations that require a high level of training. A piano tuner, for example, makes observations that are not especially intersubjective. A sentence thus may be highly occasional without being intersubjective and vice versa.

Empiricism identified observations with those sentences that were maximally occasional *and* maximally intersubjective: "Red here now" or "The dial reads ten." This is, indeed, good evidence for theory construction. Such sentences have the virtue that they are open to critical scrutiny by anyone. The problem with such evidence, as critics of empiricism have pointed out, is that one cannot do much with it. Real science needs thicker observations. According to the Quinean conception of observation we've been developing, there is no line between theory and observation. One is tempted to say that all sentences are "theory-laden," but this imports the very distinction we have worked so hard to expel. Some sentences are simply closer to the periphery of our theorizing, others more central.

What then of the problem of circularity? One might think that the Quinean conception of observation makes the justification of theory by evidence impossible. This concern arises from a holdover from empiricism, and the second part of the argument here aims to eliminate it. Classical empiricists thought of justification in foundational terms. A theoretical claim could be justified only if there were a sequence of justifications that ultimately ended in something that did not itself need justification. There must be something like theory-neutral observation if theories are to be justified at all. This idea has been criticized from the standpoint of both epistemology (BonJour 1985; Harman 1973; Lehrer 1974; Lycan 1988; Quine 1969b; Ziff 1984) and philosophy of science (Hanson 1958; Kuhn 1962; Putnam 1974). Engaging the larger issues of epistemology is beyond our purview. It is sufficient to note that this essay follows in the antifoundationalist tradition. Whether an interpretive claim is justified depends on whether it explains, is presupposed by, or is explained by or some other claim(s) in the interpretation. This conception of justification does not require that there be a realm of pure observation at the foundation of a theory. Theoretical claims at the highest level of abstraction are justified by their ability to explain claims at a somewhat lower level. Thickly theory-laden observations are made coherent by their explanatory relations to both more "theoretical" and more thinly observational claims. Claims at the periphery of the web are coherent insofar as they are explicable by more centrally located claims.

Without the twin presuppositions of the foundationalist theory of justification and the sharp distinction between theoretical and observational sentences, the theory-laden character of observation is unproblematic. With this richer conception of observation in hand, let us return to the problem of meaning. The problem was originally cast in empiricist terms. The interpreter's observations are limited to brute data descriptions of the agents, their actions, and utterances. The agents themselves are aware of a richer field for action and speech. There is no noncircular way for the interpreter to understand the significance of an utterance or action as the local agent understands it. The Quinean conception of observation, sketched above, lets us frame the issue in postempiricist terms. Since, by hypothesis, the interpreter knows nothing of the language or culture of her subjects, her initial observations must be maximally intersubjective and occasional. Native speakers also rely on intersubjective cues to judge the appropriateness of their utterances. The difference between the natives' and the interpreter's observation lies in the degree of intersubjectivity. Among the native speakers, intersubjective recognition of "observable" phenomena can depend on a great deal of cultural knowledge. To see whether a debt has been paid, for instance, depends on an understanding of money (or barter) and the ways in which such debts are incurred and settled. Among members of the culture, it may be completely obvious that Smith paid his debt to Jones. While the sentence "Smith paid his debt to Jones" would command assent from any competent speaker, the relevant conditions of utterance are opaque to the naïve interpreter.

The problem of meaning can be resolved if we take the demise of the theory/observation distinction seriously and draw on the resources of explanatory coherence. A consequence of the foregoing discussion of observation is that the interpreter's observations and those on which the native speakers rely are not different in kind. It is a difference of degree analogous to the difference between any novice and expert. In her first attempts to understand an alien group, the interpreter has nothing more than maximally intersubjective observations with which to work. She must find occasion sentences in the local language that are keyed to conditions that she can identify, even though she knows nothing of the language or culture. The (epistemically) first local sentences to be translated will be occasion sentences whose use does not depend on any cultural specifics. At its initial stage, an interpretation will be composed of very superficial claims about what the locals are saying and doing. Invoking the Ryle-Geertz metaphor of "thick" and "thin" description (Geertz 1973b; Ryle 1971), we may say that the problem of postempiricist philosophy of social science is to show how this thin description turns into a thicker, deeper, and more complete one (cf. Bohman 1991; Henderson 1993). The criterion for change, this essay has argued, is the principle of explanatory coherence.

The understanding of action is an appropriate place to begin, since a full account of the explanation of action is already on the table. As proponents of hermeneutics have long emphasized, the problem of meaning is not just a linguistic problem. In the relevant sense of "meaning," the problem arises for action too. Members of the local group can observe what a fellow member is doing in ways that must escape a naïve interpreter. They can see the sense of the action—that it was a payment, a joke, or an insult. At the opening stage of an interpretation, the interpreter has only the thinnest descriptions of action available to her. Indeed, to call a motion an "action" is already to suppose that it was intentional. The empiricists had to justify claims about intentional action on the basis of a nonintentional descriptions of the event. A coherence theorist, by contrast, is not faced with this version of the problem of other minds. The interpreter may describe the events around her in intentional terms. She will be guessing about what her interlocutors are doing, but the fact that they are guesses is irrelevant. These guesses are good insofar as they can be integrated into the rest of the interpretation. An intentional action description may be the topic for an intentional action explanation. The interpreter will have to make guesses about the possible alternative actions and motivations. These will be good hypotheses insofar as they successfully explain the observed actions. Once postulated, a claim about an agent's motivations can explain his other actions too. The success of a claim about motivation in various contexts increases the interpreter's confidence in it. Such explanatory success also links together different action descriptions. The simplest intentional action descriptions, then, are made coherent with each other by being explained by a (relatively) unified set of motivations, including beliefs, desires, wishes, intentions, plans, and so on.

An interpretation becomes thicker by deploying thicker descriptions of action in intentional action explanations and postulating complex motives, elaborate practices, and social institutions. Each new description is justified in the same way that the simplest were: it is explained or helps explain something else. The last chapter argued that intentional action explanations had semantic presuppositions. The topic and foils of an intentional action explanation must be (within limits) characterized in terms recognizable to the agents. This means that the explanation of action must go hand in hand with the development of a translation. The interpreter must be able to identify and sort actions in the way that the natives do, and this means that she must have a grip on their language for intentional action.

The explanatory coherence story about how an interpreter moves from thin translations to thick ones parallels the story about action. The (epistemically) first translations have to be sentences used in contexts where a naïve interpreter can identify the salient objects and events. They will be maximally intersubjective occasion sentences. This sort of intersubjectivity does not depend on knowledge of the culture. The (epistemically) later interpretations will translate sentences that do depend on conditions appropriate only to those who are already familiar with the culture. The transition is again achieved by a growth in explanatory coherence. Here we come up against a very difficult problem. The explanatory coherence theory of interpretive change requires claims about meaning to be explanatory. The next section will investigate how this is possible.

6.2 THE EXPLANATORY VALUE OF MEANING

In both common life and social science, there are explanatory appeals to meaning. Claims about linguistic meaning are typically not considered explanatory by philosophers because, as section 4.1 noted, most models of explanation are unable to accommodate linguistic meaning as either explanans or explanandum. Word meanings do not causally interact, and natural laws play little role in translation. Again, the erotetic model looks hopeful. Why-questions can be asked about word and sentence meaning, and claims about meaning can answer why-questions. What needs to be made clear is the structure and presuppositions of such explanations. The object of this section is to analyze explanations that deploy meaning. If successful, we will resolve two outstanding difficulties. First, we will wrap up the issues left from section 6.1 by constructing the final part of the explanatory coherence approach to the problem of meaning. And second, we will show how the erotetic model satisfies yet another criterion of adequacy from section 4.1.

6.2.1 Meaning as Explanans

We need not look far to find explanations that appeal to meaning as part of the explanantia. In section 3.1, we saw how belief and meaning "conspire" to account for utterance (Davidson 1974/1984). This conspiracy is explanatory. We explain why a person said something by appealing to what the utterance meant along with that person's beliefs, goals, and intentions. Consider an example. Over dinner, my daughter says, "Please pass the pepper." Among the why-questions that might be asked is this one: Why did she say, "Please pass the pepper" {rather than "Please pass the broccoli" or "Please pass the salsa"}? Part, but only part, of the answer is that she wanted the pepper, not the broccoli or salsa. The why-question asks why she used one linguistic form rather than another. Therefore, the full answer must both claim that she wanted the pepper and that "pepper" means pepper.

If the above example seems too contrived, consider the kind of case where we really do wonder why someone used one verbal form rather than another. It happens in politics, where subtle semantic differences can be important. At the 1992 Democratic convention, then-candidate Bill Clinton ended his acceptance speech with the image of a child. "Somewhere at this very moment," he said, "a child is being born in America. Let it be our cause to give that child a happy home, a healthy family, and a hopeful future. . . . Let it be our cause that when this child is able, she gives something back to her children, her community, and her country."[2] It was an effective piece of political rhetoric.

---

2. From the text of Clinton's July 16, 1992 acceptance speech. Special thanks to Carol Stewart for her help finding this text.

After referring to this imaginary figure as "that child" four times, he used the feminine pronoun. Why "she" rather than "he"? One might point to any one of several political factors. Perhaps he wanted to identify himself with the feminist parts of the Democratic Party. Perhaps he wanted to attract female voters. Perhaps he wanted to portray himself as sensitive and caring. Any of these is only a partial explanation without two additional semantic claims. First, "she" is a feminine pronoun. Second, the pronoun "she" is marked in traditional grammar. While linguistic habits are changing, we still expect to hear "he" in situations where the gender of the subject is unknown or unspecified. These semantic facts gave Clinton's word choice its power. The pronoun was unexpected, hence vivid. In this case, it is not just the meaning of "she," but its semantic contrast with "he" that answers the why-question.

In explanations such as these, the topic is a linguistic expression and the foils are other possible utterances. Linguistic behavior is a species of intentional action, so we would expect explanations of this sort to have a form similar to reason-giving explanations. Like reason-giving questions, the topic of a why-question about linguistic expression has to be intentional. In this context, that means that the topic is something that the agent *said,* not a belch or hiccup. There are, however, important differences. Section 5.2 argued that the foils of an intentional action explanation had to satisfy one or more of the following conditions:

i.　The alternative action is one that the agent had in mind.

ii.　The natural or social context forces a choice between the topic action and the alternative.

iii.　The alternative action is customary or normally expected under the circumstances.

iv.　The alternative is one of the typical modes, objects, or instruments of the intentional action concept deployed in the topic.

The second, third, and fourth conditions were motivated by two concerns. First, some possible contrast classes were so absurd that the why-question was rejected rather than answered. Second, while deliberate action is a paradigm of intentional action, agents do not always deliberate about all relevant alternatives. The latter three conditions tried to isolate those contrast classes that were plausible, but not necessarily deliberate. The difference between the specific interests underlying why-questions about linguistic expression and the general interest in intentional action mitigates the force of these concerns.

The final condition does not apply to why-questions about linguistic expression at all, since it invokes modes, objects, and instruments that are specific to intentional action concepts. The focus of a why-question about linguistic behavior is not the action—saying, uttering, asserting, or something of the like—but the content of the expression. (Of course, we can ask reason-giving why-questions about such actions, for example, Why did she *assert* that *P* rather than *suggest* that *P*? Such a question contrasts actions, not the contents.) With respect to the second condition, the natural or social context has less power to "force a choice" among utterances than among other sorts of action. The relationship between the natural and social context on the one hand and the alternative utterances on the other is mediated by the meaning, truth conditions, and pragmatic force of the alternatives. Similarly, whether an utterance is "customary or normally expected under the circumstances" depends on its meaning, truth conditions, and pragmatic force. Since why-questions about linguistic expression are asking about the meaning, truth conditions, or pragmatic force, (ii) and (iii) do not seem appropriate as general conditions. For example, an interpreter might legitimately ask why Jones described Smith as "challenged" rather than as "a moron." One can imagine contexts where a word like "moron" would be completely inappropriate, so inappropriate, perhaps, that its use never crossed Jones's mind. This question might be answered by describing the meaning of the words, their recent history, and their different pragmatic force in this context. However, this foil is neither forced by the natural or social environment, nor is it customary or expected. The foils of why-questions about linguistic expression, then, need not satisfy conditions (ii), (iii), or (iv).

The root of the difference between questions about intentional actions and questions about linguistic expression is that the speaker's motive may not be directly related to the content of the utterance and its alternatives. Reason-giving why-questions ask for motivations that discriminate among intentional actions. The agent's motive must therefore be directly related to the topic and foils. Why-questions about linguistic expression contrast utterances with different meanings, truth conditions, or pragmatic forces. The range of why-questions about linguistic expression is thus broader than why-questions about intentional action per se. This is the deep reason why none of the constraints on the foils of intentional action why-questions are necessary for why-questions about verbal expression. At the same time, motivation is not eliminable from the answer to such a question. Belief and other sorts of motivation conspire with meaning to account for utterance. The answer to a why-question about linguistic expression, then, must describe some of the agent's beliefs, desires, or other motivational states in virtue of which the topic utterance is relevant. To adequately discriminate between topic and foil, however, some of their linguistic features will have to be mentioned. Meaning, truth, and pragmatics is part of, but not the whole, explanation of linguistic expression.

Asking about a person's utterance is only the first of three ways in which a claim about linguistic meaning can be explained. The second is the explanation of nonverbal behavior. *Sati* provides a good example. Let us suppose, for the sake of this illustration, that Roop Kanwar was not coerced or drugged by her husband's family. We may ask why she performed *sati* rather than becoming a widow. This satisfies the presuppositions of an intentional action explanation. Like the explanation of an utterance, part of the difference between the topic and the contrasting elements is semantic. "Sati" has a rich background of meaning in Hindi. When she thinks about doing something describable as "sati," the public meaning of the word funds the content and ramifications of that description. Sati is a goddess and those who become *sati* are likewise divine. Roop Kanwar's (presumptive) desire for this status is made a relevant answer to the question because of the meaning of "sati." A relevant part of the answer will thus be claims about the meaning of the word. The point generalizes to all intentional action explanations. Section 5.2 argued that the topic must describe the action in terms recognizable to the agent. In the local language, the words designating actions will often include typical motives as a part of their meaning. Part of what makes the agent's various beliefs and feelings appropriate as reasons is thus given by the public meaning of the words in the action description. Any intentional action explanation will, then, at least *presuppose* claims about word meaning. More substantively, as in the case of *sati,* the claims about meaning may figure as part of the explanans.

A final way in which meaning can become explanatory is in accounts of how agents think about the objects of their action. In some interesting cases, the public language grounds the way in which individuals conceptualize their environment. Benjamin Lee Whorf is famous for his speculation about how language influences thought. While one may be justly suspicious of his grander claims, the examples that inspired him are instructive. Linguistics was a hobby for Whorf. His day job was fire insurance adjustment, and in "Relation of Habitual Thought and Behavior to Language" he draws on his experience (Whorf 1956: 135). Those who work around gasoline storage drums tend to exercise extraordinary care with fire. When the drums are empty, however, less care is taken. A worker may light a cigarette and toss the burning stub when finished. The worker surely knew that gasoline was highly flammable, so why did he light and throw the cigarette? Whorf suggested that the worker's mistake was to think of the drums as "empty." In English, when a container of *X* is empty, there is no more *X* in it. Whorf speculated that the worker made a peculiar inference. Since there was no more gasoline in the *empty* drums, there was no need for the care that he ordinarily exercised around gasoline. The worker's inference was guided by the meaning of the word "empty." We know (and the worker found out) that empty gasoline drums are more dangerous than full ones, since they contain the highly flammable vapor. The lack of fit between the meaning and the facts had catastrophic consequences.

The way word meaning figures into Whorf's example is more complex than what we have seen so far. It involves a chain of explanations. The primary question asks why the worker lit a match near the gasoline drums, rather than refraining. This is an intentional action and the question satisfies the presuppositions of a reason-giving explanation. His reasons presumably involved things like a desire for a cigarette, and so on. Gasoline storage drums are hazardous, and the worker knew this. So the first answer raises a further question: Why did the worker think that lighting a match was not hazardous {rather than thinking that it was hazardous}? Whorf's answer attributes the inference "if the drums are empty, they are not hazardous" to the worker. At this point, the crucial question arises. Why did he make this inference {rather than inferring that the drums remain hazardous when empty}? Now Whorf's claims about "empty" become apposite.

Whorf's claim about the public meaning of "empty" is relevant because it underlies the connection between the premise and conclusion of the inference. The meaning of "empty" is partly expressed by the claim that "if a container is empty of X, then there is no more X in the container." The conditional grounds the topic inference, but not the others in the contrast class. (It was a good inference too. The worker's mistake was to believe that the drums were empty when they were full of gasoline vapor.) Claims about meaning are quite generally relevant to explanations of inference. Inference, as distinct from implication, is an action. Many inferences, if not all, are underwritten by the meaning of our words. While the meaning of "and," "or," "not," "all," and "some" drive a class of inferences that are particularly interesting, we should not think of inference as exhausted by these "logical" words. When I hear that John is a bachelor, I may infer that he is unmarried (or a degree-holder, or a young adult male seal, depending on the context). Why-questions about this and similar inferences may be relevantly answered by appeal to the meaning of the words.

A critic might remain unimpressed by these examples and their analysis. The erotetic view permits anything as a relevance relation. Such why-questions can be asked and answered, but why should we think that they are genuine parts of social *science?* In other words, the critic might ask, why should we think that these explanations are *scientific* explanations? Other sorts of why-questions can also be raised; questions that can be answered by appeal to the agents' cognitive dispositions, their neurological make-up, or their economic system. These seem capable of more scientific answers than the sort of questions discussed above. As a compatiblist about explanation and interpretation, I would not argue that such questions are precluded. The critic's questions are interesting and useful. I want only to insist that explanations that appeal to meaning are also interesting and useful. Indeed, given the interests of the interpretive disciplines, such explanations are indispensable.

Explanations that appeal to meaning satisfy two of the interests important to the interpretive enterprise: stability (discussed in section 4.4), and understanding actions and cultures from the agent's point of view (discussed in section 5.1). The interest in understanding the agent's point of view structures the contrast classes and relevance relations of reason-giving explanations. Where the topic is a bit of verbal behavior, claims about word meaning paradigmatically capture the agent's point of view. In the explanation of nonverbal action, elements of the contrast class must be descriptions that the agents would regard as possible or appropriate in that context. What differentiates the alternatives in such explanations is partly the semantic content of these descriptions. The meaning that these action descriptions have to the agents is thus a crucial part of the explanation. The relevance of an appeal to meaning is thus a direct consequence of demanding explanations that capture the agent's point of view.

Explanatory appeal to meaning also increases the stability of the explanations. Explanations are said to be stable when small changes in the world make no difference to the explanation. Stability thus increases the predictive value of an explanation. One of the alternatives to an explanatory appeal to meaning is to rely entirely on the intentions and beliefs of the individual agent. There is a well-known program that shows how to understand the meaning of an utterance in terms of the communicative intentions of the agent (Bennett 1976; Grice 1989; Schiffer 1972). Is it possible to do all the explanatory work for meaning, as described above, by appealing only to communicative intentions? Communicative intentions of the Gricean kind are certainly sufficient in some cases. Indeed, Grice's paradigmatic examples are all plausible cases were an utterance could be explained by appeal to the communicative intentions of the speaker. As a general approach to the explanation of utterance, however, appeal to communicative intentions conflicts with the interest in stability. To do the work of meaning, a Gricean explanation must attribute rather complex, iterated intentions to the agent. If the speaker's actual intentions veer slightly from the prescribed iterations, the explanation would fail. It would be a bad strategy, then, to try to make "speaker meaning" do all of the explanatory work of an interpretation. Sentence (utterance) meaning is public and common to a group of speakers. Thus, an explanation that appeals to public meaning is not sensitive to the idiosyncrasies of individual agents. They are therefore more useful than speaker meaning for predicting how any member of the group will behave in a particular context.

It needs to be noted that the argument of the foregoing paragraph does not touch the larger issue of whether the meaning of a word or sentence in a language can be analyzed in terms of speaker meanings. That is the real thrust of the Gricean program, and this work may remain neutral on the question of its possibility. It follows that we need not choose among the various ways of analyzing word or sentence meaning in terms of truth conditions (Davidson 1984), stimulus conditions (Quine 1960), utterance conditions (Brandom 1994; Ziff 1960), or whatever. What an interpretation requires is claims of the form "'p' in language L means p." While these have an explanatory role, this work takes a position on the epistemology of language, not its metaphysics. The epistemological claim is that a translation is justified by its role in the overall interpretation of a community of speakers. We are thus at odds with the epistemological program of some of the above-mentioned philosophers of language. Insofar as critical work has been necessary to undermine these alternative epistemologies, it has been done in chapter 3. Developing an alternative epistemology is the overall goal of this book. In this section we are seeing in detail how claims about translation are integrated into an interpretation and can contribute to (or detract from) its explanatory coherence.

6.2.2 Meaning as Explanandum

In his famous "Gavagai!" example, Quine proposed that this simple utterance might have several, widely different translations. Since, as he supposed, it was uttered in the presence of rabbits (and the native speakers refrained from uttering it in the absence of rabbits), it might justly be identified with the term "rabbit" in English. Suitable adjustments of the logical syntax of the local language, however, would equally justify "undetached rabbit parts" or "instantiation of rabbithood." Nothing in the conditions of utterance could distinguish among these. Choice of translations is underdetermined, hence, he argued, indeterminate (Quine 1960; Quine 1970; Quine 1987). In the mind of an anthropologist, such choices raise the question of why the locals would have a word for undetached rabbit parts. If she could explain why they have such an odd word, then her claim that "gavagai" means undetached rabbit parts would be supported. If not, then the claim dangles uselessly. Since it is easy to explain why they have a word meaning rabbit, the straightforward hypothesis seems preferable. Rather than be stymied by possible alternative translations, a working interpreter looks to see which translations make sense in the light of what she knows about the culture, chooses one, and moves on.

The outsider's question, Why would the locals have a word for undetached rabbit parts? jumps the boundaries of Quine's thought-experiment. Quine was not concerned about the pragmatic matter of choosing the best interpretation. His quest was metaphysical. The conclusion of the indeterminacy argument is that there is nothing in the world to make one translation right and the other wrong. Word meaning is not an entity. The quick argument, above, does not refute the argument for indeterminacy. The lesson is about how anthropologists pare down real underdetermination when they are faced with it. They do so, in part, by explaining their translations. The claim about meaning is explained by statements about the social structure, cultural practices, political institutions, and so on. This indirect sort of evidence gives the interpreter good reasons for choosing among some alternatives.[3]

---

3. The argument here is consonant with Bohman's defense of "weak holism" (Bohman 1991: 125ff).

Why-questions about meaning were used effectively in structural and structural-functional anthropology. Interpreters in this tradition have an interest in categorization and its relationship to social organization. This led to a corresponding interest in semantic categories. Any talk of local categories inevitably has its roots in the translation of the local language. Local categories are reflected in taxonomies of kind terms. The categories are semantic categories in the first instance. Thus, when Bulmer asked, "Why is the cassowary not a bird?" in his well-known essay of that title, his question is semantic, not biological (Bulmer 1967). The Karam people of Highland New Guinea have a term, *kobity*, which refers to the large flightless bird known to us as the cassowary. It is not counted among the *yakt*, a superordinate term grouping 181 birds and bats. Bulmer's question is: Why does *yakt* not include *kobity* as a subordinate term?

There are apparent differences between the *kobity* and the various creatures characterized as *yakt*. The *kobity* does not fly since it has very small, featherless wings. Moreover, it is much larger than any other indigenous bird. The local species weighs upwards of 50 pounds. These and other features make it distinct from the things called *yakt*. Bulmer, however, rejects this as an explanation: "to point to these features does not explain *why* the cassowary should enjoy special taxonomic rank" (Bulmer 1967: 11 emphasis in original). None of the features that make the cassowary unique have any other use in the zoological taxonomy of the Karam. Every creature has some features that make it unique. Without evidence that the features differentiating the cassowary are used in the broader taxonomy, indicating these features fails to explain why it is treated differently. The features that differentiate things falling within a general term need to be systematic, and there is apparently no such systematic account available for the cassowary.

Bulmer turns to socio-cultural factors that might distinguish the *kobity*. Here he finds a rich source of differentiae. We can do little better than quote Bulmer's own summary of his explanation:

To recapitulate: to understand the cassowary's special status we must know:

1. That it is a forest creature, the prime game of the forest, and that there is an elaborate antithesis in Karam thought between forest and cultivation, based on the special value they attach to taro on the one hand and to *anlaw* pandanus nuts [a wild palm nut which grows in the forest] on the other, and facilitated by the seasonal cropping of both these plants.

2. That the forest-cultivation antithesis is also linked to very basic concerns with kinship roles and kinship rights, and in particular to the problems of brother-sister relationships and of relationships between cross-cousins. . . .

Lastly, I would argue that to look for an explanation of the cassowary's special taxonomic status in purely taxonomic terms, by reference to objective features of its appearance and behavior alone, could be to miss the point. Certainly it is a strange beast in many ways, and using only characters of which Karam are well aware one can isolate it as a separate taxon in any one of several different ways: as a terrestrial biped, as a hairy egg-layer, as a thick-skulled brainless monster and so on. But equally well, and still using characters which Karam are well aware of, one could fit it in with the birds (as many other New Guinea Highlanders do) or even with the wild pig and wallaby in a class of 'big game animals'. So, for me at least, 'special taxonomic status' is a function of something broader, a special status in culture, or cosmology, at large. (Bulmer 1967: 18–19)

Bulmer thus identifies an explanatory link between features of the local culture and social structure and the taxonomic relationship between *kobity* and *yakt*. The *kobity* is distinguished from *yakt* (and other taxa) because it has a special place in the culture of the Karam.

If we subject Bulmer's work to a philosopher's twist, we can see how this kind of explanatory form is directly relevant to the issue of underdetermination. Bulmer's explanation could have equally been mobilized in service of a question concerning translation. Presumably, the Karam agree to some statement that Bulmer translates as "the cassowary is not a bird." Why translate the local utterance in this way rather than some other? Given the anomalous character of this result, perhaps the translation should be changed. There is, no doubt, some Quinean tweaking that could be done with the Karam particles and adverbs which are translated as "is not a kind of." Ad hoc adjustments are easy to invent. Simply specify that the adverb translated as "not" is given special treatment in contexts including *kobity* and *yakt*. In these special contexts, the adverb functions differently, yielding "the cassowary is a bird" as the translation. Nothing in the local context of utterance could distinguish between these alternatives. The Karam speakers would assent and dissent to the same utterances in the same contexts. Bulmer's explanation gives us a compelling reason to accept his translation over the alternative. He can explain why *kobity* has a special status. To compete, the alternative translation would have to provide an explanation of why the adverb translated as "not" is given *its* special treatment.

Explanations where meaning is the topic have a variety of contrast classes. Bulmer's question asks about a relation of subordination/superordination, but any semantic relationship might be the topic of a why-question. Moreover, anthropologists often ask why cultures lack words (e.g., they have names for trees, but no general term) or why they have a multiplicity of terms (e.g., the common but spurious example of Eskimo words for snow and real examples of proliferous trade jargons). Such questions ask about a difference in possible claims about meaning. The foils, then, are alternative possible meanings or semantic relationships. Since these are claims about meaning presented by the interpreter, we can equally regard the elements of the contrast class as alternative translations. In the examples above, the explanans is a claim about some other aspect of the native speakers' behavior, culture, or society. What is the relationship between claims about meaning and claims about the culture such that the latter can discriminate among alternative translations? I suspect that there are several. Two will be characterized below, but I doubt that they exhaust the field.

First, claims about meaning may be explained historically. Words are borrowed from other languages and words have systematic histories of change within a single language. Part of the explanation of why a word has its present meaning is that it is the historical offshoot of a word with a similar meaning. The English word "scout," for example, has several overlapping senses. It can mean to examine, explore, or survey something. It also has a critical sense—to scout an idea is to criticize or reject it. In some uses, both senses are in play. When a philosopher claims to have scouted a text, she is saying both that she has looked it over and that it has been criticized. The word has this meaning because of some accidents of its history. The critical sense comes from Scandinavian roots in Old Norsk; the reconnoitering sense can be traced to Middle English and Old French. The contemporary use also depends on the accidental homophony of these two distinct words. Telling an etymological story is thus one way of explaining a meaning.

Meaning may also be explained functionally. Section 5.3 distinguished two sorts of why-question that generated functional explanations. A "disposition question" asked why something had a particular property. It was juxtaposed to "item questions" that asked about the presence of an item in the system. Functional explanations of meaning in anthropology fall most easily into the former type. The question asks why a word or phrase has a particular meaning. It is answered by showing how the word functions in a social context. Consider an example from Malinowski's *Coral Gardens and Their Magic* (1935). In this magnificent work, Malinowski examines the linguistic and sociological characteristics of the magic used by the Trobriand Islanders to guarantee the success of their gardens. The yearly gardening cycle begins with the first ground breaking and is marked with elaborate magical ceremonies. The central ritual begins with what Malinowski called the "*vatuvi* spell" (Malinowski 1935: vol. 1, 96). After appropriate preparations, a magician lays a number of stone axes before him on a mat. These axes will be used to break the ground of the gardens. Each has an amulet of herbs tied to it. The magician then utters the spell over them. It begins with the repetition of the word *vatuvi* uttered close to the axes. Malinowski describes the magician as "rubbing" the word into the axes. The magician then continues with a long repetitive list of all the garden pests and blights. The spell takes forty-five minutes to perform.

Malinowski takes the word *vatuvi* to be of central importance. The word itself is interesting. It does not appear as a part of other utterances. Rather, it seems to be a whole grammatical unit unto itself. Cognate terms suggest that *vatuvi* occupies the same semantic space as "to institute" or "to set up," and that it is more distantly related to "to heal." He ultimately decides that "this word conveys a general benediction especially directed toward the depth of the earth; it also implies firmness and permanence of the crops and conveys the idea of going down and rising again" (Malinowski 1935: vol. 2, 262). If we were to ask why *vatuvi* had the meaning of a general benediction, suggesting firmness and permanence of the crops, rather than another meaning, Malinowski would point to its role in the garden ceremony. It is repeated at the beginning of the spell, and the point of the spell is to give the axes the power to inaugurate the garden and make it well founded. Having blessed the axes, the magician can go on to enlist magical protections against particular dangers, pests, and garden blights. The word can contribute to the ceremony because it has this meaning, not another.

Bulmer's explanation of why the cassowary is not a bird seems similar. He does not appeal to the word's currency in a practice, but to the role of the cassowary in Karam society. In short, the relationship between the cassowary and humans is directly analogous to the relationship between a man and his sisters and father's sister's children (cross-cousins). The analogy is elaborated in a number of ways, including proscribed ritual language, restrictions on the way in which cassowaries may be hunted, and the symmetrical relationships between the inheritance of garden plots and the inheritance of rights to pandanus nut trees in the forest. The cassowary plays a special and important role in Karam society. Because of this special role, the cassowary is not treated as a kind of bird, or indeed as subordinate to any other biological taxon. The cassowary occupies a category all to itself, and the word for a cassowary, *kobity*, is not semantically subordinate to any other species or genus term.

In different ways, Bulmer and Malinowski both give us functional explanations of word meaning.[4] These are really nothing more that elaborate ethnographic examples of the idea that words can be central, even constitutive of human practices. This idea has been floated by a variety of venerable authors, including Wittgenstein, Winch, Taylor, and Austin. Indeed, it may seem obvious, even trite. If the idea is accepted, then we have agreed that there are functional explanations of word meaning. Words will play a role in human practices because of what they mean, and this role will constitute a system function. Functional explanations of this type may not be the only way that social and cultural factors can be brought to bear on claims about meaning. Nonetheless, they constitute a pervasive form of explanation.

---

4. It should be noted that Bulmer is not a functionalist in the sense that Malinowski was. Functional explanations as described here are distinct from the doctrines espoused by the functionalist school of anthropology.

6.3 Defusing the Double Hermeneutic

We may conclude, then, that claims about linguistic phenomena, including word meaning, translation, truth conditions, and pragmatic force, may figure in interpretation as both explanans and explanandum. One of the goals of this chapter has therefore been achieved. The challenge with which this chapter opened was to show how the principle of explanatory coherence could take the interpreter from her initial, naïve descriptions of local utterance to a sophisticated reading of the local structures of meaning. The central piece of the puzzle is that claims about meaning have a multifaceted explanatory role. The interpreter might begin with thin, behavioristic descriptions of action and utterance, but she cannot rest with them for long. Actions, even if described in behavioristic terms, need to be explained. This requires the interpreter to make some guesses about the agent's motivation and the way in which the action is conceived. These explanations, in turn, have semantic presuppositions insofar as the interpreter is claiming that the action is locally described in a particular way. Linguistic expressions need to be explained too, and we have seen how claims about meaning play a necessary part in these explanations. Finally, choices among possible alternative translations are motivated by the interpreter's ability to explain why local words mean what they do. The explanatory coherence of the interpretation increases with each of these interpretive moves. Far from leaving the interpreter stuck with brute data, the principle of explanatory coherence demands a semantically rich understanding.

An explanatory coherence view thus seems to have substantial resources for addressing the problem of meaning. We cannot claim to have resolved this problem, however, until we squarely face the so-called "double hermeneutic" of interpretation. Section 6.1 analyzed the problem of meaning as arising from limitations in the empiricist conceptions of observation and justification. Empiricist philosophy of science required both a strict distinction between theory and observation and a foundationalist conception of justification. Theoretical terms had to be constructed from and justified by observation terms. In the interpretive disciplines, this means that any understanding of meaning must be ultimately reducible to the thin, behavioristic, and superficial observations of an outsider. Dilthey, Schutz, Gadamer, Taylor, and others pointed out that what the social scientist observes is already meaningful to the participants. This level of meaning is not represented by the observations that fund all empirical theorizing. Hence, the argument concludes, empirical theorizing is incapable of comprehending meaning. Section 6.1 argued in response that an explanatory coherence view is committed to neither a strict distinction between theory and observation nor the foundationalist conception of justification. The problem of meaning does not arise for an explanatory coherence view in the way that it arose for empiricism and empiricist philosophy of science.

Others have also argued that the purported opposition between the natural and the social sciences is undermined by postempiricist philosophy of science. Rorty (1979), Giddens (1976), Bohman (1991), and others have pointed out that changes in the philosophy of natural science have fundamentally changed the dynamic of the debate over explanation and interpretation. Section 6.1 shows how the reconceptualization of "observation" is a crucial element of this change. Changes in the debate, however, have not eliminated the charge that methodologies drawn from the natural sciences have limited application to the social world. Habermas (1984: 109ff), Giddens (1976: 148–52, 158) and Makkreel (1985: 237ff) have argued that the human sciences are subject to a "double hermeneutic" that goes beyond the theory-ladenness of observation. A postempiricist epistemology wherein the theory-ladenness of observation is unproblematic does not make meaning unproblematic in the same stroke. Habermas argues:

> If the paradigm-dependent theoretical description of data calls for a stage 1 of interpretation that confronts all sciences with structurally similar tasks, then we can demonstrate for the social sciences an unavoidable stage 0 of interpretation at which there arises a *further* problem for the relation of observation language and theory language. It is not only that the observation language is dependent on the theory language; prior to choosing any theory-dependency, the social scientific "observer," as a participant in the process of reaching understanding through which alone he can gain access to his data, has to make use of the language encountered in the object domain. (Habermas 1984: 110)

The main elements of the argument seem to be these. Observations in both the natural and social sciences are theory-laden. This constitutes the hermeneutic element common to all inquiry. However, the action and speech that the interpreter encounters is already meaningful to the subjects. Before the interpreter can make observations at all, she has to speak the language. Since understanding the language is epistemologically prior to scientific observation, understanding the language requires resources that transcend the theory-laden observations of science. This is the second hermeneutic unique to social inquiry. The interpreter must draw on features of "mutual knowledge" (Giddens 1976: 149), "lived experience" (Makkreel 1985: 237), or "communicative action" (Habermas 1984: 115–17). While these authors conceptualize the additional resources of interpretation differently, they agree that interpretation relies on something that the interpreter and interpretee share. Thus, even if a postempiricist analysis of natural science is granted, the interpretive disciplines remain methodologically distinct in two significant ways. First, interpretation is epistemologically prior to theorizing of a natural scientific kind. Second, interpretation depends on a similarity between the object of inquiry and the subject who is inquiring. That both the interpreter and her subjects speak, think, and act is a condition for the possibility of interpretation and is never required by the natural sciences.

The argument of the double hermeneutic is a direct challenge to explanatory coherence. The principle of explanatory coherence, as developed here, treats both of Habermas's stages in the same way. Indeed, according to the explanatory coherence view, there is no difference in principle between "stage 1" and "stage 0." Moreover, the explanatory coherence view of interpretive change holds that there is no deep epistemic difference between the interpretive disciplines and other kinds of empirical inquiry. While the structure of the natural sciences has not been our topic, an explanatory coherence view holds that all inquiry is explanatory, and all theories are justified by their relative coherence. While speech, thought, and action make the interpretation of humans different from theorizing about rocks, it does not make interpretation epistemically distinct at a fundamental level.[5] The explanatory coherence view thus does not recognize either distinguishing feature of interpretation that the double hermeneutic motivates.

To focus the disagreement further, it will be helpful to highlight the points of agreement. From the perspective of this essay, authors in the hermeneutic tradition from Dilthey forward have rightly emphasized three ideas. First, first-person understanding of meaning is not theoretical. A speaker's ability to comprehend her native tongue is not justified by observation in the way that theoretical claims are justified by observation. A child learning her first language is not a protolinguist. While there is no space here to defend or elaborate the point, a speaker's knowledge of her language is a species of "knowing how," not "knowing that." It is practical, not theoretical. The second point of agreement is that there is a difference between the theory-ladenness of observation and the hermeneutic circle of interpretation. Observation is always theory-laden, from the immediate recognition of a friend's face to the observation of supernovae. The hermeneutic circle, strictly speaking, concerns relationships among meaningful entities. The meaning of a word, text, action, or social event depends on the larger context of meaning, and the larger context is determined by the meaning of the parts. The hermeneutic circle occurs only within the interpretive disciplines because only they investigate structures of meaning. In other words, there is a double hermeneutic of interpretation.

Finally, the explanatory coherence view agrees that interpretation requires a relationship between the interpreter's claims and the subjects' own conceptualization of their speech and action. No adequate interpretation could ignore or discount the subjects' self-interpretation. An interest in the agent's point of view is one of the defining interests of interpretation. Chapter 5

---

5. The conclusion will explore the relationship between the natural sciences and the interpretive disciplines in more detail.

showed how this interest undergirds the structure of reason-giving explanations. Intentional action explanations require a description of the action that the agent could recognize, and the explanation of belief requires the belief to be characterized in epistemically accessible terms. Moreover, the semantic presuppositions of reason-giving explanation entail that the interpretation of action and speech develop together. Chapter 3 contended that while an interpretation is not bound to find that what the subjects say is mostly true, it must presuppose that they are competent speakers of their own language. An interpretation thus cannot hold that they are mostly wrong about the meaning of their own words and the conditions of their use. Looking ahead, we will see in chapter 7 how disputes among the locals over the interpretation of social events can be crucial to interpretation. Therefore, while an interpretation is not limited to the expressive resources of the subjects, no adequate interpretation could do without them.

The hermeneutic tradition and the explanatory coherence view thus agree that first-person understanding of language is not theoretical, that the hermeneutic circle is distinct from the theory-ladenness of observation, and that an adequate interpretation must be sensitive to the agents' self-interpretation. These points of agreement encompass the premises of the double hermeneutic argument. Against the hermeneutic authors, I want to argue that these premises entail neither that interpretation is epistemologically prior to explanatory theorizing nor that interpretation depends on a special identity between the interpreter and her subjects. While the premises are true, the inference is invalid.

The conclusion that interpretation is prior to explanatory theorizing is challenged by the observation that, even at the idealized naïve stage, the interpreter must interpret both speech and action as they occur in their full social context. Section 6.2 showed how the principle of explanatory coherence demands the articulation of the relationships among speech, action, and social context. As the interpretation grows, the principle requires translation and action explanation to be integrated into the larger understanding of the culture. According to the explanatory coherence view, then, it is wrong to draw a sharp line between the investigator's learning of the language and her learning about the culture. Indeed, it is precisely because of the hermeneutic circle that there can be no separation between Habermas's "stage 1" and "stage 0." Learning the language requires theorizing about the culture and *vice versa*. One is not epistemically prior to the other. Since the premises of the argument are consistent with the explanatory coherence view, and the explanatory coherence view consistently denies the conclusion, the conclusion that understanding meaning is epistemically prior to the understanding of culture does not follow.

The second lesson that Habermas, Giddens, and Makkreel draw from the double hermeneutic argument is that interpretation requires some kind of participation of the interpreter within the meaningful life of her subjects.

Once we admit that the understanding of meaning is not epistemically prior to theorizing about the culture, there is no need to postulate a separate epistemology of meaning. However, there is a positive reason for thinking that understanding meaning might be nonetheless distinct from other kinds of inquiry. Knowledge of language is not a theoretical activity. Similarly, understanding what a member of one's own culture is doing is, in typical cases, immediately apparent. Agents do not construct and test hypotheses about their fellows' speech and action. Giddens emphasizes this practical character of cultural knowledge in his version of the argument (as does Dreyfus; see Dreyfus 1980: 7–12). Giddens argues:

> The production of action as 'meaningful', I have proposed, can usefully be analyzed as depending upon 'mutual knowledge' which is drawn upon by the participants as interpretive schemes to make sense of what each other says and does. Mutual knowledge is not corrigible to the sociological observer, who must draw upon it just as lay actors do in order to generate descriptions of their conduct; insofar as such 'knowledge', however, can be represented as 'commonsense', as a series of factual beliefs, it is open to confirmation or otherwise in the light of social scientific analysis. (Giddens 1976: 157–58)

When Giddens says that "mutual knowledge is not corrigible to the sociological observer," I take him to mean that local knowledge of meaning is not theoretical. So, if the interpreter is to comprehend meaning in the way that the natives do, her knowledge of meaning cannot be theoretical either. Again, the explanatory coherence view can agree with the premise. While this view of linguistic and cultural knowledge as practical is not entailed by an explanatory coherence view, it is certainly consistent with it. In this case, Giddens's inference is made plausible by an additional, hidden premise: the way in which the interpreter understands meaning must be similar to the way in which the natives understand meaning. At a fundamental epistemological level, the interpreter's relationship to her subjects is the same as her relationship to her colleagues.

The issue is whether what is known practically can be adequately represented theoretically. There is no indication in these arguments that the *content* of such practical knowledge is incapable of theoretical representation. The claim is that the way in which a native speaker knows her language is different from the way in which a linguist knows it. There is an analogous difference between a music teacher's knowledge that a passage is to be played in a certain way and her student's knowledge of how to play the passage in that way. The teacher can represent what the student knows. The difference between the teacher and the student lies in their relationship to what is known. Similarly, an interpreter can represent what an utterance means to the native speakers. Considered as a theoretical postulate that the utterance means so-and-so, it is tested by its coherence with the rest of the interpretation. The interpreter's epistemic relationship to the meaning of the utterance or action is thus different from the native speaker's relationship to it. The hidden premise of Giddens's argument, then, is that the structure of the interpreter's knowledge must be the same as the structure the natives' knowledge.

Expressed in this way, the hidden premise is implausible. Section 3.2 argued against the idea that interpretation must presuppose that the native speakers and the interpreter adhere to the same or similar standards of rationality. Criteria of empirical justification are species of rational standards, and it therefore follows that the interpreter need not presuppose that the native speakers employ her epistemic standards. Moreover, there is reason to think that an interpreter must appeal to evidence that goes beyond that available to the speaker. As Giddens himself emphasizes (1976: 131), the speaker may not know about the history of her language, the relationship between her action and the social conditions that make it possible, or many of the larger social factors that are crucial to interpretation. Interpretation needs an epistemology that can pull together the many kinds of phenomena that are necessary for an adequate understanding. The argument of this book is that explanatory coherence is just such an epistemology. The practical character of linguistic and social knowledge is therefore consistent with a theoretical understanding. By itself, the argument of the double hermeneutic does not entail that some commonality between interpreter and interpretee is required for interpretation.

The reflections of this section have not shown that the positive conclusions of Habermas, Giddens, or Makkreel are false. The argument has been that the features of interpretation thought to necessitate a special epistemology for interpretation do not make it necessary. Both linguistic meaning and the meaning of actions and social events can be the subject of explanation, and an explanatory coherence view can embed a rich understanding of meaning within fully explanatory theorizing. It follows that the fourth criterion of adequacy from section 4.1 has been satisfied. The erotetic model of explanation, combined with a coherence view of interpretive change, provides an appropriate and fully explanatory role for meaning in interpretation.

CHAPTER 7

Normativity

The problem of apparent irrationality arises when someone speaks or acts in ways that they ought not, given the current interpretation. To recognize the problem in the first place, not to mention resolve it, an interpreter must make some claims about what the locals ought (not) to do, say, or believe. When we analyzed the problem of apparent irrationality in section 2.5, the normative dimension of the problem was captured by two questions:

2. Is it possible for an interpreter to prefer an interpretation that attributes to the interpretees standards of rationality different from her own?

3. What are the epistemic grounds for claiming that a person or group adheres to a norm, rule, or standard?

Chapter 3 argued against a priori limitations on the standards of rationality that an interpreter might attribute to her subjects. An interpreter may claim that the locals reason or act according to standards that diverge radically from those found in the interpreter's community, if doing so increases the explanatory coherence of her interpretation. The principle of explanatory coherence thus answers question (2) in the affirmative and provides the rough outline of an answer to question (3).

The project of this chapter will be to elaborate the details of the answer to question (3) in the face of several specific challenges. As has already been discussed (section 4.1), claims about norms have to be either explained or explanatory if they are to contribute to the coherence of an interpretation. Some philosophers have argued that, on the contrary, norms cannot figure in explanations. They contend that when norms become the subject of explanation or when they are used as explanantia, they must inevitably collapse into mere descriptions. The first section of this chapter will address the problem and articulate a general account of how norms can be explanatory. We will then turn to two further challenges that arise from the examples of chapter 2. First, norms, rules, and standards are not always explicitly expressed by the group under study. When the Azande have no tradition of debate about rules for reasoning, what sense can we make of the claim that they "have" one logic or another? Section 7.2 will be devoted to the problem of implicit norms. In chapter 2, we also noticed that norms and rules are frequently contested within the group. A legitimate worry about a coherence theory of interpretation is that it artificially homogenizes a culture, since representing conflict and difference in the behavior of the locals seems to decrease the coherence of the interpretation. Section 7.3 will address this problem. The resources on which we draw will also show how an explanatory coherence view of interpretive change handles the issue of priority between "internal" and "external" characterizations of cultural phenomena. By the end of this chapter, then, we will have shown how the explanatory coherence view answers all four of the questions that established the parameters of our problem (section 2.5).

7.1 NORMS, ACTION, AND EXPLANATION

Claims about norms have already received an explanatory role in intentional action explanations. The natural place for us to begin, then, is by reviewing this role and examining its consequences. In section 5.2, we compared the erotetic model of intentional action explanation with the rationalizing model. While both gave an explanatory role to the norm of instrumental rationality, there were two fundamental differences. First, rationalizing explanations use the norm of instrumental rationality as the form of explanation. The norm serves to link the explanantia to the explanandum. Erotetic explanations do not need a norm of rationality as part of the form, since that is constituted by the logic of why-questions and their answers. The norm of instrumental rationality is part of the *content* of an erotetic intentional action explanation. The interpreter must claim that the explanantia constituted reasons for the agent. An intentional action explanation must therefore invoke some criterion of rationality. The second difference between the erotetic and rationalizing approaches is that the rationalizing approach limits itself to the norm of instrumental rationality. Other norms are applicable insofar as they can be represented as something the agent desires.[1] The erotetic model permits a subtler role for norms in intentional action explanations. Some purchase on this subtlety can be

---

1. Recall the standard objection to rationalizing explanations and the response. I do not want to take out the garbage, but I do so anyway. Does this mean that my action cannot be explained as the desire for *P* and the belief that *Q* is necessary to achieve it? The answer is that, in cases such as this, I want to fulfill my obligations to take out the garbage.

gained by reexamining the role of action descriptions and the customs or norms governing action.

In our earlier discussion of intentional action explanations, the local customs or norms and the semantics of the action description became important in two respects. Whether a foil is appropriately contrasted with an action description depends (in part) on what the words in the description mean and what norms are applicable. Also, appeal to norms and word meaning helped address the question of whether an agent has authority over the appropriate conceptualization of her action. The words and phrases that capture intentional action include, as a component of their meaning, an indication of the sort of motives that might be adequate reasons for the action. These are more or less vague, and we may arrange them on a scale from "thin" descriptions to "thick." Thicker action descriptions provide more information about the sort of motives that might constitute reasons. Thin descriptions admit almost any motive, for example, raising one's arm, moving one's toes, etc. At their thinnest, thin descriptions may not indicate whether the event was an intentional action at all.

Consider, for instance, the action of failing a student in a class. If we describe Smith's behavior in this way (say, as she fills out her final grade report), a host of possible motivations is ruled out. That Smith's car failed to start that morning is not a candidate motivation, nor is the fact that the flunked student has brown eyes.[2] These are not the right sort of motives for "flunking a student." It might be better to say that they are very poor reasons for flunking a student. This highlights the crucial point: a thick action description itself distinguishes good (appropriate, rational) motives from bad (inappropriate, irrational) motives. If we asked Smith why she flunked Jones, and her answer was that today is Tuesday, we would have reason to doubt Smith's rationality. When an interpreter explains why an agent did P, the interpreter must claim that the agent possessed motive Q *and* that Q is the sort of thing that constitutes a good reason for P. Where P is a relatively thick intentional action description, the criteria for what is to count as a good reason are part of what is understood by the phrase P itself.

One sort of norm that has an explanatory role, then, are those associated with particular kinds of intentional action. These are criteria that distinguish good from bad reasons for doing a certain type of action. Because they distinguish good reasons from bad, these criteria are directly relevant to the problem of apparent irrationality. One of the ways a problem of apparent irrationality can arise is when the interpreter loses her grip on the subjects'

---

2. One could make these relevant by telling an elaborate story, but this would simply demonstrate the point under discussion. The elaborate story turns the nonreason into a reason appropriate to the action description.

reasons for action. She can see what they are doing, but does not comprehend their reasons. Alternatively, she knows what reasons they give, but cannot see how the avowed reasons could be sufficiently motivating. To resolve this sort of difficulty, the interpreter needs to identify what counts as a good or bad reason (for the locals) in such a context. These will be local criteria of rationality. Claims about such criteria increase coherence by permitting the explanation of behavior that was otherwise inexplicable.

Local customs and rules have an explanatory role similar to the criteria associated with action descriptions. They are less fine-grained than the latter, and are associated with social contexts of action rather than the semantics of the action description. Consider a very thin action description—raising one's hand. There is very little in this description that differentiates good from bad reasons for the action. In the right context, the presence of the rules and customs help determine what sort of reasons can be appropriate. At an auction, raising one's hand (at the right time) constitutes making a bid, and there is an identifiable range of reasons for performing this sort of action. Strategic maxims can forge obvious links between motives and actions. To shift the example, it is considered good strategy in chess to control the middle of the board. In light of this value, some possible moves become better than others and the moves of a player can be explained. Norms, rules, values, and customs are of particular interest because they can directly govern action across a vast range of contexts. Moral rules do precisely this. Their applicability across contexts does not diminish their usefulness to the explanation of a specific action. If, among a group, air pollution is regarded as something to be avoided, then the fact that his bicycle does not pollute might explain why Michael chose to ride his bicycle to work rather than drive his car. Norms governing inference can have similar explanatory value. We will explore some examples in the next section. For now, the point to be highlighted is that these norms are among the explanantia of intentional action and belief formation.

Before moving on, we must pause to countenance a fundamental objection. Henderson (1993) has argued that norms, qua norms, can have no such role in explanations.[3] Intentional action explanations appeal to the agent's reason as the explanation of his action. The explanation attributes the reason to the agent and claims that the agent takes it to be a good or sufficient reason for the action. The agent must thus either believe that a reason of this type is a good reason or have a corresponding disposition to act when presented with reasons of this type. In either case, the norm has been replaced by something without normative force. What seemed to be a norm with an

---

3. What follows is a generalized form of the argument Henderson presents. Henderson's own formulation relies on causal relevance relations. Since section 4.4 argues for laissez-faire contextualism, Henderson's argument has to be slightly recast here.

explanatory role turns out, on close examination, to be nothing more than a belief or disposition. Conversely, if the agent had no disposition to act when presented with such reasons, or if he did not believe that reasons of this type were sufficient for action, then the purported explanation would be undermined. Henderson writes that "once we appreciate what it takes to answer a why-question, and thus to provide an explanation for an action or intentional state, we find that normative principles, qua normative principles, have nothing to contribute here" (Henderson 1993: 168). We will call this the Henderson problem: when they are used as explanantia, claims about norms collapse into descriptions of belief or habit. Norms qua norms have no explanatory role.

The Henderson problem gets its bite from the fact that we expect reasons to be effective determinants of action. If reasons are causes, as many believe, then the agent must have the disposition to act in a certain way under those circumstances. We may deny that reasons are causes, however, and end up with the same difficulty. The agent has to take the reason *as a reason*. She has to believe that reasons of this sort are sufficient reasons for action. In either case, the reason is explanatory only because there is a correlated fact about the agent. Without this fact, the reason is not explanatory. With this fact, the norm of instrumental rationality collapses into a description of the agent's beliefs or dispositions. The root of the Henderson problem, then, is the individualistic character of intentional action explanations. Whether conceived as answers to why-questions, practical syllogisms, or deductions from covering laws, intentional action explanations always explain what an individual does. The explanation must appeal to salient facts about that individual. What seems to be important, in the end, is *not* whether the agent's reasons were good, but whether she believed them to be good (or had a disposition to act on them).

The Henderson problem arises, I suggest, because we have focused on the agent alone. To see the explanatory force of the norms, we must raise our eyes from the individual and gaze upon the social context in which she acts. This diagnosis suggests a possible resolution. The primary role for norms in social scientific explanation is in the explanation of group-level phenomena. In other words, claims about norms—such as instrumental rationality, moral injunctions, practical maxims, and so on—are, in the first instance, answers to why-questions about a social group. Claims about norms have a secondary role in the explanation of intentional action. They provide the normative standards in light of which a particular agent's motives are good or bad reasons. Articulating the agent's motives is a large part of explaining her action. That the motives were good (or bad) reasons for this sort of action requires reference to the agent's community. The normative aspects of an individual's action, including its rationality, only appear when the action is viewed against the background of group activity.

To make this suggestion plausible, one must show first that there are social-level explanations of social phenomena that invoke norms as explanantia, and second that these resist reduction to individualistic explanations. A likely class of candidates for such explanations arise from what Clifford Geertz called "models for" behavior. In his landmark essay "Religion as a Cultural System" (1973a), Geertz distinguished between "models of" and "models for." All human groups articulate a model *of* their natural and social environment. This is a body of conceptions and generalizations used to describe, predict, and explain natural or social phenomena. A model *of* natural or social phenomena is descriptive. A model *for* behavior is normative. It is a collection of normative conceptions and generalizations dictating how one ought to behave. Any human group, according to Geertz, will have both models for behavior and models of behavior. Models of behavior provide a way of understanding the social world— how society works, how its members are interdependent, and so on. A model for behavior says how members of the group ought to interact. Pragmatic prescriptions, moral prohibitions, or canons of reasoning may express the local models for behavior. The local models may also be encoded in ritual life and religious symbolism.

Geertz hypothesized that one of the functions of religious symbolism is to establish "powerful, pervasive, and long-lasting moods and motivations" (Geertz 1973a: 90). Geertz himself characterized these moods and motivations as "dispositions." There is, on Geertz's view, a relationship between the models for behavior embedded in religious symbolism and the actual behavior of the members of the group. The religious symbolism and ritual life of a group constitutes or encodes a model for behavior. The model for behavior is a set of norms. In the light of these norms, individuals form dispositions to act in the proscribed ways. Systems of religious symbols and rituals, then, influence the behavior of the group through the dispositions of the individuals. A model for behavior thus relies on two levels of explanation. The individuals in the group share "powerful, pervasive, and long-lasting moods and motivations." In philosopher's jargon, these are the "dispositions to act" or "beliefs and desires" that figure in intentional action explanations. The agent is not alone in having such dispositions (beliefs and desires), and this fact raises its own why-questions. Why do the members of the group all have *this* disposition (belief, etc.) rather than another? Why do only *these* members of the group, and not *those,* end up with such-and-such dispositions (beliefs, etc.)? That there is a particular model for behavior encoded in laws or hidden in the religious symbolism is a relevant part of the answer to these questions.

A straightforward sort of case will be one where the model for behavior is an explicit set of norms, such as regulations or laws. Consider, for example, the relationship between traffic laws and the intentional actions of individual drivers. It is the law in the United States that one drives on the right–hand side of the road. The laws express the norm that one ought to drive on the right-hand side of the road. For an agent behind the wheel, however, this norm may not be a proximate reason for sticking to the right-hand curb.

Perhaps you are different, but my reason for driving on the right is that *I don't want to die.* Even in this simple case, then, there is a complex interplay of explanations. For any driver, one might ask why she is now driving on the right, rather than the left. The likely explanations will appeal to her immediate motivations: the desire to avoid those cars over there, the belief that driving on the left is likely to cause a collision (even if that lane is presently empty), or perhaps the belief that it is illegal. There is, however, a remarkable regularity of behavior. We may thus ask why drivers in the United States drive on the right-hand side, rather than on the left. A straightforward answer is that driving on the left is prohibited. The norm, expressed by the laws and enforced by the police, is that one ought to drive on the right and one ought not drive on the left except under specific circumstances.

We have, then, a class of examples where norms play a role in group-level explanations. Proponents of individualistic explanations will object that this explanatory role for norms is an illusion. On close examination, claims about norms dissolve into claims about individuals. With this dissolution goes any robust normative status for claims about laws, rules, or reasons. We must therefore turn to the second task of showing that group-level explanations appealing to norms do not, in general, reduce to individual-level explanations. The argument will have two parts. The first concerns the general issue of explanatory reduction. Borrowing an argument from Garfinkel (1981: 62–66),[4] I will argue that group-level explanations do not always reduce to individualistic explanations. I will then argue that the normative explanations mentioned above are among those that do not reduce.

A group-level explanation appeals to some feature of the group or relationship among individuals in its explanantia. Group-level explanations have two possible explananda. The topic and contrast might concern some property of the group, such as the distribution of a disposition. The question of why United States drivers are mostly disposed to drive on the right, rather than the left, has a group-level explanandum. Alternatively, the topic and contrast might describe an individual, her actions, thoughts, and so on. The question of why Jones is driving on the right side, not the left, would be an example. A group-level explanation of this individualistic explanandum would answer the why-question by describing some feature of the group. The hypothesis floated in response to the Henderson problem is antireductionistic about both sorts of explanation. It proposes that claims about norms are claims about a social group, and that they can be necessary for full, relevant answers to questions about both individuals and groups.

---

4. The details of the formulation below are my own. While the argument was inspired by and draws heavily on Garfinkel's work, I do not claim that it accurately represents his view.

While group-level explanations of group-level phenomena are a bit un-settling, group-level explanations of an individual's action are downright spooky. They seem to require an ontology of social entities with the power to control individual choice. The most famous group-level answer to a question about individual action is Durkheim's explanation of suicide, and Durkheim's onto-logical commitment to "social facts" is notorious. Garfinkel's antireductionist argument is interesting because it is ontologically neutral. The argument con-cerns the conditions for explanatory reduction. It is consistent with the argu-ment to suppose that a society is nothing more than a number of individuals with their psychological states. Even so, *explanations* pertaining to social matters are not always replaceable by explanations appealing solely to individuals. Garfinkel's argument thus permits a commitment to explanatory holism that is independent of doctrines about ontological holism.

The deflationary challenge is that explanantia describing features of a group or relations among its members can always be replaced by explanantia that mention only individuals and their properties. According to the erotetic model, group-level and individual-level explanations compete only if they answer the same why-question. To argue for an explanatory antireductionism, then, one needs to show that some why-questions are not adequately answered by claims about individuals and their properties.

Garfinkel's argument depends on the conception of a structural presup-position. Section 4.3 gave this notion an extended treatment. Structural pre-suppositions arise out of the relevance criteria of some why-questions. Where a why-question has a structural presupposition, the relevant answers have to say something about how the members of the group were related. Structural presuppositions are satisfied by structural conditions. Structural conditions are features of the group that serve to limit the real possibilities of individuals. That is, the possibilities for group behavior are smaller than the joint possibilities of individual behavior. Garfinkel's antireductionist argument, then, is this. Where a group exhibits a structural condition, why-questions about the group will have structural presuppositions. Answers that describe atomic states of the individuals will not be relevant answers to why-questions with structural pre-suppositions. Therefore, where a structural condition is present, explanations cannot be given in terms of the individuals and their atomic properties alone.

To put some flesh on the bones of this argument, consider the grading example again. Consider two professors, Professor Reed and Professor Pauley. Reed uses a noncompetitive scale where the total number of points earned determines a student's grade. Pauley grades on a strict curve. She determines in advance that there will be 15 percent As, 25 percent Bs, 45 percent Cs, 10 percent Ds and 5 percent Fs. Suppose Sam is a student in both classes, and earns an A from both Reed and Pauley. In each case, we can ask: Why did Sam get an A, rather than any other grade? This question admits of an individu-alistic answer when asked about Professor Reed's class. For instance: Sam worked hard and earned ninety-three points. This answer might not be adequate to answer the question when we turn to Professor Pauley's class. Even if it is true that Sam worked hard and earned ninety-three points here too, he had to do better than 85 percent of the class to get an A. Professor Pauley's curve is a structural condition of the grade distributions. Questions about the grade distribution or about individual grades must have structural presuppositions built into their relevance relations. The two why-questions about Sam's grade have the same contrast class, but they have different relevance relations. Relevant answers to the question, Why did Sam get an A? when asked about Professor Pauley's class have to mention the relationship between Sam and his fellow students.

Similar considerations distinguish group-level questions asked about the two classes. In each class, there is a distribution of grades. Suppose that in Professor Reed's class, Sam, Mary, and Paul received As, Beth, John, . . . received Bs, and so on through the class. We may ask why there was this distribution rather than another. In the context of Professor Reed's class, facts about individual performances are again sufficient to answer the question. This is not so in the context of Professor Pauley's class. Given the curve, individual performance is not a sufficient answer because not every combination of individual grades is a genuine possibility. No matter what the individual performances are, the top 15 percent will get As.

Where there is a structural condition, some questions about the group and the individual members cannot be answered in individualistic terms. As a general thesis, then, explanatory reductionism fails. It is not the case that every why-question about a group can be answered by appeal only to features of the individual members. Notice that the argument shows only that explanatory reductionism is not possible in *every* case. There will be some cases, namely those that lack structural conditions (or where the structural conditions are irrelevant to the question) where the why-questions about the group can be answered by appeal only to the properties of individuals. Professor Reed's noncompetitive grading system is such a system. In general, explanatory reduction will be successful when the possible states of the group are the same as the joint possibilities of the individual states. Each possible group state corresponds to a possible arrangement of individual states and vice versa. Explanatory reduction will fail when there is a possibility of joint behavior of the individuals that is not a possible state of the group.

Having argued the general case, we need to see how explanations involving norms fare. If claims about norms figure as answers to why-questions with structural presuppositions, then we may conclude that these explanations do not reduce to explanations that appeal to facts about the individuals alone. Let us return, then, to the earlier questions about driving and traffic laws. To neutralize the ontological issues, let us assume an underlying determinism. Each driver acquires her motivation to drive on the right through her unique history of experiences. The pattern of driving behavior is nothing more than the joint occurrence of individual motivations and actions. The individual motivations need not all be the same, nor need they be constant for an individual over time. Nonetheless, there is a remarkable regularity in these motivations, so we may ask why there is this distribution of motivations rather than another. The answer floated above was that a legal norm prohibits driving on the left. Is this a case where the group-level phenomenon can be explained in individualistic terms? It is much more like the curved grades than the noncompetitive scale, since not all distributions of motives are genuine possibilities. While each driver gets her motivations through a specific history of experiences and interactions, they (almost) all end up driving on the right-hand side. There is a structural condition in play, since the possibilities for group behavior are smaller than the joint possibilities of individual behavior. In this context, why-questions about the distribution of individual dispositions to drive on one side or another will have structural presuppositions. The relevant answers must say something about the relationship among the drivers, and cannot mention only their atomic properties. Explanatory reduction fails in this case.

In general, when a norm is invoked to explain a group-level phenomenon, there will be structural conditions in the social context and structural presuppositions to the why-question. Regardless of their personal history, individuals in the group mostly end up in the same place. Not all joint possibilities of individual belief or action are real possibilities for the group. Models for behavior are invoked precisely because a regularity is found among the dispositions, beliefs, etc. of individuals. Therefore, explanations that invoke norms to explain group-level phenomena will not generally be reducible to individualistic explanations.

We are now in a position to address the Henderson problem. The problem rests on the insight that when norms are treated as reasons for action, they become beliefs about norms. They no longer function *as a norm* in the explanation. To resolve the Henderson problem, we need some slippage between what is a good reason for acting and what the agent believes is a good reason for acting. The role of norms in the explanation of group-level phenomena provides the flexibility we need. I thus suggest we distinguish two dimensions of an intentional action explanation. In what we might call the psychological dimension, an intentional action explanation appeals to the beliefs, goals, etc. of the agent. These are the agent's motives. To say that these motives are sufficient or good reasons is not to attribute another belief to the agent. Rather, it is to say that the agent is acting in accordance with some norm whereby such reasons are good reasons for her action. That there is such a norm is an additional claim with two explanatory roles. The claim that there is such a norm explains some aspect of the group's behavior. It also is a part of the answer to an intentional action why-question: that the agent's motives constitute sufficient or good reasons for the action. We may call this the social dimension of the intentional action explanation.

There is a possible response to this resolution of the Henderson problem.[5] It is important dialectically and because it raises some deep-running issues. One might argue that the Henderson problem recurs at the social level: as long as the group-level claims are *normative,* they are explanatorily impotent. To use such claims in explanation, they must be transformed into group-level descriptions. Thus, for example, imagine a sociologist who came to the American South during segregation. Suppose she noticed the regularity of behavior that dark skinned people sat in the back of the bus. The social norms of segregation are one explanation for this pattern of dispositions: "negroes" ought to sit in the back of a bus. It may be granted for the sake of argument that this claim relevantly answers a why-question in the way discussed above and that the explanation does not reduce to individual-level explanations. Nonetheless, the interpreter does not thereby *endorse* the second-class citizenship of blacks. She can condemn segregation and consistently appeal to the "norm" in her explanations. This shows that the claim about the norm is not functioning *as a norm* in the interpretation.

The argument above touches an issue that runs through our discussion of rational norms, all the way back to section 3.2. Many philosophers find neo-rationalist arguments for the principle of humanity persuasive because to call an inference or action "rational" is to evaluate it. The ramifications of this evaluative character of claims about rationality has been most clearly and forcefully expressed by Habermas. Understanding an action, belief, or utterance, according to Habermas, requires understanding the agent's reasons for it. The relationship between a motive and the action it motivates, or between a belief (or utterance) and the beliefs that support it is normative. On these points, this essay is in complete agreement with Habermas. He argues further:

> But if, in order to understand an expression, the interpreter must *bring to mind the reasons* with which a speaker would if necessary and under suitable conditions defend its validity, he is *himself* drawn into the process of assessing validity claims. For reasons are of such a nature that they cannot be described in the attitude of a third person, that is, without reactions of affirmation or negation or abstention. (Habermas 1984: 115)

Habermas concludes:

> An interpreter cannot, therefore, interpret expressions connected through criticizable validity claims with a potential of reasons (and thus represent

---

5. Henderson has pressed this response in conversation and correspondence. The argument and example below are drawn from his comments.

knowledge) without taking a position on them. And he cannot take a position without applying his *own* standards of judgment, at any rate, standards that he has made his own. (Habermas 1984: 116)

Habermas thus joins with the "neo-rationalists" in arguing that criteria of rationality are not discovered empirically (cf. section 3.2). If seeing something as rational is to endorse it, an interpreter could not understand action, inference, or belief without evaluating the larger pattern in which it occurs. If the interpreter must evaluate the larger pattern, then she could not also hold that it includes forms of rationality different from her own. Criteria of rationality, therefore, are presupposed by the very activity of interpretation, they are not discovered through it.

Henderson, of course, is neither a Habermasian nor a neo-rationalist. As discussed in section 3.3, he makes common cause with this work in arguing that the methodology of interpretation is fully explanatory and there is no asymmetry between explanations of rational and irrational belief, utterance, or action. Henderson and Habermas agree that claims about rationality are evaluations, but they draw antithetical conclusions. Where Habermas concludes that the interpreter must normatively engage with her interlocutors, Henderson concludes that normative claims, qua normative, have no place in interpretation. In one respect, the position developed here must agree with Henderson in this dispute. Evaluation is not explanatory. So, according the principle of explanatory coherence, the interpreter's evaluation of her interlocutors is irrelevant to the choice of interpretation. We need to distinguish, then, between the interpreter's evaluation of local belief, behavior, and utterance, and the interpreter's claim that the native speakers are bound by such-and-such norms.

The central question, then, is whether reasons, rules, norms, and values "are of such a nature that they cannot be described in the attitude of a third person, that is, without reactions of affirmation or negation or abstention" (Habermas 1984: 115). Habermas's principle would require that every representation of a norm, rule, or prescription would itself have to be a prescription. It appears easy to generate counterexamples to Habermas's principle. Institutions, for instance, are shot through with norms, rules, and prescriptions, and there seems to be little difficulty in characterizing those norms without endorsing them. Suppose that a student government has the rule that spending proposals ought to be considered by the Executive Committee before going to the Student Senate. Suppose this rule is written down in the Book of Rules. This is a norm in the sense that it does not describe the de facto operations of the student government. It is consistent with the claim that, say, only 75 percent of the spending proposals are actually considered by the Executive Committee before going to the Student Senate. The first is a norm because it says how members ought to proceed, the second is a description because it says how they do proceed. If Habermas were correct, then the interpreter could not formulate this rule without endorsing or criticizing it. Yet it seems that a person may say (truly) that "one norm of this institution is that spending proposals ought to be considered by the Executive Committee before going to the Student Senate" without either endorsing or criticizing the norm.

Habermas's principle and the apparent counterexample conflate two ways of distinguishing norms from non-norms. The first is a distinction among kinds of speech act. In this sense, a single sentence might be either a prescription or description, depending on the context and speaker's intentions. Thus, "John will go home at 7:00" can be uttered as a prescription of what should happen or as a description of what will. In this sense, norms are always endorsed or criticized, and if recognizing reasons is normative, then the interpreter must evaluate them. The apparent counterexample relies on a different way of distinguishing norms from non-norms. This second distinction differentiates among kinds of semantic content. This is the difference between "75 percent of the proposals go to the Executive Committee before the Student Senate" and "proposals ought to go to the Executive Committee before going to the Student Senate." In this sense, norms are statements about what ought to happen in a given situation. They are marked by the occurrence of words like "ought," "should," "good," and their cognates. Unlike descriptions, norms are not falsified by their violation: if only 74 percent of the proposals really go to the Executive Committee before the Student Senate, then the first sentence, but not the second, must be false.

Habermas's principle that norms cannot be described without "reactions of affirmation or negation or abstention" is undermined by the fact that the two ways of distinguishing norms from non-norms are independent. A sentence of the form "S ought to do P" can be uttered with either the force of a description or of a prescription. Similarly, "S does P" may be descriptive or prescriptive. Yet semantically, the first is a norm and the second is not. Contrary to Habermas's view, then, it *is* possible to describe norms without affirming, denying, or abstaining from them. We can therefore agree with Habermas that recognizing a reason requires recognizing its normative status. According to this essay, a reason has normative status insofar as the reason is given within the context of a body of norms, and that according to those norms it is a good or bad reason. The interpreter can describe what the norms are, and how the reason satisfies (or fails to satisfy) them without thereby endorsing either the norms or the reason. Reasons can be recognized as reasons without the interpreter thereby endorsing them.

With these distinctions in hand, let us return to the concern that the Henderson problem arises again at the group level. We can see now that Henderson's conclusion that "normative principles, qua normative principles, have nothing to contribute" to explanation is two sided (Henderson 1993: 168). In the sense that norms are evaluative speech acts, they do not contribute to explanation. The mere fact that the interpreter agrees with the locals does

nothing to explain their action. Both Habermas and the proponents of rationalizing explanation make this first sort of normativity central to interpretation. If Henderson's arguments and the arguments of this essay are correct,
then such views of interpretation fail. In the second sense, where norms are
distinguished from descriptions by their content (not their pragmatic force),
Henderson's argument applies differently at the individual and group levels.
Considered at the individual level alone, a norm is not explanatory. An intentional action explanation needs a motive, and if a norm is to serve as a motive,
it must be translated into a belief. Doing so, Henderson rightly argued, strips
the claim of its normative content. At the social level, this section has argued,
no such transformation occurs. If those arguments are sound, then the
interpreter's claim that "in this group, one ought to do P under conditions C"
is a relevant answer to a why-question. This section argued that the why-
question is not adequately answered by the corresponding description that
people in the group usually do P under conditions C. Only the first, and not
the second, version of the Henderson problem arises at the group level. But
since group-level explanations do not depend on the interpreter's evaluation,
norms can explain patterns of behavior exhibited by a group.

7.2 Norms, Rules, and Mistakes

The foregoing section argued that claims about norms explain patterns of
group behavior. Sections 5.2 and 7.1 argued that claims about norms make
positive contributions to the explanation of intentional action. In response to
the Henderson problem, I insisted that we distinguish between hypotheses
about an agent's actual motivations and the assertion that her motives are good
(adequate, sufficient) reasons for her action. The appeal to norms substantiates
the second claim, not the first. This latter point thus needs further unpacking.
What is the relationship between an intentional action and the norms governing rational action? Does the agent have to consciously recognize and accept
every norm to which she is bound?

    One possibility would be to follow Winch and simply identify "mean-
ingful" action with rule-governed behavior (Winch 1958: 52). Winch argued
that rule-following was a necessary element of a wide range of examples,
including using a word to refer (25), expanding a mathematical series (31),
voting Labour in the General Election (45), forgetting to post a letter (47),
economic exchange (50), a monk following the prescripts of his order (52),
and an anarchist eschewing rules altogether (53). Winch assimilates all of
these cases because he is arguing for the metaphysical point that meaningful
action is made possible by a social context. Wittgenstein's analysis of rule-
following provides the ultimate basis for this relationship. Section 7.1 made
a similar point on epistemic grounds. But, while his point is well taken,

Winch's assimilation of such different cases is problematic from our point of view. When we turn from the metaphysics of the social world to its episte-mology, the anarchist and the voter are misunderstood if they are interpreted as following rules in the same sense that the monk is. There is a difference between claiming that there is a rule for doing such-and-such and that the agent is following the rule, and simply saying that the agent has reasons for her action. Given the demands of this project, we need a more fine-grained analysis of meaningful behavior.

When thinking about rules, it is helpful to distinguish two ways in which the rules may be related to actions (cf. Taylor 1971). In one paradigm, games, the rules are constitutive. A chessman can move from one square to another if and only if the move corresponds to the rules. A pawn cannot move one square to the left, since this is not a move in the game. The rules of chess are constitutive in the sense that they define the possibilities for action. The limit for constitutive rules is seen in a computer game. Here the rules are built into the program. One literally cannot play the game without following the rules. Not all rules are constitutive. The limits of the notion are visible when we recognize that many of our games are more flexible than chess. Some games leave space for regular violations of the rules. In the card game we used to call "Bull," for example, the *point* is to cheat. Of course, this cheating occurs within a rather well-defined domain.[6] Hence, even if we restrict ourselves to games, there is a range of ways in which the rules are related to the behavior they govern. Chess and computer games fall on one end of a range. At the other end of the range is rule-governed behavior. An action is rule-governed insofar as the rules do not exhaustively define the possibilities for action. The rules are applied to a preexisting domain of action. Traffic laws are rules that govern, but do not constitute, behavior. Someone is driving whether or not he follows the local traffic laws.

The notion of rule-following is not sufficiently fine grained for our purposes, even with the distinction between rule-constituted and rule-gov-erned behavior in hand. When I walk across the College Quad, I stay on the sidewalks. This is a bit of regular behavior with a normative element. In some sense (yet to be articulated), I ought to stay on the sidewalk. Is this "ought" the product of a rule that governs my behavior or constitutes it? It does not fit happily into either category. If I veer onto the grass, I have not ceased

---

6. In this game, the players take cards from their hands and place them face down on the stack. A particular card is supposed to be played, but players may "cheat" by putting down a different card or more than one card. Other players have an option of calling "Bull!" and penalties are assessed on either the cheater or, if there was no cheating, on the whistle-blower. Not all forms of cheating are countenanced, such as hiding cards under the table, stacking the deck, and so on.

walking. And unlike some universities, Emory does not have a rule about walking on the grass. We seem to need another category.

Rules have a distinctive function in human practices. They are linguistic formulations that have some authority. It makes sense to consult the rules, to look them up, and to appeal to rules in adjudicating a dispute. If the rules are constitutive, then one must internalize the rules in order to engage in the activity (such as playing chess or baseball). One's possibilities for action (in that setting) become exactly those sanctioned by the rules. Where some behavior is rule-governed, the agents regard themselves as bound by the rules and treat them as authoritative. In order to have this feature, rules have to be formulated, either verbally or in writing.

Winch, of course, had a much more generous conception of a rule. Let us use the term "norm" to capture the more general notion. A norm is a regularity of behavior with which the agents ought to comply. It need not be formulated explicitly, and it need not be treated as an authority. Given this terminological convention, rules are explicit norms. Because they are explicit, they can play an authoritative and adjudicative role in social practices. To make sense of meaningful action, however, we also need to recognize *implicit* norms.[7] The distinction between rules and implicit norms makes it possible to articulate the difference between Winch's examples of the monk and the anarchist. For the monk, there are many rules that dictate the pattern of his life. Part of the point of a monastic order is to submit oneself to this kind of discipline. The anarchist rejects this way of life, but cannot reject all norms. The implicit norm under which the anarchist acts requires that he eschew such rules, forging his own way without appeal to that sort of structure. When interpreting the monk's activity, it is essential to understand the rules of his Order. When interpreting the anarchist, it is essential to interpret him as trying to live without rules. The distinction between rules and implicit norms is thus of primary importance in interpretation. The different points to these ways of life can become clear only when the distinction is in place.[8]

The distinction between rules and implicit norms helps resolve a rather nasty difficulty that we uncovered at the end of section 2.3. In that section, we were contrasting Cooper's hypothesis that the Azande use a three-valued logic with Evans-Pritchard's view that they used inferential principles much like our own. Two questions emerged. First, in a culture where there is no tradition of reflecting on principles of logical inference, what does it mean to

---

7. The modifier "implicit" will be dropped when it is clear from the context that implicit norms are intended.

8. The distinction between norms and rules does not necessarily undermine Winch's claims about meaningful behavior. He would view it as a distinction among kinds of rule (Winch 1958: 52).

say that they are "using" one logic or another? Second, what is the difference between using a logic different from the interpreter's and simply making mistakes while using a similar logic?

The first question arises because of the status of logic in our own culture. Since antiquity, Western intellectuals have appealed to the authority of explicitly formulated rules for reasoning. The importance of these rules makes logic the very model of rule-following for us. We cannot grasp what it means "use" a logic in a nonliterate society until we loosen the grip of this picture. To begin prying things apart, recall that only a small segment of our own society recognizes logic as a system of authoritative rules. Consider a person who has never encountered a class in formal logic. Surely, he reasons, and his reasoning conforms to some norms. These norms are exhibited by the patterns of his reasoning and by his normative judgments. He will take some reasons as *bad* reasons. He will reject some inferences. He may even say of himself that he was mistaken, misled, or confused. While there are norms of reasoning implicit in his practices, the relationship between his practice and the logical norms is very different from the relationship between, say, *my* practice and the rules of first-order logic. If someone demonstrates that one of my arguments is formally invalid, I have two possible responses. I can contend that my argument has not been properly represented. (In other words, the argument does conform to the rules and was misunderstood by the critic.) Alternatively, I must take this as a reason for striking the argument from my text.

This attitude toward the rules of formal logic is not universally shared, even among people who (in a sense to be articulated) share this logic. Outside of the academy, displaying the formal invalidity of an opponent's argument is taken as mere pedantry. This is not a superficial response. Rather, it shows the different role that norms of reasoning play in the practice of professional academics and others. Someone who has never encountered a class in logic reasons—and let us suppose he reasons well—but he does so without appealing to rules. There is a group of inferences that he is disposed to make, and there is a group of inferences that he is inclined to eschew. The distinguishing feature of the latter class is that he is sensitive to criticism when he makes an inference of this kind, and he is inclined to criticize others when they make such inferences. What makes it the case that the academic and the nonacademic "use" the same logic is that they share, to a large extent, this way of discriminating good inferences from bad. The difference between them is not in the norms they use, but in their different attitudes toward the rules of first-order logic.

Norms of inference need not take the form of explicit rules. Norms of inference may be implicit in the practice of making inferences, judging them to be good or bad, and correcting oneself and others. Understanding what the norms are is a matter of finding the best explanation of these practices. When an interpreter investigates groups that, like the Azande, do not have a rule-based tradition of inference, she will have to attend closely to the local habits of making and criticizing inferences. The Azande's refusal to be moved by the inconsistent triad is just one bit of the pattern. To determine whether the Azande are adhering to norms that are different from the ones we recognize, the interpreter has to decide how this refusal fits into their overall practice of making inferences. The interpreter's project is to determine which of the various ways of formulating the norms provides the best explanation of the inferential habits of the group. This will require a body of explanations, that is, an interpretation of the Azande inferential practice. To be ultimately acceptable, this set of explanations has to be integrated into the larger interpretation of Azande life. The norms themselves may be questioned: Why *these* norms and not some others? To the extent that this question can be answered, the explanatory coherence of the interpretation is increased.

The conceptual difference between a group that uses a distinctive logic and one where a particular kind of mistake is pervasive should now be clear. It depends on the choice of the best overall interpretation from two interpretive possibilities. Where a group employs a logic different from the interpreter, the interpretation will attribute either implicit norms or explicit rules of inference to the local group. These cohere with the rest of the interpretation insofar as they explain the local habits of inference. Explanations of why they have these norms ought to be forthcoming too, if this interpretation is to have the most explanatory coherence. As argued in chapter 3, the norms attributed to the group may be different from the norms to which the interpreter is committed. Attributing a different logic to a group does not preclude local mistakes. Indeed, it is very likely that some individuals will violate the local rules or norms. Such violations also need to be explained. That the individual was tired, not paying attention, or is just plain stupid are obvious candidates. The second interpretive option is that the norms of reasoning used by the local group are the same as the interpreter's, but that mistakes are widespread. An interpretation that attributes pervasive mistakes will need to explain why the individuals deviate from the norms present in their group. In this case, the individualistic explanations will be less satisfactory. A pervasive or systematic mistake cries out for a systematic answer. If answers are forthcoming, this interpretation may have more explanatory coherence than the first alternative. Ultimately, of course, it is an empirical question whether mistakes are prevalent in a group or whether they employ a genuinely different form of logic.

7.3 CONTESTED NORMS AND THE COMMUNITY OF AGENTS

The line of thought developed in the foregoing section has important implications for the fourth question of section 2.5. Under what conditions are interpretations that include descriptions and evaluations from the subjects' point of view to be preferred over interpretations that employ ideas or evidence to which the subjects do not have access? It turns out that the answer is rather complex. Part of the answer arises out of the discussion of intentional action explanation in section 5.2. There it was argued that an interest in the agent's point of view is constitutive of interpretive inquiry. The agent's conception of his action, the alternative possibilities for action, and criteria for good and bad reasons are all essential parts of an intentional action explanation. Therefore, some descriptions and evaluations from the agent's point of view are ineliminable parts of an interpretation. In a sense, the agents' view of themselves is the wellspring of all further interpretation.

It does not follow that an interpretation is limited to the agents' view of their social world. We have seen several ways in which the agents' point of view must be supplemented. First, our discussion of intentional action explanations showed that there are circumstances where the foils of an intentional action why-question might not be those that the agent has in mind. Also, the agent's own view of her action is not necessarily authoritative. The agent's self-conception is more or less irrelevant in some contexts. Second, the discussion of norms has revealed cases where the interpreter's explanation might have to go beyond what the locals say about their own behavior. What makes the agent's psychological states *reasons* depends on the norms for action present in her culture. While those norms are determined by the regularities of intentional action found in the group, there is no requirement that the agents themselves must be able to characterize these regularities. Some relevant norms may be implicit. Claims about such norms explain the observed patterns of behavior. Since, by hypothesis, the locals do not formulate these norms, the explanation must be external to their view of themselves. Finally, the most coherent interpretation is likely to include functional or other group-level explanations, and these often appeal to phenomena described from an external point of view.

We have to accept, then, a rather complex answer to question (4) of section 2.5. An interpretation will necessarily include claims that represent the agents' view of themselves, their actions, and their reasoning. However, the best overall interpretation is almost certainly going to include claims that do not represent the agents' view of themselves. Minimally, such external claims will characterize social regularities that the locals have not articulated. In some cases, the difference between the internal view of the culture and the interpreter's may be even greater. If the individuals exhibit some kind of self-deception, as in the case of bloodsucking witchcraft, the overall interpretation may have to run contrary to the agents' manifest self-understanding. In the most extreme case, the local agents *could* not accept the best overall interpretation of their behavior without undermining the very possibility of living their lives as they do.

The possibility of interpretations that run counter to local self-conceptions opens an important interpretive space. Within this space, we may construct solutions to the two remaining difficulties raised by apparent irrationality. One lesson from the examples in chapter 2 was that an interpretation must not portray a group of people as *always* acting rationally. This is a real danger for a methodology, such as the one proposed here, that permits the attribution of local standards of rationality. If the interpreter is permitted to invent standards to rationalize local behavior, then people will always turn out to be rational by their own lights.[9] On the contrary, the problems of apparent irrationality sometimes yield real irrationalities, as we saw in the case of bloodsucking witchcraft and the Purrinton murders. The problem is this: How can the best interpretation show that the agents are acting irrationally or that they have mistakenly applied the local norms that govern their action? The second difficulty raised by the examples of chapter 2 was best illustrated by the discussion of *sati*. There we found real conflict about the events and their interpretation. Part of this conflict was the result of conflicting norms within Indian society. How can an interpretation represent such conflict, particularly when the primary epistemological virtue of an interpretation is its coherence?

Nutini and Roberts's explanation of bloodsucking witchcraft entailed that someone must place the body of the infant near the door. As we noticed in that discussion, this presents the Tlaxcalan witchcraft beliefs as an elaborate ideology of self-deception. How is such an interpretation possible? Let us begin by reviewing its salient features. First, Nutini and Roberts detail the system of ideas that informs the belief in *tlahuepuchis*. Second, while the Tlaxcalans distinguish carefully between natural and supernatural causes of death, and have clear epistemic criteria for identifying each kind of case, they do not subject the belief in witches itself to such scrutiny. Nutini and Roberts thus need to explain why the Tlaxcalans continue to believe in the witchcraft system and why they do not hold it open to criticism. Third, Nutini and Roberts explain the deaths of the infants as the result of unintentional suffocation. The system of belief about *tlahuepuchis* acts to defuse the mother's (and the family's) feelings of guilt. In this part of their account, Nutini and Roberts appeal to putatively universal psychological processes. These processes help explain why the belief system is maintained. They also explain, finally, how the person who moves the infant's body can continue to believe that witches exist.

On Nutini and Roberts's full interpretation, then, the Tlaxcalans do not have an accurate understanding of the social, cultural, or natural world in which they act. They have false beliefs about why some children die and about the actions of some of their fellows. Moreover, they are mistaken about their own reasons in a certain respect. After an incident of bloodsucking witchcraft, the members of the family will recount experiences that fit into the pattern—

---

9. Jarvie (1970) and MacIntyre (1967) argued that Winch's work suffered from just this defect.

strange dogs or turkeys, soporific vapors, bright lights, and so on. If Nutini and Roberts are right, then these reports are either false or badly misconstrued versions of actual events. The Tlaxcalans, however, do not (and perhaps, cannot) understand themselves as lying in this situation.[10] Nutini and Roberts's interpretation can have these striking features because it satisfies the conditions that all interpretations must satisfy. First, they explain the agents' behavior as intentional action, and these explanations appeal to reasons and possibilities for action of which they are aware. These reasons include the system of beliefs about *tlahuepuchis*. Second, the Tlaxcalan behavior has some striking anomalies, even when understood in the agents' terms. To explain these events and the actions that surround them, Nutini and Roberts appeal to psychological, social, and physical facts of which the agents are not aware. These external factors are integrated into the interpretation because they help explain some of the puzzling features of this culture. Under these dramatic conditions, it is possible to form an interpretation that attributes a kind of systematic self-deception to the local agents.

   Sati presents us with a different sort of relationship between norms and the persons who realize them. Whereas the bloodsucking witchcraft example included subjects who misunderstood their own actions in a systematic way, *sati* shows us subjects who have more than one way of understanding their own action, and the norms are hotly disputed. An adequate interpretation of Roop Kanwar's death and the events that surrounded it has to account for a variety of relevant facts. First, there is a complex of myths, doctrines, and rules that are relevant to the status of women in the society, relationships between husbands and wives, the spiritual and ritual possibilities for women, and so on. These bear on the question of whether women who have lost their husbands ought to commit *sati*, but they do not endorse it unequivocally. Second, there is an ancient tradition in India of interpreting myths, doctrines, and rules that includes careful textual exegesis and argumentation (Nussbaum and Sen 1989; Sharma 1983). Moreover, this tradition of dispute is intertwined with political issues. The British outlawed *sati* in 1829. The colonial reform was supported by the arguments of Hindu scholars like Raja Rammohun Roy. The debates were directly concerned with whether *sati* was sanctioned by Vedic texts, but the clear political undercurrent was resistance to colonial rule and the preservation of traditional Hinduism against reformism (Georgeson 1992; Sharma 1983; Yang 1989). These polarities have been transformed into the contemporary political concerns of feminists or secular reformers against traditionalism. The third aspect of *sati* that any interpretation needs to accommodate is the

---

10. This is consistent with the possibility that some members of the group do lie about these events. Once the beliefs and practices are in place, it is possible for an individual to exploit them for his own advantage. The point is that, given this interpretation, all reports of bloodsucking witchcraft cannot be intentionally deceptive.

social and economic position of the women themselves, both as a general pattern and as a particular circumstance that influences the individuals involved. Widows have a marginal social, spiritual, and economic status. Even those Indian reformers who argued against *sati* on religious grounds recommended the harsh life of an ascetic as the alternative to *sati* (Sharma 1983;Yang 1989). The prospect of being a widow was so bleak that one can argue that *sati* is a form of rational suicide, at least in some cases (Yang 1989).

Finally, when considering the reasons that an individual might have for participating in *sati,* we must not forget that *satis* were not all voluntary. There is historical evidence of women being drugged, or tied to the pyre. In some regions, legal regulations governing inheritance may have given the widow's in-laws some motivation for doing away with her. The normative sanction for *sati* probably provided a convenient cover. Moreover, the practice of prearranging marriages and marrying young meant that some of the widows were little more than children when their husbands died. Combining this with the fact that the environment in which Hindu women lived was highly coercive and controlled, one might argue that no *sati* was a full-blooded free choice.

Sati is a complex social phenomenon with individual, historical, social, economic and religious dimensions. Any interpretation of *sati* will have to limit itself in some way—to a particular time or geographical region, to the *sati* of one woman or to the fate of all women in a caste. The limitations are selected by the interpreter on the basis of her interest, and as we have already seen, these interests structure the why-questions at the core of her inquiry. Regardless of the limits set by a particular interpreter, the explanations that constitute her interpretation are very likely to invoke both individual and group-level explananta. If the interpreter is trying to understand the motives of a particular woman, like Roop Kanwar, or the people around her, the interpreter will have to explain their actions. The above arguments force the conclusion that even these individualistic explanations will have to appeal to norms of some sort, and therefore to the wider social context of action.

The particular difficulty presented by *sati* is that there seems to be no univocal set of rules or norms in terms of which to make sense of the individual's action. Multivocality occurs both at the level of implicit norms and at the level of explicit rules. Consider first the norms. In the years before its prohibition (1815–1828), the British recorded the number of *satis* committed in each administrative district. Apparently, the practice of *sati* was much more common in some districts than in others. Even in the district with the highest incidence (averaging ninety-four per year), only 1.2 percent of the women who became widows died as *sati* (Yang 1989: 23). Thus, during this period at least, individual women were presented with a conflicting pair of norms. A small number of widows were venerated as exhibiting ultimate virtue. Independently of what scholars or the elite said about it, the rituals that surrounded the event and the continuing role of the *sati* in local ritual life itself constituted a model in terms of which widows might guide their own action. At the same time, the vast majority of widows did not participate. This pattern of intentional action supported a conflicting norm, forceful simply because of its popularity. Moreover, the explicit rules promulgated by the elite were as equivocal as the implicit norms. As we have already noted, there was a long-standing tradition of textual interpretation in India. While various texts were taken to be authoritative, the Hindu scholars were aware that the regulative pronouncements had to be distilled from texts. Moreover, the sacred texts did not agree about *sati* (Georgeson 1992). Arguments both for and against *sati* were thus made on the basis of authoritative texts. When an individual widow was wondering whether to mount the pyre, then, there were justifications available for both committing *sati* and for refusing. In that context, one could have good reason for either action.

What makes interpretation possible at all in this messy environment is the slippage between norms and their behavioral basis. The behavior that undergirds rules or norms always outruns the rules or norms themselves. More than one set of norms might be exemplified in a group precisely because the underlying pattern of action is fissured. When explaining the group-level events, an interpreter may make use of these internal differences to postulate the existence of divergent, or even conflicting, norms. When the locals begin to formulate rules for their own behavior, the behavior outruns their rules just as it does for the interpreter. There is therefore more than one way for the locals to make explicit the norms that govern their behavior. The possibility for alternative rules is enhanced when there is a tradition of deliberating and disagreeing about the rules, as there is in India.

Far from making local conflict unintelligible, an explanatory coherence approach seems like the only method for choosing interpretations in a context like this. An interpretation must attribute norms, rules, and reasons to the agents. The problems involved in interpreting *sati* show that the most coherent interpretation might have to attribute substantial incoherence to the local group. Divergences among the behavior of the agents might be best explained by appealing to norms that license divergent actions. Such divergent norms may even be encoded in alternative models for behavior that have widespread appeal. In addition, some conflicts among the locals might be best explained by their own appeal to the authority of divergent rules. Such explanatory moves are possible because what makes the interpretation coherent is different from what makes the behavior of the local group coherent. An interpretation is a body of claims woven together by explanatory relationships. Conflict among the agents is the sort of phenomenon that requires explanation, and we have seen how attributing inconsistent norms can help explain conflict. Attributing inconsistency might be the best way of maximizing explanatory coherence. Far from homogenizing a culture, the explanatory postulation of local norms is the best way to make sense of real tears in the social fabric.

CHAPTER 8

Conclusion

The primary object of this work has been to articulate an account of interpretive change. What epistemic criteria should guide an interpreter as she changes her interpretation? What makes one interpretation better than another? The answer to these questions amounts to an *interpretive dynamics,* that is, an account of the ways in which interpretations develop. It provides a model of how an interpretation ought to grow from a superficial reading to a deep and comprehensive understanding. An interpretive dynamics should also show how breakdowns in understanding—like the challenges of apparent irrationality—are to be overcome. This section will sketch the interpretive dynamics made possible by the foregoing chapters and highlight its most interesting features.

Interpretive change is determined by (at least) three factors: the natural and social events observed by the interpreter, the interpreter's interests, and the demand for explanatory coherence. The first two constitute the determinants of change, and the principle of explanatory coherence governs how the interpretation evolves. Likening the epistemology of interpretive change to a mechanical system, we might say that the interpreter's interests and the natural and social events are the forces behind interpretive change, and the principle of explanatory coherence constitutes its kinematics.

The role that natural and social events have in determining interpretive change deserves emphasis. Talk about coherence emphasizes the relationships among elements of the interpretation. We have paid little attention to the relationship between the interpretation and the reality it represents. It is therefore easy to lose sight of the fact that the world is the primary determinant of interpretive change. Coherence epistemologies often arise when some form of "the given" or epistemic certainty is undermined. However, it would be a mistake to think that our knowledge loses touch with its object when the foundation is lost. A coherence epistemology insists that knowledge does not

175

require a self-justifying realm of experience. Every belief stands in need of justification, even those that result from immediate perception. Another way to put the same point is that all observation is theory-laden. Admitting this lack of an undeniable foundation does not leave justification to the whim of the knowing subject. Quine's metaphor of the web helps make the point. What empiricist philosophy of science took to be basic observational statements become sentences at the periphery of the web of belief. The knowing subject does not create these peripheral sentences from whole cloth. The interpreter's subjects act, refrain from acting, talk among themselves, and respond in particular ways to her queries, her presence, and her behavior. If the interpreter wants to understand the people with whom she is working, she must describe these actions.

Of course, the interpreter's descriptions always are theory-laden. She will have some kind of working interpretation in terms of which she can describe behavior and translate utterance. This is true even at the ideal epistemic limit of "radical interpretation." Where the interpreter knows nothing of the language or culture of her subjects, her understanding of action, motivation, and speech must be modeled on her own culture. She has no choice but to regard them as saying what she takes to be true and doing what she would do under the circumstances. (In the light of the above arguments, it should go without saying that this preliminary interpretive scheme is not privileged in any way. Any part—or all of it—may be revised for the sake of more coherence.) Thus, even the ideal limit, interpretation is theory-laden. Real interpreters, of course, never begin from this position. Radical translation is an epistemologist's idealization. A real interpreter always knows something about her subjects when she begins her research. Or, even if the interpreter knows nothing about the particular community she is to study, she might know about neighboring groups, related languages, and so on. This is the interpretive platform from which she describes action, makes hypotheses about motivation, and translates speech.

Theory-laden as her understanding always is, the interpreter is obligated to describe what goes on around her. This is how the social reality she is studying ultimately determines the shape of her interpretation. If explanatory coherence is to be maintained, these claims on the periphery of the interpretation must be given some explanatory role. This means that the interpreter must keep adjusting her interpretation to accommodate new data. Indeed, since no interpretation is going to be so seamless and comprehensive that it can explain everything that the locals say and do, one can say with justice that local action and speech is constantly decreasing the coherence of the interpretation. The interpreter's burden is to maintain and even increase coherence in the face of the torrent of observation.

While interpretive claims at the edge of the web determine the shape of the interpretation from the side of social reality, interest exerts its influence from the side of the interpreter. The interpreter's interest partly determines whether one interpretive claim can be the explanation of another. One claim, Q, explains another, P, if and only if Q is the (best) answer to a why-question with P as topic. Q can be the best answer to the question, Why P? only if Q satisfies the relevance criterion, and thereby discriminates between P and some foil(s). Therefore, whether Q explains P depends on the choice of relevance criteria and the foils. We saw in section 4.4 that the interests of the interpreter partly determine these choices. This means that the coherence of a claim with an interpretation depends in part on the interests of the interpreter. This essay has already illustrated some of the ways in which interests influence interpretation. There are, we have argued, interests constitutive to the interpretive enterprise. Such interests are stable and shared by interpreters. They include an interest in the agents' point of view (section 5.1), the structure of the society in which they live (section 5.1), the stability of explanation (section 4.4), and causal relationships among events (section 4.4). This is by no means an exhaustive list. The whole range of interests that structure social inquiry are well worth a detailed investigation, but that project lies beyond our present scope. We have argued that these constitutive interests demand that any interpretation include certain forms of explanation, including reason-giving and intentional action explanations, functional or other social explanations, explanations of meaning, and explanations that invoke norms. An interpreter may also have idiosyncratic interests, for instance, an interest in ritual forms, economic life, or the relationship between present social structures and those of the past. These interests will motivate the choice of particular forms of explanation. In their light, the interpreter will make particular phenomena the center of her interpretation, seeking to explain them fully while leaving other parts of the agents' world less well understood.

The interpreter's interests are influenced by the social phenomena she encounters. An interpreter may begin with a set of interests that precludes or marginalizes some kinds of explanatory relations. All alone, of course, the fact that an interpreter's interests are limited is not problematic. We cannot demand that interpreters be interested in everything. The interpreter's interests become criticizable, however, when failure to adopt a particular explanatory form prevents the interpreter from explaining a range of phenomena. There may be cases where adopting or modifying her interests would permit the development of an interpretation with greater explanatory coherence. Given the phenomena confronted, changing interests might make for more coherence. Therefore, the interpreter may have good reason to modify her interests in the light of increased knowledge of the culture.

The observed social phenomena and the interpreter's interest are the two forces that push interpretive change. The principle of explanatory coherence determines how an interpretation ought to change, given the existing explanations and interpretive claims, the new observations, and the interpreter's interests. While it is beyond the scope of this essay to articulate a detailed set of criteria for interpretive change, section 4.5 presented a rough model.[1] There we identified a set of ranked criteria that count in favor of coherence and a set of criteria that count against it:

One interpretation is *less* coherent than another insofar as it has more claims, P, such that:

1. P neither answers, nor is the topic, nor is presupposed by any why-question.

2. P either answers a why-question or is presupposed by a why-question, but not both, and is not the topic of any why-question.

3. P answers one why-question and is presupposed by another, but is not the topic of any why-question.

One interpretation is *more* coherent than another insofar as it has more claims, P, such that:

4. P answers one question, is the topic of another, and is presupposed by a third.

5. P answers one question and is the topic of another, or P is the topic of one question and the presupposition of another.

6. P is the topic of a why-question.

The list is ranked, with lower numbered criteria counting more strongly for (or against) relative coherence than higher numbers. It is important to recognize that these are *comparative* criteria. They permit us to say whether one interpretation is better than another, and whether a proposed change in an interpretation will make it more or less coherent. It makes no sense to apply these criteria to a single interpretation and say that it is coherent simpliciter. The remainder of this section will outline the broad ramifications of this account of interpretive change.

8.1.1 Nothing is Sacred

A common view of the dynamics of interpretation is that interpretive change must be based on something the interpreter and her subjects share. While

---

1. I imagine that this list could generate counterintuitive examples, and that the criteria could be chisholmed into a more adequate and fine-grained analysis. Again, doing so is beyond the horizon of this work. This essay has tried to construct the framework for a fully explanatory model of interpretation. Getting all of the fine detail right must be left for the future.

Hollis's "bridgehead" of true and rational belief is a particularly vivid form of this commitment, the general idea is shared by many philosophers with otherwise different positions. This essay has agreed that as a starting point of interpretation, the interpreter may assume that the native speakers believe and reason (mostly) as she does (section 3.1). However, the principle of explanatory coherence permits virtually any part of this initial interpretation to change. While thin descriptions of speech and behavior—the claims on the edge of the web—must remain, their explanatory import is always open for reevaluation. More deeply, that the native speakers reason according to a pattern familiar to the interpreter is treated by the principle of explanatory coherence as an explanatory hypothesis. It is no different in kind from the hypothesis that they believe in tree spirits or prefer to marry their matrilateral cross-cousins. If positing an unfamiliar pattern of reasoning would expand the explanatory power of the interpretation, then the interpretation should be changed. In principle, nothing is immune from revision.

8.1.2 Rationality is Explanatory

The principle of explanatory coherence permits the interpreter to attribute patterns of reasoning and rational action different from her own because it treats claims about rationality as *explanatory* posits. This is an unpopular idea in the philosophy of social science. Staking out and defending the alternative claim has occupied much of this work. Proponents of rationalizing explanations took instrumental rationality to constitute the form of intentional action explanations. By contrast, this work places claims about rationality among the explanantia of intentional action (section 5.2). Some proponents of the principle of humanity have argued that rationality is constitutive of the conception of an intentional agent and thus that they cannot be part of the empirical content of the interpretation (section 3.2). After arguing against this position, chapter 3 adopted a symmetrical principle of interpretive change: true and false, rational and irrational beliefs are all equally explained (section 3.3). Henderson argued powerfully that no normative claims, including claims about rationality, could be explanatory (section 7.1). To resolve this difficulty, chapter 7 argued that claims about criteria, standards, or norms of rationality are, in the first instance, part of the explanation of group-level patterns of action. To see an action or inference as rational, on this view, is to see how it fits into the local patterns.

   The idea that claims about rationality cannot be explanatory is one of the primary reasons why philosophers have thought that interpretation must rely on some shared foundation of true belief and rational action. Undermining these arguments and articulating the way in which claims about criteria, standards, or norms of rationality can be explanatory makes possible a view of interpretation wherein rationality is central and yet not imposed a priori on the interpretation. Interpretation would be impossible without the postulation of some criteria of rationality. An interpretation must deploy reason-giving explanations (section 5.1), and these invoke criteria of rationality among their explanans (section 5.2). Because criteria of rationality also explain patterns of speech, thought, and action (section 7.1), they constitute a crucial explanatory link among different parts of the interpretation. This is the sense in which criteria of rationality are central, even necessary, for an interpretation. At the same time, it is always possible for the interpreter to revise her understanding of the local standards of rationality. Because of their centrality, this sort of revision has profound ramifications for the relative coherence of an interpretation. Nothing in the epistemology of interpretation precludes the replacement of every familiar criterion of rational thought and action. Thus, whether the local criteria of rational thought and action are in any way similar to the interpreter's is ultimately an empirical matter. It depends entirely on whether the familiar criteria survive the changes demanded by the social reality and the principle of explanatory coherence.

8.1.3 Multiple Explanatory Perspectives

One of the distinctive features of the interpretive dynamics provided here is that it does not force all social phenomena into a single pattern of explanation. As articulated in chapter 4, the logic of question and answer constitutes the logical form for all explanation. Within this form, however, there are many explanatory patterns. The foregoing chapters have examined the details of several patterns central to interpretation. An important result of these analyses is that the interpretive dynamics motivated by the principle of explanatory coherence permits, and in most cases requires, multiple explanatory perspectives on an action, a social event, or an institution. The interests constitutive to interpretation demand both intentional action and social-level explanations (section 5.1). In some cases, this means that a single action or event will be the topic of different why-questions. This is reinforced by the multifaceted explanatory role of criteria of rationality. Even explaining an individual action requires the identification of the person's motives and placing the action in the wider social context. Action explanations thus depend on explanations at the social level. Moreover, the interpretation of most social phenomena will require both explanations invoking the agent's point of view and the concepts with which he operates *and* explanations appealing to patterns, phenomena, or concepts outside of his ken (sections 5.4 and 7.2). The interpretive dynamics that this work defends is therefore not restrictive about the explanations that constitute interpretation. It integrates a variety of explanatory patterns and perspectives. While it is pluralistic about explanations, this essay has recognized that explanations with different forms can conflict. The analysis is powerful enough to distinguish between cases where different explanatory perspectives are complementary and those where the perspectives conflict (section 5.1).

8.1.4 No Knowledge of Language without Knowledge of Culture

Perhaps no philosopher has unequivocally held that one could know everything about a language and yet know nothing about the people who spoke it. Nonetheless, many have thought that the knowledge of language and the knowledge of culture are relatively independent. This essay has argued that understanding a language and understanding the action and society of its speakers are two aspects of a single inquiry. This is partly the result of giving an explanatory role to claims about linguistic meaning (section 6.2). It also follows from the presuppositions of reason-giving explanations. As we saw in section 5.2, reason-giving explanations presuppose claims about linguistic meaning insofar as the action or belief has to be described in local terms. Claims about meaning may also figure prominently in the explanation of social phenomena (section 6.2). The translation must therefore fit with both the individual and social aspects of the interpretation. Coherence increases as this integration becomes more complete and systematic. The best translations, then, will be those that are deeply intertwined with the rest of the interpretation. The upshot for interpretive dynamics is that there are powerful constraints on translation that come from the other parts of an interpretation. An interpreter is not free to make translational hypotheses as she wills.

8.1.5 No Homogenization

Interpreters are sometimes criticized for imposing an artificial consensus on their subjects. Local disputes about the way to apply rules, about the significance of a social or natural event, or about what is good, right, and just are often papered over by the interpreter for the sake of a tidy interpretation. One might think that a coherence theory encourages this kind of homogenization of local opinion. Doing so would confuse the coherence of the interpretation with the coherence of the group interpreted. Where subgroups exhibit different patterns of action or where a minority rejects, criticizes, or subverts the dominant view, a responsible interpretation must represent the observed differences in speech and action. The best explanation of these observed differences might be that they reflect real disagreements in the community. Hence, claiming that the community is fractured by discord, inequitable power structures, or conflicting understandings can make an interpretation more coherent than the alternatives. The interpretive dynamics of an explanatory coherence view therefore does not demand that interpretive change progress toward local consensus.

8.1.6 No Over-rationalization

Like the homogenization of local opinion, over-rationalization is a real danger for any interpretive dynamics. Some views of explanation and interpretation in the social sciences take the better interpretation to be the one that shows more behavior to be rational. The consequence of this would be that all behavior is rational when fully understood. Since not all behavior is fully rational, an interpretive dynamics must have some way of blocking this consequence. What keeps the interpretive dynamics presented here from over-rationalizing action is the permissibility of multiple explanatory perspectives. While the interpreter cannot eliminate or replace all reason-giving explanations, and thus cannot completely expunge reasons from the interpretation, the principle of explanatory coherence does not demand that all action be explained as rational. There are some examples—the Purrinton murders—where the best account might portray the action as profoundly irrational, even by local standards. The best explanation in this sort of case may appeal to subintentional psychological facts. These terms are probably unfamiliar to the agent, and they are certainly not the way in which he conceived of his action. The principle of explanatory coherence is therefore not committed to interpreting all action as rational. The best interpretation might portray substantial irrationality. In less striking cases, interpretations may explain an action in terms of the agent's motivation *and* in terms of its social function. Within a part of the interpretation, the actions are explained neither as rational nor irrational. As long as the interpretations are consistent with other reason-giving explanations, this sort of interpretation does not transgress against representing the agents' point of view (section 5.4). Therefore, the interpretive dynamics supported by the principle of explanatory coherence do not lead to the over-rationalization of thought and action.

8.2 On the Relationship between the Social and Natural Sciences

One of the primary theses of the foregoing chapters has been that an interpretation is an interlaced body of explanations. An interpretation is not thereby identical to an explanation, any more than a jigsaw puzzle is identical to one of its parts. An interpretation is a holistic account of some social complex. The claims that constitute the interpretation are structured by explanatory relationships. The view defended here thus effaces some of the differences between the social and natural sciences. It thereby takes a position in the venerable debate over the relationship between these two branches of inquiry. This section will survey the debate's territory and situate the explanatory coherence view of interpretation within it. It will contend that the entry of explanatory coherence and allied views transforms the debate over the relationship between the social and natural sciences. The old battle lines have been overrun and new ones formed. The philosophy of social science has a new configuration, and this work is one among several that are shaping it.

Is there a single methodology that unifies the social and the natural sciences? Those who answer in the negative are *methodological separatists*.[2] They divide into several camps, depending on how they conceive of the relationship between the different sorts of inquiry. The first kind of methodological separatism arose in response to empiricism and positivism. These philosophers argued that there is a deep epistemic difference between inquiry into human subjects (as meaning-generating, self-interpreting, norm-following beings) and inquiry into other sorts of object. Inquiry into the social world must be interpretive or hermeneutic, while inquiry in to the natural world is theoretical or explanatory. Interpretation and explanation are thus mutually exclusive and independent. Recent proponents of this sort of separatism (often called "exclusivism") include Dreyfus (1980), Davidson (1970/1980), Winch (1958), and Taylor (1971). A second sort of methodological separatism denies that interpretation and explanation are mutually exclusive. They may, like Lawson and McCauley (1990) and Sperber (1985), contend that interpretive and explanatory methods are mutually dependent. While epistemologically distinct, neither can give a complete account of the social world without the other. Lawson and McCauley call their position "interactionism." Finally, there are separatists who, like Bohman (1991), Little (1991), and Roth (1987), resist the program of unifying and generalizing methods of inquiry. To think that inquiry divides neatly into the social and natural sciences is already too much unity. On this kind of view, each discipline develops forms of explanation and methods of interpretation in response to the phenomena they confront. There is little or nothing to be said about methodology at a high level of abstraction. Both Roth and Little call their view "methodological pluralism."

Those who think that the natural and human sciences have a unified methodology we may call *methodological assimilationists*. Like the separatists, methodological assimilationists take several forms. Historically, the most common view is that the social sciences need to adopt the methods of the natural sciences. Assimilationists of this stripe disagree among themselves about just how far the methods of the natural sciences can be driven into the traditional domain of interpretation and in their attitude toward the remainder. Hempel, for example, thought that intentional action could be explained on the model of natural scientific explanations. He also held that appeals to meaning, function, and social structure were not explanatory, and hence not properly scientific. Henderson, as we have seen, argues that appeal to norms can never be explanatory. Henderson is pluralistic about explanatory forms, and thus embeds the interpretation of the language within a larger explanatory framework that includes psychological and functional explanations. Finally, eliminativists regard

---

2. The term "methodological separatist" is Henderson's (1993).

scientific methodology as properly ranging only over some domain (for example, behavior or neuro-physiology) and contend that the remaining intentional phenomena are mere appearance to be explained away. Opposed to all
these naturalistic sorts of methodological assimilationists is a small minority
who see a unity to inquiry without insisting that the natural sciences are the
only model for inquiry. The demise of logical positivism and the rise of
postempiricist philosophy of science made space for this kind of view. Rorty
(1979), perhaps, fits this description.

The relationship between the assimilationists and the separatists, and among
their subgroups, is quite complex. To comprehend the overall field, we need
to identify those specific ideas that have divided antagonists. There are, broadly,
four main fault lines among the positions: the role of causality or laws in
explanation, meaning, normativity, and the relevance of the agents' self-interpretation. These four are closely related, and arguments in one area quickly
spill over into the others. The most vivid difference between humans and other
subjects of inquiry is that the words and actions of an agent mean something
to him and to his compatriots. Methodological separatists often point to this
fact when defending the necessity of interpretive methods in the human
sciences. An adequate epistemology of the social world must recognize that its
subjects reflect on their own action, interpret it, and have their own ways of
understanding it. Moreover, it must have some way of interpreting the meaning of the subjects' utterances. Naturalistic assimilationists have typically
downplayed the importance of norms and the agents' self-interpretation, and
shunted off linguistic meaning to the empirical, but not truly scientific, enterprise of translation. The remaining three points of dispute in these debates—
meaning, norms, and the agents' self-interpretation—constitute three of the
ways in which human subjects are importantly different from other objects of
inquiry.

In the traditional debates over the status of the social sciences, models of
explanation presupposed that explanation necessarily involved either causes or
laws. Explanation either subsumed the explanandum under a law or identified
the explanans with the cause of the explanandum. As a result, some forms of
methodological assimilationism insisted that the social sciences could yield
scientific knowledge only if they found causal models or universal laws of
human action. Against this, defenders of a distinctive methodology for the
human sciences argued that hermeneutic methods produced nonexplanatory
understanding. A third position in the debate was articulated by Collingwood
(1946), Dray (1957), and von Wright (1971). They contended that human
action could be explained, but the form of explanation was neither subsumptive
nor causal. Rationalizing explanation shows an intentional action to be the
rational outcome of the agent's beliefs and desires.

If the erotetic model of explanation, as defended in chapter 4, is correct,
then the foregoing three-way debate about explanation dissolves. Explanations

that appeal to laws or causes are fully legitimate, but they are not the only patterns of explanation. Laws and causes are characteristic explanantia of many explanations in the natural sciences, but this fact provides no support for the naturalistic assimilationists. Nor should it worry those who want to preserve the distinct character of the human sciences. There are, this essay has argued, patterns of explanation that fit the phenomena unique to the social sciences. The fact that explanations appealing to laws and causes have not been useful in the interpretive disciplines, therefore, shows neither that these disciplines are epistemologically suspect nor that they need a nonexplanatory methodology. They share an explanatory epistemology, according to this work, but the social and natural sciences are not thereby forced into a single mold. Finally, as argued in section 5.2, the character of motivation and the role of rationality in the explanation of human action does not give intentional action explanations a completely unique form. They too may be represented by why-questions. Of course, motivation and rationality give such why-questions distinctive presuppositions and demand particular contrast classes and relevance criteria. The erotetic view can thus preserve what is special about the explanation of human action without forcing an epistemic break between the explanation of action and the explanation of events.

Understanding linguistic meaning has usually been taken to be a nonexplanatory enterprise. This has funded many forms of separatism. Those who think that interpretation and explanation are distinct but mutually dependent have thought so because explanations of social events and human action often presuppose translations, and the latter are not explanatory. Similarly, hermeneutics recognizes the importance of linguistic understanding and models all interpretation upon it. The presumption that claims about linguistic meaning have no explanatory role has forced some assimilationists toward an eliminativist stance: meaning is a murky business best left out of the ultimate scientific picture. Henderson (1990; 1993) is a noteworthy exception. His form of naturalistic assimilationism makes interpretation, including the interpretation of language, fully explanatory. This essay has argued similarly that linguistic meaning is within the purview of an explanatory epistemology. Claims about word meaning can be the topic of why-questions (section 6.2.2), and may be invoked as part of the answer to questions about patterns of action and social structures (section 6.2.1). If these arguments are sound, then many forms of methodological separatism rest on a false presupposition. The importance of understanding the language does not show that the interpretive disciplines require a nonexplanatory epistemology. Moreover, as against the eliminativists, there is no need to suppose that meaning will be explained away as inquiry progresses.

The capacity to recognize norms, rules, and values is another distinctive feature of human beings that provides grounds for methodological separatism. One way to depict the debate is to see all parties to the debate as assenting to the conditional "if norms have an explanatory role, then the social and natural sciences must have distinct methodologies" and disagreeing over the truth value of its components. Naturalistic assimilationists, including Hempel (1963) and Henderson (1993), have denied the antecedent. Similarly, philosophers like Gadamer (1975), Taylor (1971), and Winch (1958) contend that normativity puts human activity beyond the reach of explanation. These separatists and their assimilationist opponents agree that norms are not explanatory, and are arguing over the consequences of this fact. Proponents of rationalizing explanation take both the antecedent and the consequent of the above conditional to be true. As discussed above, they think that the social sciences have a distinct form of explanation because the norms of rationality have an explanatory role. Chapter 7 argued that norms and rules can be the topic of a why-question and that they can form a part of the relevant answer to a why-question. Explanations invoking norms were thus shown to have an explanatory role without invoking a novel explanatory form. This work therefore denies the truth of the conditional that the traditional explanation/understanding debate presupposes.

Finally, many separatists have contended that the agents' self-interpretations are central to understanding the social world. No adequate interpretation could eliminate the agents' point of view. In many ways, this point is fundamental to methodological separatist appeals to the importance of meaning. Not only words, but also actions and social events are meaningful to the agents. They conceptualize their social environment and act on that basis. The locals may disagree about the way to understand features of their own society, and such disputes may be a crucial part of the social fabric. Explanatory methodologies, separatists argue, do not capture the reflexivity of human life. Explanation typically employs concepts that are not drawn from the group studied. Both reductionistic psychological explanations and holistic sociological explanations appeal to things about which the agents know nothing. The methods of the natural sciences do not need to reflect their objects' self-interpretations, because their objects do not understand themselves. The social sciences must have a methodology different from the natural, the separatists have argued, because the human capacity for reflection makes us fundamentally different from the objects of natural science.

From the point of view of this essay, methodological separatists are right to demand a methodology that captures the agents' understanding of their own action. Nonetheless, if the arguments of this essay are sound, the separatists are wrong to suppose that a fully explanatory methodology necessarily obscured the agents' point of view. Section 5.1 argued that understanding the locals' view of their own action and society is one of the constitutive interests of the interpretive disciplines. This interest motivates the structure of reason-giving explanations, demanding that the topic characterize the action in terms recognizable to, or epistemically accessible to, the agent. This, in turn, means that an interpretation must deploy the local conceptualization of actions and the local criteria of good reasons for action (or belief). Since the interest is constitutive, no adequate interpretation could eliminate the natives' conceptualization of their own actions. At the same time, the local understanding need not be univocal. Section 7.3 showed how contested norms and differing local interpretations can be represented in a coherent interpretation. That different individuals or subgroups have divergent interpretations of social events might be the best explanation of their various actions and utterances. The most coherent interpretation of a group might thus posit conflict and discord. An explanatory coherence view of interpretive change *must* therefore capture the agents' reflexive interpretation. However, as sections 5.4 and 7.3 have argued, an interpretation is not limited to the local conceptual resources. It is possible for an interpretation to consistently combine the agents' conceptualization of their own action with explanations of that action that are completely external. Section 5.4 argued that explanations appealing to latent social functions can be compatible with intentional action explanations. Similarly, explanations that relate word meaning to claims about the social structure do not presuppose that the locals are aware of such relationships (section 6.2). What makes this combination of internal and external explanations possible is the unity of their explanatory form and their integration by the principle of explanatory coherence.

It should be clear that the explanatory coherence view defended here does not join either the separatist or the assimilationist side of the traditional disputes. On each of the four central issues, this essay either argues against a presupposition of the debate or admits the significance of the phenomena without agreeing to its purported ramifications. This result is possible because the methodology defended herein is globally assimilationist and locally separatist. At the highest level of abstraction, all inquiry is explanatory. All explanations are answers to why-questions. The dynamics of explanatory coherence govern theory change in all empirical inquiry.[3] Therefore, there is no deep epistemic or methodological distinction between the social and the natural sciences. This is the sense in which explanatory coherence, as articulated here, is globally assimilationist. To argue that inquiry is unified at this level, however, does not efface all differences among disciplines. The erotetic model of explanation entails that features of the phenomena investigated and the constitutive interests of the investigators may dictate different patterns of explanation. There are, therefore, broad differences between interpretation and other sorts of theorizing. Interpretations require explanations that invoke norms, reasons, and

---

3. Since we have only been concerned with the interpretive disciplines, this broad claim is not fully supported by the foregoing chapters. Nonetheless, the existing application of the erotetic model to the natural sciences and the continuing development of coherence epistemologies support the claim that a similar explanatory coherence view could be developed for natural scientific theorizing.

meaning. Theorizing about nonagents does not require these patterns. Various forms of causal, historical, structural, and functional explanation may suffice. The methodological separatists were therefore right to argue that features of human beings made social inquiry distinct. Their mistake was to take these differences to require a radically different form of understanding.

To talk about the difference between interpretation and noninterpretive theorizing is to remain at a very high level of abstraction. When we consider specific disciplines and subdisciplines, like medical anthropology, cognitive linguistics, developmental psychology, art history, and so on, we find clusters of explanatory forms. At this local level, explanatory coherence does not demand methodological unity. Again, the investigator's interests and the phenomena investigated interact to motivate the structure of why-questions. We would expect to find different structures of explanation in these various domains, and thus that the theories and interpretations proposed take different shapes. Thus, for example, some projects in medical anthropology may rely heavily on causal explanation and care little about the local conceptualization of disease. By contrast, art historians might rely entirely on meaning-based explanations. At the most fine-grained level of analysis, then, this view unites with methodological pluralists such as Bohman, Little, and Roth.

This work should be seen as joining the voices calling for a new way of approaching the philosophy of social science. If the arguments of the foregoing chapters are sound, then the old debates over explanation and understanding must be transformed. The old positions are no longer tenable. The problem is not whether there are explanations in the interpretive disciplines. The new problem is to understand the explanations we find in the practice of historians, ethnographers, sociologists, economists . . . ; to understand their structure and presuppositions; and to uncover the interests that motivate them. If we want to understand the methodology and epistemological status of a discipline, it will not do to merely ask whether it is explanatory or interpretive. Inquiry does not neatly divide into natural and social kinds. We need to look at the details, and when we do, the disciplines explode into clusters of similarities and differences. If we want to understand the conflict between kinds of explanation, we need a close analysis of the explanations and the specific disciplines in which they are found. If we want to critique a line of inquiry, we must examine the details of the practitioners' web of explanations. Real epistemological critique has to be local.

References

Anscombe, G. E. M. 1963. *Intention.* 2nd ed. Ithaca: Cornell University Press.

Barnes, Eric. 1994. "Why P rather than Q? The Curiosities of Fact and Foil." *Philosophical Studies* 73:35–53.

Bar-On, Dorit, and Mark Risjord. 1992. "Is There Such a Thing as a Language?" *Canadian Journal of Philosophy* 22:163–90.

Belnap, Nuel. 1966. "Questions." *Journal of Philosophy* 63:597–611.

Belnap, N. D., and J. B. Steel. 1976. *The Logic of Questions and Answers.* New Haven: Yale University Press.

Bennett, Jonathan. 1976. *Linguistic Behavior.* Cambridge: Cambridge University Press.

Bohman, James. 1991. *New Philosophy of Social Science.* Cambridge, Mass.: MIT Press.

BonJour, Laurence. 1985. *The Structure of Empirical Knowledge.* Cambridge, Mass.: Harvard University Press.

Brandom, Robert. 1994. *Making It Explicit.* Cambridge, Mass.: Harvard University Press.

Bromberger, Sylvain. 1966. "Why Questions." In *Mind and Cosmos: Essays in Contemporary Science and Philosophy,* edited by R. Colodny. Pittsburgh: University of Pittsburgh Press.

Bromberger, Sylvain. 1992. *On What We Know We Don't Know.* Chicago: University of Chicago Press.

Bulmer, Ralph. 1967. "Why Is the Cassowary Not a Bird? A Problem of Zoological Taxonomy among the Karam of the New Guinea Highlands." *Man* 2:5–25.

Churchland, Paul. 1970. "The Logical Character of Action Explanations." *Philosophical Review* 79:214–36.

Collingwood, R. G. 1946. *The Idea of History.* Oxford: Oxford University Press.

Cooper, David. 1975. "Alternative Logic in 'Primitive Thought.' " *Man (N.S.)* 10:238–56.

Cooper, David. 1985–86. "Anthropology and Translation." *Aristotelian Society Proceedings* 86:51–68.

Courtright, Paul B. 1994. "The Iconographies of Sati." In *Sati, the Blessing and the Curse: The Burning of Wives in India,* edited by J. S. Hawley. Oxford: Oxford University Press.

Cross, Charles B. 1991. "Explanation and the Theory of Questions." *Erkenntnis* 34:237–60.

Cummins, Robert. 1975. "Functional Explanation." *Journal of Philosophy* 72:741–64.

Cummins, Robert. 1983. *The Nature of Psychological Explanation.* Cambridge, Mass.: MIT Press.

Davidson, Donald. 1963/1980. "Actions, Reasons and Causes." In *Essays on Actions and Events.* Oxford: Clarendon Press.

Davidson, Donald. 1973/1984. "Radical Interpretation." In *Inquiries into Truth and Interpretation.* Oxford: Oxford University Press.

Davidson, Donald. 1974/1984. "Belief and the Basis of Meaning." In *Inquiries into Truth and Interpretation.* Oxford: Oxford University Press.

Davidson, Donald. 1970/1980. "Mental Events." In *Essays on Actions and Events.* Oxford: Clarendon Press.

Davidson, Donald. 1984. *Inquiries into Truth and Interpretation.* Oxford: Clarendon Press.

Dilthey, Wilhelm. 1996. *Hermeneutics and the Study of History.* Translated by R. A. Makkreel and F. Rodi. Princeton: Princeton University Press.

Douglas, Mary. 1966. *Purity and Danger: An Analysis of the Concepts of Pollution and Taboo.* London: Routledge and Kegan Paul.

Dray, William. 1957. *Laws and Explanation in History.* Oxford: Oxford University Press.

Dray, William. 1963. "The Historical Explanation of Actions Reconsidered." In *Philosophy and History: A Symposium,* edited by S. Hook. New York: New York University Press.

Dretske, Fred. 1973. "Contrastive Statements." *Philosophical Review* 82:411–37.

Dreyfus, Hubert. 1980. "Holism and Hermeneutics." *Review of Metaphysics* 34:3–23.

Evans-Pritchard, E. E. 1937. *Witchcraft, Oracles and Magic Among the Azande.* Oxford: Clarendon Press.

Feleppa, Robert. 1988. *Convention, Translation, and Understanding.* Albany: State University of New York Press.

Gadamer, Hans-Georg. 1975. *Truth and Method.* New York: Seabury.

Garfinkel, Alan. 1981. *Forms of Explanation.* New Haven: Yale University Press.

Geertz, Clifford. 1973a. "Religion as a Cultural System." In *The Interpretation of Cultures.* New York: Basic Books.

Geertz, Clifford. 1973b. "Thick Description: Toward and Interpretive Theory of Culture." In *The Interpretation of Cultures.* New York: Basic Books.

Gellner, Ernest. 1970. "Concepts and Society." In *Rationality,* edited by B. R. Wilson. Oxford: Basil Blackwell.

Georgeson, Hanne. 1992. "Representation of Some Hindu Women Through Some of the Rewritings on Widow-burning." *Australian Journal of Anthropology* 3:150–74.

Giddens, Anthony. 1976. *New Rules of the Sociological Method.* New York: Basic Books.

Gould, Steven J., and Richard C. Lewontin. 1979. "The Spandrels of San Marco and the Panglossian Program." *Proceedings of the Royal Society of London* 205:281–88.

Grandy, Richard E. 1973. "Reference, Meaning, and Belief." *Journal of Philosophy* 70:439–52.

Grice, Paul. 1989. *Studies in the Way of Words*. Cambridge, Mass.: Harvard University Press.

Grimes, Thomas. 1987. "Explanation and the Poverty of Pragmatics." *Erkenntnis* 27:79–92.

Habermas, Jürgen. 1984. *The Theory of Communicative Action*. Vol. 1, *Reason and the Rationalization of Society*. Translated by T. McCarthy. Boston: Beacon Press.

Habermas, Jürgen. 1988/1967. *On the Logic of the Social Sciences*. Translated by S. W. Nicholsen and J. A. Stark. Cambridge, Mass.: MIT Press.

Hanson, N. 1958. *Patterns of Discovery*. Cambridge: Cambridge University Press.

Harman, Gilbert. 1973. *Thought*. Princeton: Princeton University Press.

Harman, Gilbert. 1986. *Change in View*. Cambridge, Mass.: MIT Press.

Harris, Zelig. 1960. *Structural Linguistics*. Chicago: University of Chicago Press.

Hawley, John S., ed. 1994. *Sati, the Blessing and the Curse: The Burning of Wives in India*. Oxford: Oxford University Press.

Headland, Thomas, Kenneth Pike, and Marvin Harris, eds. 1990. *Emics and Etics: The Insider/Outsider Debate*. Frontiers of Anthropology, Vol. 7. Newbury Park: Sage.

Hempel, Carl. 1942. "The Function of General Laws in History." *Journal of Philosophy* 39:35–48.

Hempel, Carl. 1963. "Reasons and Covering Laws in Historical Explanation." In *Philosophy and History: A Symposium*, edited by S. Hook. New York: New York University Press.

Hempel, Carl. 1965. *Aspects of Scientific Explanation and Other Essays in the Philosophy of Science*. New York: The Free Press.

Henderson, David. 1990. "An Empirical Basis for Charity in Interpretation." *Erkenntnis* 32:83–103.

Henderson, David. 1993. *Interpretation and Explanation in the Human Sciences*. Albany: State University of New York Press.

Hintikka, Jaakko. 1977. "The Semantics of Questions and the Questions of Semantics." *Acta Philosophical Fennica* 28.

Hitchcock, Christopher R. 1996. "The Role of Contrast in Causal and Explanatory Claims." *Synthese* 107:395–419.

Hollis, Martin. 1967a. "The Limits of Irrationality." *Archives Europeenes de Sociologie* 7:265–71.

Hollis, Martin. 1967b. "Reason and Ritual." *Philosophy* 43:231–47.

Hollis, Martin. 1982. "The Social Destruction of Reality." In *Rationality and Relativism*, edited by M. Hollis and S. Lukes. Cambridge, Mass.: MIT Press.

Horton, Robert. 1967. "African Thought and Western Science." *Africa* 37:50–71, 115–87.

Horton, Robert. 1982. "Tradition and Modernity Revisited." In *Rationality and Relativism*, edited by M. Hollis and S. Lukes. Cambridge, Mass.: MIT Press.

Humphreys, Paul. 1989. *The Chances of Explanation*. Princeton: Princeton University Press.

Jarvie, Ian C. 1964. *The Revolution in Anthropology*. London: Routledge and Kegan Paul.

Jarvie, Ian C. 1970. "Understanding and Explanation in Sociology and Social Anthropology." In *Explanation in the Behavioral Sciences*, edited by R. Borger and F. Cioffi. Cambridge: Cambridge University Press.

Jarvie, Ian C. 1972. *Concepts and Society*. London: Routledge and Kegan Paul.

Jarvie, Ian C, and Joseph Agassi. 1967. "The Problem of the Rationality of Magic." *British Journal of Anthropology* 18:55–74.

Kitcher, Philip, and Wesley Salmon. 1987. "Van Fraassen on Explanation." *Journal of Philosophy* 84:315–30.

Koura, Antti. 1988. "An Approach to Why-Questions." *Synthese* 74:191–206.

Kuhn, Thomas. 1962. *The Structure of Scientific Revolutions*. Chicago: University of Chicago Press.

Lawson, Thomas E., and Robert N. McCauley. 1990. *Rethinking Religion*. Cambridge: Cambridge University Press.

Lehrer, Keith. 1974. *Knowledge*. Oxford: Clarendon Press.

Lehrer, Keith. 1990. *Theory of Knowledge*. Boulder: Westview Press.

Lipton, Peter. 1987. "A Real Contrast." *Analysis* 47:207–8.

Lipton, Peter. 1991a. "Contrastive Explanation and Causal Triangulation." *Philosophy of Science* 58:687–97.

Lipton, Peter. 1991b. *Inference to the Best Explanation*. London: Routledge.

Little, Daniel. 1991. *Varieties of Social Explanation*. Boulder: Westview Press.

Lukes, Steven. 1967. "Some Problems about Rationality." *Archives Europeenes de Sociologie* 7:247–64.

Lukes, Steven. 1982. "Relativism in its Place." In *Rationality and Relativism*, edited by M. Hollis and S. Lukes. Cambridge, Mass.: MIT Press.

Lycan, William. 1988. *Judgment and Justification*. Cambridge: Cambridge University Press.

Macdonald, Graham, and Philip Pettit. 1981. *Semantics and Social Science*. London: Routledge and Kegan Paul.

MacIntyre, Alasdair. 1967. "The Idea of a Social Science." *Proceedings of the Aristotelian Society, Supplementary Volume* 61:95–114.

Makkreel, Rudolf. 1985. "Dilthey and Universal Hermeneutics: The Status of the Human Sciences." *The Journal of the British Society for Phenomenology* 16:236–49.

Malinowski, Bronislaw. 1935. *Coral Gardens and Their Magic*. 2 Vols. New York: American Book Company.

Melden, A. I. 1961. *Free Action*. London: Routledge and Kegan Paul.

Merton, Robert K. 1957. *Social Theory and Social Structure*. Revised ed. Glencoe, Ill.: Free Press.

Millikan, Ruth G. 1984. *Language, Thought and Other Biological Categories*. Cambridge, Mass.: MIT Press.

Morton, Adam. 1970. "Denying the Doctrine and Changing the Subject." *Journal of Philosophy* 70:503–10.

Neander, Karen. 1991. "Functions as Selected Effects: The Conceptual Analyst's Defense." *Philosophy of Science* 58:168–84.

Nussbaum, Martha C., and Amartya Sen. 1989. "Internal Criticism and Indian Rationalist Traditions." In *Relativism: Interpretation and Confrontation*, edited by M. Krausz. Notre Dame: University of Notre Dame Press.

Nutini, Hugo G., and John M. Roberts. 1993. *Bloodsucking Witchcraft: An Epistemological Study of Anthropomorphic Supernaturalism in Rural Tlaxcala*. Tucson: University of Arizona Press.

Preston, Elizabeth. 1998. "Why is a Wing like a Spoon?: A Pluralist Theory of Function." *Journal of Philosophy* 95:215–54.

Putnam, Hilary. 1974. "The 'Corroboration' of Theories." In *The Philosophy of Karl Popper*, edited by P. Schilpp. La Salle: Open Court.

Quine, Willard van Orman. 1960. *Word and Object*. Cambridge, Mass.: MIT Press.

Quine, Willard van Orman. 1969a. "Ontological Relativity." In *Ontological Relativity and Other Essays*. New York: Columbia University Press.

Quine, Willard van Orman. 1969b. *Ontological Relativity and Other Essays*. New York: Columbia University Press.

Quine, Willard van Orman. 1970. "On the Reasons for Indeterminacy of Translation." *Journal of Philosophy* 67:178–83.

Quine, Willard van Orman. 1975. "On Empirically Equivalent Systems of the World." *Erkenntnis* 9:313–28.

Quine, Willard van Orman. 1986. *Philosophy of Logic*. 2nd ed. Cambridge, Mass.: Harvard University Press.

Quine, Willard van Orman. 1987. "Indeterminacy of Translation Again." *Journal of Philosophy* 84:5–10.

Ramberg, Bjorn. 1989. *Donald Davidson's Philosophy of Language*. Oxford: Basil Blackwell.

Risjord, Mark. 1993. "Wittgenstein's Woodcutters: The Problem of Apparent Irrationality." *American Philosophical Quarterly* 30:247–58.

Risjord, Mark. 1998. "Norms and Explanation in the Social Sciences." *Studies in History and Philosophy of Science* 29:223–37.

Risjord, Mark. Forthcoming. "The Politics of Explanation and the Origins of Ethnography." *Perspectives on Science*.

Root, Michael. 1986. "Davidson and Social Science." In *Truth and Interpretation*, edited by E. LePore. Oxford: Basil Blackwell.

Rorty, Richard. 1979. *Philosophy and the Mirror of Nature*. Princeton: Princeton University Press.

Rosenberg, Alexander. 1988. *Philosophy of Social Science*. Boulder: Westview Press.

Roth, Paul. 1987. *Meaning and Method in the Social Sciences*. Ithaca: Cornell University Press.

Ruben, David-Hillel. 1987. "Explaining Contrastive Facts." *Analysis* 47:35–37.

Ruben, David-Hillel. 1990. *Explaining Explanation*. London: Routledge.

Ruse, Michael. 1971. "Function Statements in Biology." *Philosophy of Science* 38:87–95.

Ruse, Michael. 1973. *Philosophy of Biology*. London: Hutchinson.

Ruse, Michael. 1981. "Teleology Redux." In *Scientific Philosophy Today*, edited by J. Agassi and R. S. Cohen. Dordrecht: D. Ridel.

Ryle, Gilbert. 1949. *The Concept of Mind.* Chicago: University of Chicago Press.

Ryle, Gilbert. 1971. "Thinking and Reflecting." In *Collected Papers.* New York: Barnes and Noble.

Salmon, Merrilee. 1978. "Do Azande and Nuer Use a Non-Standard Logic?" *Man (N.S.)* 13:444–54.

Salmon, Wesley. 1984. *Scientific Explanation and the Causal Structure of the World.* Princeton: Princeton University Press.

Schiffer, Steven. 1972. *Meaning.* Oxford: Oxford University Press.

Schutz, Alfred. 1967. "Concept and Theory Formation in the Social Sciences." In *Collected Papers,* edited by M. Natanson. The Hague: Martinus Nijhoff.

Sharma, Arvind. 1983. "The *Gita,* Suttee and Rammohun Roy." *Economic and Social History Review* 20:341–47.

Sintonen, Matti. 1984. "On the Logic of Why-Questions." *Proceedings of the Philosophy of Science Association, 1984* 1:168–76.

Sintonen, Matti. 1989. "Explanation: In Search of the Rationale." In *Scientific Explanation,* edited by P. Kitcher and W. Salmon. Minneapolis: University of Minnesota Press.

Sober, Elliott. 1986. "Explanatory Presupposition." *Australasian Journal of Philosophy* 64:143–49.

Sperber, Dan. 1985. *On Anthropological Knowledge.* Cambridge: Cambridge University Press.

Taylor, Charles. 1971. "Interpretation and the Sciences of Man." *Review of Metaphysics* 25:3–34, 45–51.

Teller, Paul. 1974. "On Why-Questions." *Nous* 8:371–80.

Temple, Dennis. 1988. "The Contrast Theory of Why-Questions." *Philosophy of Science* 55:141–51.

Thagard, Paul. 1978. "The Best Explanation: Criteria for Theory Choice." *Journal of Philosophy* 75:76–92.

Thagard, Paul. 1992. *Conceptual Revolutions.* Princeton: Princeton University Press.

Tichy, Paul. 1978. "Questions, Answers, and Their Logic." *American Philosophical Quarterly* 15:275–84.

Travis, Charles. 1978. "Why?" *American Philosophical Quarterly* 15:285–93.

Tuomela, Raimo. 1980. "Explaining Explaining." *Erkenntnis* 15:211–43.

Ulrich, Laurel T. 1990. *A Midwife's Tale: The Life of Martha Ballard, Based on Her Diary, 1785–1812.* New York: Random House.

van Fraassen, Bas C. 1980. *The Scientific Image.* Oxford: Oxford University Press.

von Wright, George H. 1971. *Explanation and Understanding.* Ithaca: Cornell University Press.

Whorf, Benjamin L. 1956. *Language, Thought, and Reality; Selected Writings.* Cambridge, Mass.: MIT Press.

Wilson, Bryan R., ed. 1970. *Rationality.* Oxford: Basil Blackwell.

Winch, Peter. 1958. *The Idea of a Social Science.* London: Routledge and Kegan Paul.

Winch, Peter. 1964. "Understanding a Primitive Society." *American Philosophical Quarterly* 1:307–24.

Wittgenstein, Ludwig. 1956. *Remarks on the Foundations of Mathematics.* Translated by G. E. M. Anscombe. 2nd ed. Oxford: Basil Blackwell.

Wright, Larry. 1972. "Explanation and Teleology." *Philosophy of Science* 39:204–18.

Wright, Larry. 1976. *Teleological Explanations.* Berkeley: University of California Press.

Yang, Anand. 1989. "Whose Sati? Widow burning in Early 19th Century India." *Journal of Women's History* 1:8–33.

Ziff, Paul. 1960. *Semantic Analysis.* Ithaca: Cornell University Press.

Ziff, Paul. 1984. *Epistemic Analysis.* Dordrecht: D. Reidel.

Index